Lawlaka lama khalaqtul aflak,
Wa lawlaka lama azhartu ilayahi rububiyaii

"If it were not for thee. I would not have created the heavens and manifested the sovereignty"

—A Hadith-i-Qudsi.

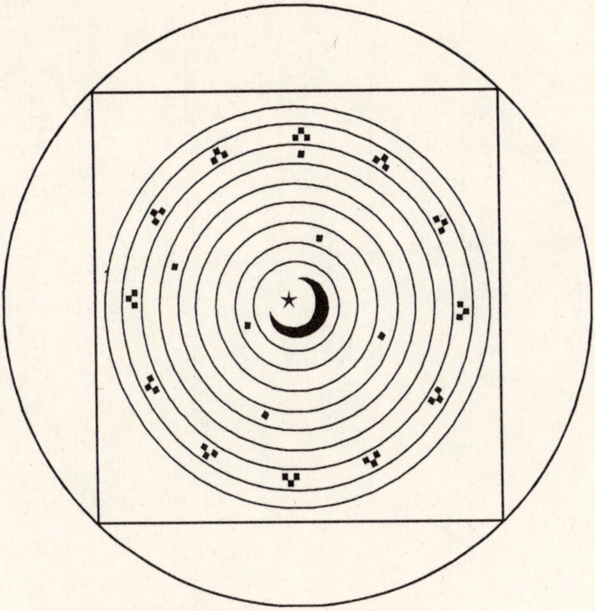

Ashabi kan nujumi, Bi-ayyihim
Iqtadaytum ihtadaytum.
My companions are stars;
Whomsoever any one of them you follow, you
will be rightly guided."—A Hadith.

(Frontispiece, pp. 71-72 and *74-75)*

STUDIES IN TASAWWUF

Khan Sahib Khaja Khan, B.A.,

Forward by:

Nawab A. Hydari Hydar Nawaz Jung Bahadur

KITAB BHAVAN
NEW DELHI-110002

Kitab Bhavan
Publishers, Distributors, Exporters & Importers
1784, Kalan Mahal, Darya Ganj
New Delhi-110002 (India)

Phone : (91-11) 23277392/93, 23274686
Fax : (91-11) 23263383
E-mail : nasri@vsnl.com
Web Site : www.kitabbhavan.com

First Edition : 1923
New Typesetting : 2003

ISBN : 81-7151-333-6

Laser Typesetting at:
Laser Track
Darya Ganj, New Delhi-2

Published in India by:
Nusrat Ali Nasri for Kitab Bhavan
1784, Kalan Mahal, Darya Ganj
New Delhi-110002 (India)

Printed in India at:
Nice Printing Press
Khureji Khas, Delhi-110051

CONTENTS

FOREWORD

Whilst the esoteric side of the other great religions is made more and more accessible to English readers, it is a matter of great misfortune that similar service is not being rendered to Islam, with the result that the majority of non-Muslims and even many Muslims, who have been brought up entirely under a European cultural environment, remain ignorant of that particular side in Islam which is its core and centre, which really gives life and vitality to its outward forms and activities, and which most can appeal to followers of other faiths owing to the universal character of its content. Mussalmans will therefore, be grateful to a competent scholar like Mr. Khwaja Khan, who has in these pages thrown a great deal of illuminating light on various points in esoteric Islam, popularly known under the name of Tasawwuf (Theosophy). 1 hope Mr. Khwaja Khan will continue to dig in the fertile and consecrated field he has chosen for his labours and make available from time to time the treasures, he finds.

A. HYDARI

PREFACE

In the preface to my book on "The Philosophy of Islam," I expressed the hope to bring out an enlarged edition of that book; but this was given up, for the present, in favour of this book, which also is a collection of metaphysical Essays—written in the same way as my above mentioned book. It may be observed that a thread of connection is running throughout the essays, although outwardly they appear to be disconnected. The very first essay "Esoteric Narratives" may appear to have no bearing on the subject; but really, it underlies the subject-matter of all the essays; for here, we are dealing with the Esoteric side of Islam; and this essay proves how far an Esoteric meaning underlies the formalism of Islam, and how such a meaning is justifiable in the eyes of the "Elders of the Church" of Islam, and of the great Islamic thinkers. If Islam is denuded of Esotericism, it becomes a mere skeleton of formalities which people of a rationalistic turn of mind would accept only as formalities. Unless this skeleton is clothed with flesh and vivified, the real beauty of Islam cannot be appreciated. Chapter II to V deal with the descent of man— *Tanazzulāt-i-Sitta* (the six devolutions); and Chapter VI to XI relate to his ascent; Chapter XII treats of the history of the subject, and Chapter XIII is a comparative study of the same. A life of the makers of Tasawwuf, or at least of those eminent men mentioned in the book was also a desideratum. As a few books already exist in English, e.g., Claud Field's *"The Mystics and Saints of Islam,"* Dr. R.A. Nicholson's *"Mystics in Islam"* (on the lines more or less of Fariduddin 'Attār's *Tadhkiratul-Auliyā* and Mullā Jāmi's *Nafhatul-Uns),* this has been postponed. Lives of these thinkers with a comparative study of their thoughts—philosophical, ethical and illuminational—and of their particular *ashghāl* (practices) and *adhkar* (repetition *of* Divine names and formulas) and *mālfuzāt* (sayings) is, however, still a desideratum.

The Elders of the Church of Islam who have dealt with Tasawwuf have so far done it in detached essays; whether they be those who have treated it as philosophy, or whether they be those who have treated it as *Kashf* (illumination), like Shaykh, Mahiyyuddin ibn-ul-'Arabi and 'Abdul Karim Jili.

The works of writers on Tasawwuf are generally in poetry; because it was not thought advisable in those days to deal with the subject in a plain matter-of-fact way, and lay bare the truths before ordinary people, whose minds were not prepared to receive them, and who mismanipulated the same, and made use of them as a dangerous weapon; secondly, propaganda work was best done in those days, by means of poetical effusions. Poetry could not put a philosophical subject in a precise and mathematical style. Subjects were often repeated with a view to drive home the truths and to make them clearer and more understandable. As they thought with Talleyrand that speech was meant to conceal thought, they did not, like Carlyle and Hegel, hesitate to speak in paradoxes. Of course there have been differences of opinion, but these differences of honest opinion are considered to be a real blessing in Islam : *Ikhtilāf- ul- 'Ulamā rahmatun.*

Again poetry is the best medium of expression for Ahl-i-Kashf (people of illumination). Their Kashf finds a ready and enthusiastic, and forcible expression in poetry; while the best of prose is too dull for the purpose. That which one sees with his inner eye finds expression in conscious measured language. Some people who are not under this occult influence also use poetry as a matter of mimicry; but their effusion appears hollow. It may be that they are trying to advance from the unreal to the real. The poetry of Rūmi, Sa'di, Ibn-ul-'Arabi clearly shows that the forcibleness of their poetry had its *fons et origo* in the realization of the realism of their ideas, and in the genuineness of their feelings. The effusive languages of David, St. Paul and Sri Krishna bear a clear testimony to the fact that they had realized what they expressed. The living pictures in the 'Ālam-i-Mithāl and Barzakh could only be expressed in poetry. The Qur'ān. too, is in the effusive language of the Arabs, but it is not considered to be poetry, as the elements of pre-determination and determined effort are wanting in it (as held by Imām Fakhrud-din Rāzi). In poetry, these elements! must be present; the words of God merely passed out of the lips of the Prophet.

Gur chi Qu'rān as, labi-Payghambar ast
Her ki gouyad Haqq na gufta kafir ast.

(Mathnawi)

Although the Qur'ān is from the lips of the Prophet,
Whoever says it is not God's word, hides the truth
And God has said, "We have not taught him poetry."

(Sūra xxxvi: 69)

The writings of ancient writers are of a synthetical character; they are long discourses which one has to wade through to get at the kernel of the matter, they appear to have purposely done, to make themselves difficult for the ordinary work-a-day intellect to understand. To understand a complicated and long discourse, the reader has to analyse the subject-matter. Herbert Spencer's *Synthetical Philosophy* is based on an analytical basis. You cannot take away a single sentence or a single paragraph, without obscuring the meaning of a whole chapter. Here our great thinkers have made themselves purposely obscure; perhaps by not dealing with each subject separately. Shaykh Sadruddin of Qoniah was a disciple of Ibn-ul-'Arabi, as Schelling was of Hegel; and he was one of the few persons who lectured on *Fūsus-ul-Hikam,* and yet he confessed not to have understood his master properly as Schelling had confessed in the case of his own master; the difference, however, was that the Shaykh's writings were in a vein of *kashf* (illumination), and Hegel was a purely speculative philosopher.

I have tried to put the thoughts of these elders in such a way that the different parts of the system harmonized with one another, at least to the best of my understanding. At the end of the book, I have given explanations of technical terms. The significance of some of these terms is not yet definitely settled, just as is the case in respect of technical philosophic terms used by different English writers. Writers sometimes use these terms in different senses; sometimes the definitions are not clear cut.

Some terms found in the book like Ahadiyyat, Wahdat, Wāhidiyyat do not find a place in the glossary; since they have been explained at some length in the body of the book itself. I have tried to fix these explanations on to well-established and accredited usages.

Some thoughts in the realm of philosophy are to be ordinarily realised by revolving them in one's mind; (specially if they are to accord with particular schools of thought;) I have made a study of this subject for some years, and leave it to the reader to judge how far I have been able to make my exposition of it understood on these lines. The object of the treatise is not controversial; a few quotations have been made from the scriptures of Christianity and Hinduism, to show the identity of aim of all religions, and how far these have common basis.

Kufr Kāfir ra wa din dindar ra,
Dharra-i-dardi dil-i-'Attār ra.

Infidelity (welcome) to an infidel and piety to the pious man,
An atom of ache to the heart of 'Attār.

The transliteration system generally used by Orientalists has been adopted. It is desirable, no doubt, to have a definite system of spelling; but intonation, and even pronunciation differ in different places—say in India and Persia, India and Arabia; and it is difficult to fix on anyone intonation as the standard. An Englishman's intonation sometimes differs from that of a Scotchman or Welshman. The question in transliteration is not the spelling of written words; but of the spelling of words as pronounced.

Chapters III, XIII and Appendix II originally appeared in the *Theosophist;* and the rest in the 'Muhammadan' of Madras. I have to thank the Editors of these journals for their courtesy in allowing me to make use of these publications, I am also indebted to Maulvi Muhammad Na'im-ur-Rahmān Sāhib, M.A., H.P, Professor of Arabic in the Government Muhammadan College, Madras, for revising, in proof, the transliteration of Classical and Vernacular words according to the system of the Royal Asiatic. Society; and to Nawab A Hydari Hydar Nawāz Jung Bahādur. Finance Minister to H.E. Highness the Nizām, for his encouraging Foreword.

Royapettah, Madras. **KHAJA KHAN**

Chapter 1

ESOTERIC NARRATIVES

Gar zi sirri marifat agah shawi,
Lufz bu guzari sua maana shawi.
(Mathnawi)

If thou wouldst be acquainted with inner meaning, Drop the letter and adopt the spirit.

Direct exposition of a spiritual theme is avoided in the holy scriptures of most religions. The glare of the sun is too strong and blinding to the watery eye. If one wishes to have a view even of its penumbra, one must use coloured glasses. Direct facts are misleading and confusing to the ordinary man; esoteric writers and speakers have all along clothed realities' in many-hued garbs, so that those who have eyes to see may see. Sri Krishna has not laid his truths in their simple nakedness. Jesus Christ has spoken in parables; he, even said, that pearls should not be thrown before swines. Common people, not realizing the drift of argument, go astray; it requires a certain amount of leavening in one's temperament to grasp facts; culture is not a correct word hereto use, as that implies only intellectual ploughing and sowing; leavening implies fermentation of feelings to the proper degree, in addition to training of the intellect. Not possessing this leavening, they either go astray or are led to make the confusion of the world worse confounded.

Great teachers have therefore hit upon ceremonials as the basis on which training is fixed. These ceremonials are their *shari 'at* or exoteric laws *Shari 'at* is from *shar,* the beaten-out path in the desert, which leads to a watering *ghãt.* If you take this way, it leads you straight to the *ghãt,* where the water of life is found—the *haqiqat* (truth) lies enveloped in this *shari'at* to cut through the shell to get at the kernel of the truth is a laborious task. In the Qur'ãn itself, the verses are of two kinds—*Āyāt-i-Bayyināt,* plain verses; they are writ large, so that one that runs may read, *e.g.* the stories of the former Prophets, laws about the division of property *('ilm-i-farā'yid),* commandments—positive and negative, etc. Then there are *Āyāt-i-Mutashabihāt* (verses involving doubt); which can be interpreted in as many as seven different ways.

These latter kind of verses have given rise to as many as seventy two sects. They relate to the essence and attributes of God, the mysteries of prophetship—in fact to the Greater Mysteries of Islam *('Ilm-i-Haqā'yaq)* and the Lesser Mysteries (*'Ilm-i-Daqā'yaq).*

Not only in the Qur'ãn are there such narratives, but Sūfi writers have exposed their facts in the form of stories.

The *Mathnawi* of Jalāluddin Rūmi is full of stories; and moral is drawn only for those who have eyes to see; the lesser writers of mysteries—Shaykh Sa'di, for example, also sometimes draw out their truths in the form of stories. While this form of exposition obscures the mental horizon of those who have no taste for the deeper truths of life, it becomes most palatable to those who are in for it.

Dhauq-een bada na da u ba khudi ta ni crashi.

The intoxication of this wine you do not relish, until you have tasted of it.

"Verily we have cast veils over their hearts, lest they should understand the Qur'ãn, and into their ears caused thickness of hearing." Moses asked God whether there was anyone man more knowing than himself; and he was directed to go to Khizr. Khizr is supposed to be one Balya ibn Malacan, who having drunk of the water of life had become immortal. Moses with his servant, Joshua, proceeded to the place where the two seas met. When they arrived at the meeting of the two seas, they forgot the fish (the roasted one) which they had brought for their dinner; and the fish took its way freely to the sea. When Moses called for dinner, Joshua told him what had actually happened. They then returned to the place from which the fish had jumped into the sea. Here Moses met Khizr and requested him to be allowed to follow him "that thou mayest teach me part of that which thou hast been taught." Khizr answered: "Verily thou couldst not bear with me: for how couldst thou patiently suffer those things, the knowledge whereof thou dost not comprehend." Moses replied: "Thou shalt find me patient if God please." (The Qur'ãn continues).[1]

"So they both went on by the seashore, until they got aboard a ship; and Khizr made a hole therein. And Moses said unto him: "Hast thou made a hole therein, so that thou mayst drown those who are aboard? thou hast done a strange thing." He answered, "Did I not tell thee that thou couldst not bear with me?" Moses said : "Rebuke me not, because I did forget, and impose not on me a difficulty which I had not anticipated." Wherefore they left the ship and proceeded until they met with a youth; and Khizr slew him. Moses said: "Hast thou slain an innocent person, without his having killed another? Now hast thou committed an unjust action." He answered, "Did I not tell thee that thou couldst not bear with me." Moses said: "If I ask thee concerning anything hereafter, suffer me not to accompany thee; now hast thou received an excuse from me." They went forward, therefore, until they came to the inhabitants of a certain city; and they asked food of the inhabitants thereof; but they refused to receive them. And they found therein a wall, which was ready to fall down, and Khizr

---

1 Sūra Kahf, XVII.

set himself to put it upright. Whereupon Moses said unto him: "If thou wouldst, thou mightest doubtless have received a reward for it." He answered, this shall be a separation between me and thee; but I will first declare unto thee the significance of that which thou couldst not bear with patience. The vessel belonged to certain poor men, who did their business in the sea; and I was minded to render it unserviceable, because there was a King behind them, who took away every sound ship by force. As to the youth, his parents were true believers; and we feared, lest he being an unbeliever should oblige them to suffer his perverseness and ingratitude: wherefore we desired that their Lord might give them a more righteous child in exchange and one more affectionate towards them. And the wall belonged to two orphan youths in the city; and under it was a treasure hidden, which belonged to them, and their father was a righteous man; and thy Lord was pleased that they should attain their full age and take forth their treasure, through the mercy of thy Lord; and I did not what thou hast seen, of mine 'own will, but by God's direction. This is the interpretation of that which thou couldst not bear with patience."

Khizr met Moses at the junction of the rivers; Love and Humanity—the unmanifest and manifest of Nirguna and Sarguna or exotericism and esotericism. The Qur'ãn says: "We have issued two seas that never mingle with one another; there is a partition between them that is irremoveable."

Marajal-bahrayni yaltaqiyan baynā-huma barza-khun lā yabghiyan.[1]

David too refers to this partition: "Deep calleth unto deep at the noise of thy water spouts; all thy waves and billows are gone over me."[2]

---

1 Sūra Rahmān. LV : 19 : 20.
2 Psalm, 42:7, (I).

When one is on this cataract, one requires a boat and a boatman to tide over it. Moses met the boatman in the person of Khizr and the boat was the boat of spiritual training. When the boat reaches the other side of the river, there lives a King who confiscates all sound boats. To save his ship, Khizr, the spiritual guide springs a leak in it. This is the hole of Love in the bottom of Humanity. Satan is unable to confiscate it, a leaky boat is of no good to him. In such a boat Humanity passes over to Spirituality.

Khizr and Moses, the *guru* and disciple, it may be, landed on the other side of river, in the country over which the tyrant ruled. Khizr took hold of a youth, *i.e.,* desire and slew him outright. This youth was Nafs (desire-body). In the second stage of the journey one has to kill his desire body; unless desires are killed, there can be no progress, this demon in the shape of a youth will be shadowing our steps. The two then leave this country and enter another country—a country inhabited by plunderers no doubt—and in a state of ruin. Here Khizr and Moses have to satisfy their creature comforts, but nobody would give them a crumb of bread. Khizr, however, sets about repairing a wall in imminent danger of falling. Under the shadow of this wall, two precious treasures lie buried—Treasure of Prophetship and Saintship, the two orphans referred to. In this country of plunderers, the wall of *shari 'at* is protecting these two treasures. Under the protection of ceremonial institutions, the peace of the country was maintained. If the wall of *shari 'at* had collapsed, the two treasures would have fallen into unworthy hands. *Hence shari 'at* (ceremonial institution) protects spiritual treasures.

Here is another story from Shaykh Sa'di's 'Gulistan' (Chap. I). A king was travelling in a boat with his 'Ajami slave; the slave who had not seen the troubles of the sea, began to tremble and wail and gnash his teeth. A physician was sitting in the same boat. He said: "If your Majesty order me. I shall make him quiet by a device." The king agreed. The physician ordered that the slave should be thrown into the sea, and after he had two or three dippings to be pulled up by the hair of his head. The slave was accordingly pulled up after this trial. He then went and sat quiet in a corner. The king asked the physician what was the wisdom of this experiment. He replied that the slave had not realised the danger of drowning, and was excited. When he actually went through the danger, he realized the safety of being on board a ship. Similarly a man does not understand and realize the doctrine of *Hama ust* or Divine Immanence, until he is involved in a variety of dangers and comes out safe. The 'Ajami slave (other than Arabs are 'Ajamis) is a term for an uninitiated man; such a man is subject to "affections of the heart," Khatarāt) ; and he gets confused and his mental balance is upset. Even when he is told that all saints had realized this doctrine, he does not resume a mental equilibrium. The Perfect Pir throws him overboard into the sea of doubts and infidelity, and then pulls him up towards the shore of safety and a correct appreciation of the underlying reality. It may be objected to, that this story has no perceptible application to the doctrine of *Hama ust.* The intention of Shaykh Sa'di is plain from his concluding verses: "There is difference between a man whose beloved is in his bosom and one whose eyes are expectant at the door." The believer in *Hama ust* has observed the Truth with the eyes of certainty and the non-believer is looking forward to the prospect of a beatific vision in a future life.

Chapter II

PHILOSOPHIC SCHOOLS OF ISLAMIC THOUGHT

There are three main schools of thought—Ijādiyyah, Wujūdiyyah and Shuhūdiyyah. The Ijādiyyah are the Creationists or Transcendentalists, who believe in a God separate from His Creation, an extra-cosmic God who created the heaven and the earth in six days, and took rest on the seventh. "Praised be God Who created the heavens and the earth and brought into being the Darkness and Light" (Sūra xvii: 1) When "the hand of God" is mentioned "as being on the hand of the Prophet" Sūra xxvi: 13), there is no metaphorical sense. When God descends to the Fourth Heaven in the latter part of the night, that too is to be taken literally; only that we do not wish to examine it. He is the maker, the engraver, and painter. Everything is "from Him". (Hama-azust). This is the belief of the ordinary people. "The simple belief of Musalmans," says Sir Sayyid Ahmad,[1] "is that God is one. He exists by his own holy essence. He brought all things from nothingness into thingness. All things are dependent on him for their existence. He is not dependent on anything. He is unique in His essence and in His attributes and in His works. Nobody takes part in his actions; His essence and His knowledge are not like our essence and knowledge. His hearing is not like our hearing, nor are his intention. His power, and His speech like our intention, our power, and our speech." There is no resemblance between

1 "Tasanifi-Ahmadiyyah," p. 139.

these except in name. Creating is his special attribute, for nobody can create a thing out of nothing. Even the action of a man is created by Him, only that in the nature of a man. He has created independent intention, and will, to do good and evil works. He is not contained in anything; nor does anything contain Him. He surrounds everything by His Essence and is near and with everything; but His proximity and propinquity are not understood by us." This is the philosophical aspect of the Asharia school. Since the essence of created is according to them, a "nothingness" and since they go according to the exoteric teaching of the Qur'ãn, and since also they practice certain *Adhkār,* they are counted as a sect of Sūfis.

The second great school, which exerted a great influence on the philosophy of Islam was that of Wujūdiyyah. The great thinker, Shaykh Muhiyyuddin ibn al-'Arabi (ob 1241) was a native of Spain. Although he died in Syria, he is counted amongst the philosophers and Sūfis of the West. His doctrine was that man (or the world) comes out of the knowledge of God, and gains the experience of the world and then returns to his own *'ayn* (or reality). Here duality is struck at its very root. There is only one essence, which has manifested the "many" out of its own knowledge; which knowledge in the second stage of Emanation is itself. Having gained experience, it travels back to its own reality in the knowledge of God. "Everything is him" (*llama ust).* Some people confound this with Pantheism. The difference is obvious. Although the One exists, the essence of things are in his knowledge, much as there are forms or plans in the knowledge of the builder. When a plan exists as a plan in knowledge, it is no longer the builder itself. Identity no longer exists, and in reverting, the plan reverts to its type. Pantheism even in the case of the Hindu philosophy is a much abused word. Every stock and stone is not God—it simply means that everything is instinct with consciousness, which the researches of Babu Chandra Bose and others have amply testified to a wondering world. Pantheism may be a doctrine of Divine Immanence, which the Mussalman sect of Mu'tazilites believe in (*i.e.*, God pervades His universe). But the original philosophy of Ibn 'Arabi is of a loftier kind. The world was not created causally but existed in the knowledge of God, and His knowledge is as eternal as His *Dhāt* itself.

'Abdul Karim al-Jili (ob. 811 A.H) the renowned āuthor of *Insān-ul-Kāmil* and several other books, was the founder of the next important sect of Shuhūdiyyah. Unlike Ghazzāli, who believed that attributes alone are in evidence and essence is an unknown quantity (a zero), he believes that essence itself is in evidence, and attributes are always hidden; you have no cognizance of benevolence, which is always hidden in the benevolent one, who alone is in evidence.

Al-haqqu mahsūsun, wal khalquq ma'qūlun.

The essence is sensed, the world is only inferred. He believed that God created the world out of nothingness. *Ex-nihilo nihil fit* ?—of the Greek philosophy did not find favour with him. For don't you see forms coming out of nothingness, and receding into nothingness ? Wax is moulded into forms, which therefore come out of nothingness. Forms come out of the knowledge of God ; but before they come out they existed in God Hāfiz, the Persian poet, was in his poetry, an exponent of Jili. When attributes become manifest, they receive names (asmā). Names are therefore mirrors. For without names, attributes would not have manifested themselves. The names (asmā) are therefore mirrors, which reveal all the secrets of Divine being; this is the theory of Divine Immanence. The names are mirrors for yet another reason. God created the world out of nothingness. The Divine attributes became manifest by contrast with the attributes of "nothingness". "Nothingness" has no speech, no-sight, no-hearing, no providence, no-good, etc. The power of speech, sight, hearing and the goodness of God become manifest, by contrast with lack of the same in this "nothingness" or form (*'ayn).*

The essence possesses the attributes of completion and permanency and the *'adam* (nothingness) has the attributes of "imperfection" and degeneracy and decay. The Wujūdiyyahs have only one Essence, that of God; and the *Dhāts* of God like the juggler's rupee becomes the *Dhāts* of the created in manifestation. The *Dhāts* of created is *'abd (banda)* or bounded *(i.e.)* by attributes and names. The Tauhid (Unity) consists in merely "dropping off limitations or indications" *(At-tauhidu isqāt-ul-ishārāt).* The first binding or circumscription was in God descending in His own knowledge; this is the stage of the reality of Muhammad—as the Sūfis call it or Christos, as the Gnostic Christians call it. The Shuhūdiyyahs, however believe in two *Dhāts*, the one of the Reality and the other of the non-reality, the one of God and the other of the *banda;* that of the *banda*, however, is zero (*'adam*), this *'adam* is, however, *idafi* (relational); it is not *Haqiqi* (real). If there is an essence called *'adam,* then there will be two *Dhāts* which will be dualism. The *'adam-i-idāfi* is only relatively an *'adam.* It is a mere zero. If any number of *zeros* are added to a number by plus sign, the value of that number does not change. This *'adam* is, therefore, an emblem in the knowledge of God. Since perfection appertains to Dhāt, God is goodness itself. Imperfection relates to *'adam;* and hence Evil is the manifestation of *'adam.* "The judgment that we give, when we judge an action to be foolish or wicked a statement false, a work of art ugly, are all metaphorical. We do not mean to say that there is an existence called error, ugliness, or foolishness; but only that there is a given existence and that another is wanting." There are several verses of the Qur'ān to support the Wujūdiyyah. "For God is in the East and the West, so wherever thou turneth thy face, there is the face of God (Sūra ii : 115). "God is with you wherever you are," (Sūra xx: 46). "We are nearer to man than you, but you do not observe" (Sūra xxvii: 18). "He is the first and the last—the apparent and the real— and He knows everything." (Sūra iv: 26). The Shuhūdiyyah have the following further support: "God is the light of the heavens, and the earth. He is like a lamp in a glass, and the glass in a niche, etc. (Sūra xxiv : 35). "Have you not seen how the Lord has lengthened his shadow." "Have you not seen how mountains look solid, though they are moving like clouds."

The idea of co-existence of God and matter was debated by Aristotle, who held that both are co-existent, only that God is unchangeable and matter changeable.

Abu 'Ali ibn Sinā, of Spain (ob. 1037) readily fell in with the doctrine of Aristotle. Plato with his doctrine of Archetypes, held that there is one world-soul, of which souls of men are transient parts. For him, the Universal existed before the individual. This was Plato's doctrine of Realism. The doctrine of Archetypes has its vague counter-part in Sūra iii: 6, where mention is made of *Ummul-Kitāb* (Mother of books) and *Kitābu'l-Mubin* (the clear prototype). What there is in the *Ummul-Kitāb* (the essence) becomes manifest in the *Kitābu'l-Mubin* or *Lawh-i-Mahfūz* (the Preserved Table).

"All are parts of one stupendous whole,
Whose body nature is and God the soul."

A Persian poet has said:

Huq jāni jahān-ast wa jahān jumla badan.

God is the soul of the world! and the world is His body.

The Neo Platonists of Alexandria led by Philo and his pupil Plotinus appear to have been the founders of the doctrine of emanation. But their emanation consisted in *Nous* (the Cosmic soul, the *Intelligentsia primus* of Aristotle) coming out of the

Divine. They accounted for the ten Intelligences *('Uqūl-i-'Ashara).* Nous or the First Intelligence first came out, then it created the first angel. This angel created the second Intelligence, and so on up to the tenth. These angels work on the four elements, and have produced the whole world. The angels are called *Abāi-'Ulawi* (the superior fathers) and the elements on which they work are the *Ummahāti-Sifti* (the inferior mothers). Beneditto Croce criticises,[1] this doctrine in the following terms: "On the one hand is postulated a Logos, a thought *inse* (one does not understand how this can ever think and be thought); and it is made to adopt a resolution (which does not understand how it can ever adopt) of coming forth from itself and creating a nature in order to be able to return finally to itself, by means of this alienation, and to be henceforth *per se* that is to say, able to think and will." It was, however, reserved for Abū Nasr Fārābi (ob, 950) to throw a more consistent light on the point. It was the gradation of the reflection of God, that comprised the internal and the external worlds—the reflection is transient, and the essence is eternal. The last great Muslim philosopher, Shaikh Muhiyyuddin ibn 'Arabi, put on the topmost stone to this superstructure by saying that the Divine one descended into his own knowledge. Just as by switching a gas light in a dark Museum, the contents of the Museum are illuminated all at once, so when knowledge illuminated the being, the world evolved (to outward appearances), gradation by gradation, and became manifest. This want of knowledge is not, however, a deficiency in the essence. In one aspect, it is absorbed in itself and there is no manifestation; and in another it frees itself from itself, and then the attributes become manifest.

As off-shoots of the Wujūdiyyah school, there are the schools of Anawallahs and Fanawallahs. They are not schools of thought properly so-called, but are considered the aim and object

1 *Philosophy of the Practical,* translated by Douglas Ainlie, p. 295.

of contemplation (Murāqaba) of certain schools of Sāliks, ("pilgrims on the path of spirituality") Abū Sa'di Ahrār appears to have given currency to the word "Fanā" and "Baqā". The Anawallahs are really subjective idealists, resembling the school of Fitche of the modern German Philosophy, who maintain the identity of being and knowing. "I alone exist," said Fitche, "the tree and the image of it are one thing and this one is the modification of my own mind." The thing of itself *(Ding an Sich* of the. Germans) is a mere fiction. The Anawallahs assert that in the unlimited expanse of consciousness, a point (*nuqta)* appears: this is my Ego. When other similar points appear (and they are legion), they are the same as this my Ego, and so they are my own manifestations. This point is Euclid's point which has no outward existence *in loco,* but exists in its internal aspect in the mind of the thinker. When it expands, it becomes existence itself. The Fanawallahs assert that it is the Truth that exists, and I am "nothingness". These are the objective idealists, akin to the school of Schelling. "The contemplation of Anawallahs of which, the sect of Shuttaris are prominent exponents, leads through a thorny path. Imagination and judgment are upset, and a man is liable to become an Egotist (Self-expressionist). This path is therefore abjured. The path of *Fanā* (self-annihilation) adopted by most schools is readily pursued, as there are not so many pit-falls in it. But where are the authorities for these latter in the Qur'ān? When the Prophet threw a handful of dust at the army of the enemy at the battle of Uhud, "it was not thou that didst throw it, it was God himself" (Sūra viii: 18). "The hand of God is on thine hand" (Sūra xxvi: 31). In this stage, God is actor and *'abd* His instrumentality. This is called *Qārbi-Farā'yid* corresponding to subjective Idealism. When, however. God is the instrument and *'abd.* His actor. God is the internal of the *'abd,* and *'abd* is manifest, it is *Qurbi-Nawāfil,* corresponding to objective idealism.

The *'abd* sees, hears, and touches by the sight, hearing and touch of God. It must, however, be remembered that this annihilation is only "insight." The school of Hegel appears to be between and betwixt Subjective and Objective idealism—it is subject-to-objective self-consciousness; the Absolute is manifest in both mind and matter. Knowing and being are the same Hegel said:[1] "God has no independent existence; He exists only in us. God does not know Himself; it is only we that know him; while man thinks of and knows God; God knows and thinks of Himself and exists. God is the truth of man, and man is the reality of God." "The course of human history is frankly identified with the course of self-revelation." This appears to be an interpretation of the *Hadih-i-Qudsi: Al-insānou-sirri-* wa na *sirruhu:* "Man is my secret; and I am man's secret," *i.e.,* Man is a manifestation of God's names (*asmā*). He sees man in the mirror of His own names and attributes.[2] Man sees himself, in the mirror of God's names and attributes." Names are mirrors cither ways. Shaikh 'Abdul Karim al-Jili, the author of *Insān-ul-Kāmil,* has. however, gone a step further than Hegel. The latter would circumscribe the knowledge of God of the outer world to the same extent as the knowledge of man himself. This would be a shortcoming in the knowledge of God which is unthinkable and incompatible with His Omniscience.[3] "Let it be known," says the Shaykh, "that God has many and innumerable worlds, upon whichsoever of these. He looks through man, it is called *Shahādat-i-Wujūdiyyah* (existence in evidence); and upon whichsoever He looks without the instrumentality of Man, it is called *Ghayb* (the unseen). Of this *Ghayb,* there are two kinds, and *Ghayb* is detailed in the knowledge of man, and the other is abstract. The detailed *Ghayb*

---

1. Hegel quoted in. Luthards" *Fundamental Truths,* p. 66.
2. Al-Insan-ul-Kamil, part II, p.106.
Ibid, p. 108.

is the unseen in evidence in the knowledge of man like his cognizance of angels, etc., which go to form *'Alam-i-Malakut* (the angelic world) and the abstract *Ghayb* is the unseen in *'adam* (or nothingness) which man has no cognizance of; God alone has knowledge of this."

Since the unseen world governs and controls the seen world, more and unlimited knowledge is implied as possessed by God than what he possesses through the instrumentality of man, although so far as the seen world is concerned. God's knowledge of it may be only co-extensive with the knowledge of man himself. It may however be stated that the author of the Mathnawi appears to be of the same mind as Hegel, when he wrote:

> *'Ilm i-huq-dar ilm-i-sūfi gum shawad*
> *Kin sakun khi bawar-i-mardum shawad*
>
> God's knowledge becomes hidden in the knowledge of the sūfi;
> How can this statement find credence with the common people.

Man's knowledge is God's knowledge in limitation. When man's knowledge is apparent. God's knowledge is hidden. When ice (water in limitation) is apparent, water itself is hidden.

Besides the schools enumerated above, there are the schools which hold God to be, (1) Thought, (2) Will, (3) Beauty or Love, (4) Light.

Those who take it to be Thought are similar to Shuhūdiyyah. *An-huwa al-anā kama kāna."* (He is now just as he was before.) Thought makes no change in individuality. The worlds may come, and the worlds may go, but He goes on forever, unchanged and unchangeable.

Shaqiq Balkhi, Ibrāhim Adham, Rābi'a Basri and some others were the exponents of the Will system. The whole is the manifestation of Will. Shaykh Muhiyyuddin ibn al-'Arabi held that it is God that is manifest through forms in His knowedge: the fromer held that if there were no Will. The forms could not be, manifest.

The "Love" School held that the Universe is a mirror in which God sees Himself; and hence the Universe is the manifestation of Beauty and Love. Ma'rūf Karkhi, Hāfiz, the renowned poet of Shirāz, etc., were the exponents of this doctrine.

Shaykh Shihābuddin known as Shaikh-ul-Ishrāq al-Maqtul ("the Slain"), the great commentator of Aristotle held that God is Light, "God is the Light of the heavens and the earth. He is like a lamp in a glass case and the glass case in a niche" (Qur'ãn, viii:18).

It may be observed that all these latter schools arose from the fact that the *I'tibārāt* (suppositions or hypostasis) were exalted to the rank of *Dhãt*. They take their origin at a lower source (Ahadiyyat). The followers of Zoroaster exalted the two aspects of *Jalāl* and *Jamāl* (glory and beauty) to the rank of Essence itself; and believed in a God of good and in a God of evil (Ormuzd and Ahriman). So these systems of Sūfi thought appear to have exalted the *I'tibārāt* of the *Dhãt* (or suppositions) to the rank of the *Dhãt* itself.

They say, in the words of Hadith-i-Qudsi, "God was a hidden treasure, and He loved to be known and created the world to be known." In this awakening, four aspects are found; Wajūd (Essence), 'Ilm (knowledge of self), Nūr (Light, *i.e.,* dawning of Essence in the knowledge or Ego) and Shuhūd (Observation of self). In the next stage, these become existence or life, and knowledge (of attributes) or Love, Desire, and Power. The schools of will (Shūhad), of Love (knowledge) and of Nūr (Light) have thus had their origin in I'tibārāt.

The great Sufis like Ibn 'Arabi, Jili, Ghazzāli, have mostly written in prose, but others specially the Persian poets have expounded their philosophy in poetry. Philosophy must be compressed into compartments, to be rightly and clearly understood. Poetical effusions, however elevating to the feelings, do not readily lend themselves to such expression. *Mathnawi* the magnum opus, of Jalāluddin Rūmi is a conglomeration of all schools. His idea was to teach a central Truth, and all paths leading to his hilltop were mentioned and expatiated upon. On a close examination, it will be found that the theories contradicting each other exist in the excellent epitome of the Maulānā.

Chapter III

DHĀT AND SIFĀT

These two terms signify respectively the Essence or Reality, and the attributes, or predecables, of the Divine Being. *Dhãt* is the feminine form of the Arabic word, *Dhū* (possessor). Hence *Dhāt* is that which possesses *sifāt,* and is feminine in significance; it is that about which something can be predicated; and a predicate is what can be affirmed about *Dhãt.* This is reasoning in a vicious circle. Indeed, the definition in the *Dictionary Al-Mughrab, viz.,* that *Dhãt* is "that by being, which a thing is what it is," it, as vague and nebulous as it could possibly be.

Shaykh-ul-Ishrāq (Shaykh Shihābuddin Maqtūl), the critical commentator of Aristotle, objected to Aristotle's definition of a definition, *viz.,* "that is the naming of *genus* and *differentia,* on the ground that the hearer may be unacquainted with the *differentia:* and hence, without a knowledge of *differentia,* the definition of a thing in the terms of *genus* and *differentia* becomes unintelligible. He substituted for it "the summation of all the known attributes of a thing." If the attributes alone are given, and nothing asserted about *Dhãt,* the *Dhãt* entirely vanishes. "A substance is a collection of qualities—taste, odour, colour, which in themselves are nothing more than material potentialities." It is the same as the Buddhist idea, which reduces *Dhãt* to a zero. On this ground Imām Ghazzāli ignored *Dhãt* altogether, and concerned himself entirely with *sifāt.* Though a theologian of high standing and a moralist who has exerted immense influence on the morality of

Islam, so much so that he has been given the title of *Hujjat-ul-Islam,* (the proof of Islam)—he has yet been called a "sceptical philosopher."

It is as if the reality is *Dhãt* from an internal point of view, and *sifãt* from an external point; as if the *Dhãt,* circumscribed within circle after circle, shows itself as *sifãt.* It is also a point of contention whether God can be called a *shay* (a thing). A *shay is* that "about which something could be known and of which something could be asserted; "*shay* becomes *Dhãt* in this sense. In the Qur'ãn it is written: *"Kullu shayin halikun illa wajhullah"*—"Everything is liable to annihilation except the face of God." Then the inference is that the *Dhãt* of God is a thing, for no exception could be made from a group, except of a thing of its own nature.

But thinkers have, however, given three *Bātini* (internal) gradations or emanations of God : (1) *Lā bi-sharti-shay,*—"without condition of anything," (2) *Bi-sharti lā shay. i.e.,* with condition of nothing," and (3) *Bi-sharti shay, i.e.,* "with condition of a thing." Shaykh Muhiyyuddin ibn al-'Arabi asserts that God is not *shay,* and depends for his authority on the Qur'ãnic verse: *Laysa-kamislihili shayun*—"He is not like the example or model of a thing." A *shay* is that which comes under wish, *Shā Sha'in* (the wisher wished). God is the wisher and not what is wished. This may mean that He is the thing itself. The Shaykh has, however, distinctly said: "He is in manifestation" and yet not the *Dhãt* of things, "He is He, and *shay* is *shay,*" *Ana ana, wa anta anta* (I am I, and thou art thou), *i.e , shay* has a separate *Dhãt* in manifestation.

In the first case, the *Dhãt* is above all conditions; imagination cannot soar up to it. In the second, its existence is implied without further assertion. In the third, something could be asserted about it. The second assertion gave rise to the sect of

Mu'tazilites, founded by Wāsil ibn al-'Atā, who asserted that *Dhāt* is predicateless and rejected separate attributes. The assertion of predicates militates against the Oneness of God.[1] The predicates are His essence itself. The first four suppositions in the *Dhāt,* namely, *'ilm* (knowledge), nūr (Light), *wujūd* (existence), and *shuhūd* (self-consciousness), are essence itself and not superimposition on essence. In manifestation, the attribute of existence was superimposed by God on the preexisting atoms, *i.e.,* on centres in the unlimited expanse of Consciousness. Nazzām, the disciple of Abu Huzal-Allaf, who fourished in the middle of the ninth century, called these by the name of *wujūb* (modes) of the Divine being. These are the believers in the Doctrine of Immanence, *i.e.,* that *Dhāt* pervades and permeates the whole creation.

In the above summations of the predicables of an attribute, nothing has been said about the eternity of an attribute. Only so much is said, that it is either hidden or manifest. It is considered sufficient to say that in the above gradation of emanations, no reference is to be made to an attribute. It is the stage of *La bi sharti shay*—"without condition of anything". It is called by different names—*Munqatul-ishārāt* (the stage at which all indications are dropped), *Ayn-ul-kāfūr* (fountain of camphor), *i.e.,* whatever enters into camphor becomes camphor itself, *Dhāt-i-sadhaj* (colourless Reality). In that stage attributes themselves are unheard of and so nothing can be asserted about them. It is only in the fourth stage of manifestation that attributes are in evidence, and anything can be asserted about them.

It is said that a companion of the Prophet, named Zarrāra,

---

1 'Abdul Karim Jili in his I*nsan-ul-Kāmil* (p. 61) says that *sifat* are always hidden in *Dhāt.* For if *sifāt* appear by themselves, they become separate entities. They are that which convey knowledge to the understanding. Benevolence is never seen as an entity, but it is only the *Dhāt* that is benevolent.

asserted that the attributes are not eternal. His sect goes by the name of Zarrārins. Imām Hanbal and the Mu'tazilites were persecuted by the Caliph of their times for having asserted that the Qur'ãn (the speech of God) was created, *i.e.,* non-eternal. The other Imāms asserted that it was not created. The assertion of Eternal attributes implied a multiplicity of Gods. The knower, the known and knowledge are one in the stage of *Dhãt* like the painter, the picture and his knowledge are one in the *Dhãt* of the person who paints.

However, the sects of Ash'aris (founded by Abul-Hasan-al-Ash'ari, 873-935) assert that attributes are not identical with *Dhãt;* nor are they separate from it. It is as if the attributes cannot be compared to anything. There can be no *via media;* God is the ultimate necessary existence. Who carries His attributes in His own being, and whose existence and essence are identical. Their tenets are as follows: (1) The essence ranks first the attributes come next; (2) the essence is self-existing and the attributes depend on the essence (like wax and its softness); (3) the essence is unity and the attributes display diversity; (4) the essence has self consciousness, the attributes have none; (5) the essence is always hidden, the attributes are sometimes hidden and sometimes manifest; (6) the attributes must be in their proper locality; (7) the manifestation of one attribute conflicts with or suppresses the manifestation of another.

The question is often asked whether the *Dhãt* of God is the same as the *Dhãt* of the created. In the 85th Sūra (Al-Burūj) God swears by the *Dhãts* of the Constellation of the Zodiacs, so the *Dhãt* of God is different from that of the *'abd* (created).

In manifestation, the two are different, and the Qur'ãn used the words most easily understood by the people. But there can be no two *Dhãts,* any more than there can be two swords in a scabbard. The *Dhãt* of the creature is the rupee of the juggler, who takes up a disc of broken pottery, throws it up in the air, and brings down for the bystander the real rupee of silver.

In manifesting Himself through His own ideas *(a'yān),* the *Dhãt* of the Creator becomes known as the *Dhãt* of the created. In the non-manifest state, there is one *Dhãt;* but in manifestation, it is known as the incalculably immense number of *Dhãts* of the created.

Hamidūddin Nāgori (Nagore of Rajputānā) has said:

Zi darya mouji gun gun bar āmad
Zi bay chuni bi rangāi chun bar āmad
Gāhi dar kiswat-i-Layla furou shud
Gāhi dar sūrat-i-Majnu bar amad.

In the ocean, innumerable waves of different colours arise
And from namelessness assume a name,
Sometimes in the garb of Majnūn
And sometimes in the shape of Layla.

The identity of the Ocean and waves is real identity, and the dissimilarity is only phenomenāl.

A controversy as to the creation or eternity of the Qur'ãn *(Kalām-i-Lafzi* or *Kalām-i-Nafsi)* raged round the throne of Al-Mūmūn; and many were the tortures inflicted by the Mihna, (Inquisition) on those who denied the eternity of the Qur'ãn. It was said that the attributes were, in the first instance, either *Jalāli* (majestic) *or Jamāli* (beautiful); that when the *Jalāli* attributes appear, all manifestations recede into "nothingness," and when *Jamāli* attributes are in evidence, the beautiful world comes into being. The first is *tanzih* (getting rid of phenomena) and the second is *tasbih* (assuming of the same). Something like this is found in the philosophy of Zoroaster (Zardusht), who asserted that good and evil are the primary manifestations of the Deity (Yezdān). They were called Ormuzd and Ahriman. The Persian Monists, *i.e.,* the Magi who, guided by a rising star, were led out in search of the birth-place of Christ, were true *Muwahhids (i.e.,* Unitarians). Some of the followers of Zoroaster construed those to be two gods, and they were called the Zindiqs, *i.e.,* those who did not pay regard to rank. The Zarwanians alone remained true to the colours.

However, the *Jalāli* and *Jamāli* attributes are in evidence in the cult of Islam. Again, the attributes may be "personal," "relational," or "verbal": the first are like Pure, Sacred, Living; the second are those that involve the manifestation of an attribute, like creator, destroyer; and the third are those that show action, like providence, etc. So far the philosophical aspect of *Dhāt* and *sifāt* has been based on the teaching of the Qur'ān; the philosophers speculated and theorised on the doubtful verses of the Qur'ān (Āyāt-i-Mutashābihāt). Some of the verses has been mentioned above; others are the following:

For God is in the East and West, so wherever thou turnest thy face, there is the face of God— (Sūra Baqara, ii: 128).

Really God surrounds everything—(Sūra Nisā v:116).

God is with you, wherever you are—(Sūra Hadid vii: 5).

We are nearer to man then his jugular vein— (Sūra Wāqiya, lvi: 78).

I am in your individuality, but you do not observe.—*(Sūra Dhāriyāt,* li: 19).

He is the first and the last—the apparent and the real—and He knows everything—*(Sūra Rahmān* lv:26).

God is the light of the heavens and the earth, etc. (sūra Anfāl, viii : 18).

The Qur'ān is full of the attributes of God; such as speech, seeing, hearing, knowing, etc. The best definitions given are all negative; indeed, as in the definition of a point, nothing could be positive. The *Kalima;* or the first article of the Muslim faith asserts:

"There is no Allāh, but Allāh." The word Allāh is from *al-Alah. Ilah* is simply "that which is worthy of worship." So the *Kalima* means: there is no one worthy of worship excepting the One who is worth of worship. Some people worship several things; some worship anything and everything that are believed to help them in the realisation of their objects. Some worship their good *selves;* some have, in the words of Bacon, the idols of the market place, the idols of the forum, the idols of the cave, and the idols of the theatre to worship. Some worship the phenomena of the Universe. The Muslim *Kalima* declares that none of these are worthy of worship. These are all transient, illusory appearances. The one deserving of worship is the God on whom these depend; and this he testifies as in evidence *(shahāda)* unlike the Jewish *Kalima (Shema Isrā'il)* where the testimony is of the ear: "Here, O Israel, Jehovah, our Elohim, is one Jehovah."

Again, the *Sūra,* which is the quintessence of the Qur'ãn *(Sūra Ikhlās)* gives negative definitions. God is *Ahad, i.e.,* His *Dhãt* is homogeneous. Here He is not *wāhid,* if that means one as opposed to two, three and any other number—implying contrast and comparison—but He is *Ahad.* A pile of grain of the same species illustrates the nature of *Ahad:* where His *Dhãt* is concerned, it is homogeneity, or, more correctly, oneness of homogeneity. Heterogeneity is in manifestation. Then he is *Samad* (independent). Everything depends on Him; He does not depend on anything. Though positive in appearance, these are really negative in nature. Also the saying, "He is un-begetting and unbegotten," is obviously negative in nature. It is the same as the definition of a point, out of which the whole world is formed.

Chapter IV

THE ONE IN THE MANY
(*Wahdat-dar-Kathrat*)

Human nature is perforce compelled to acknowledge the existence of a Superior Power which guides and moulds its destiny. All religious books make a direct appeal and home-thrust to the heart and intuition of man, which results in a universal acknowledgement among mankind, thinking and unthinking, of the existence of this guiding Power *(argumentum ex-concesur gentium)* or as Sinā'i puts it.

Kufr-o-din har du dar rahat puyan
Wahdu lā sharika-lah guyan.

David summarised this appeal to intuition, when he sung : "The heavens declare the glory of God; and the firmament showeth his handy work" (Ps 19-1.)

The Qur'ān has also directly appealed to this inner sense: "Do they not consider the camels how they are created, and the heaven how it is raised and the mountains how they are fixed and the earth how it is extended?" (*Sūra ; 88*).

It is only when the question of relationship between God and man, between the absolute and the limited, between the infinite and finate, between the unseen and the seen—between Rabb and '*abd* is debated, that opinions and beliefs differ. The debate is as old as the hills. Aristotle taught that God and matter (or more literally the reality of the word—*māhiyat)* are co-eternal; only that God was unchangeable and māhiyat was changeable. His followers—the Peripatetics *(Mashshain)* are the advocates of his theory. Their motto was, as Mullā Jāmi has put it:

Qabiliyat-bijali-jail-nist
Fili fail khilafi qabil nist

> Aptitude is not the product of the action of the actor. The action of the actor is not contrary to the aptitude of the acted.[1]

According to them there are two essences from the very beginning—the actor did not produce *'māhiyat,'* but He only bestowed His own existence upon it. Take for example, the reality of fire. God bestowed upon it His own Existence. Fire has its own peculiar properties and angularities. These manifested themselves, when fire clothed itself with existence. When Abraham was slung into the bonfire by order of Nimrod (Numrūd), God commanded fire thus *"ya naru kuni bardun wa salamun ala Ibrahima"* (O Fire, become cold and protective towards Ibrãhim). God did not command the Essence of Fire to change, it being co-eternal with God, He commanded its property or quality (heat) to be changed into cold—the extension was changed and not the essence; like in the Catholic Church doctrine of Transubstantiation, in which the substance of bread and wine changes and not their essences.

This school says that the knowledge of God is co-eternal with Him, the known in the first stage is the "known unknown" *(ma'lūm-i-ma'dūm)*. The *a'yan* are the known *(ma'lum)*, so far as the knowledge of God is concerned; and they are the *(ma'd ūm)* (non-existent), so far as their own existence is concerned. A triangle, for example, is there in the knowledge of God; but it has no external or concrete existence (so to speak.) One aspect of the triangle is "beingness" in the knowledge of God;

1 See also "Jawãhir-as-Sulûk," p. 31.

and co-eternity with Him, and the other side is its triangularity in externality— which is *'adam.* God cannot alter its triangularity or anything else. Its *māhiyat* is therefore co-eternal with God. Its *māhiyat* were absolute *'adam,* then the *Dhãt,* of God would become an absolute '*adam* like 1x 0=0. But it is '*adam* in the sense of *mal 'um-i-ma 'dūm,* there being distinction in knowledge of Himself from *māhiyat;* so by adding this cypher, there is no charge in *Dhãt* like 1+0=1. This cypher with the addition of any number of cyphers with *plus* sign before them does not affect the oneness of one; but gives it distinction. In their inward aspect, the a'yān possess *Imtiyāz-i-sulbi* and in their outward aspect, *Imtiyāz-i-'Ilmi.* God can, however, manifest any particular aspect of a'yān, at His Will. A potter cannot alter the shape of a *Kūza* into a Jug and still call it *Kūza,* 'but he could mould clay into either a jug or a kūza as he likes. While *a'yān* could not be altered, their particular properties (*or muqtaziyat)* could be suppressed or brought into prominence by God's Will. The poet Hāfiz has sung:

Dar kuyi naik nami mara guzar naadan
Gar tu nami pasundi ta ghyir kun kaza ra

They did not allow me to enter the path of rectitude
If thou dost not approve, change Thy will.

That is, manifest Thyself in the approvable and approved points of my *a'yān*—

Those who maintain two eternal essences, one of God—real essence, and the other of 'abd an *'adam*— nothingness, neither preceding the other are the Ahli-shara (people of ordinances), and Ash'aris (of which Sunnis are the prominent sect). They bring forward the following documentary evidences in their support.

1. God does not tyrannize over His creatures *(Wullahu laysa bi Zallamel abd).*

2. Kalima-i-Shahādat; "there is no god, but God and

Muhammad is His Prophet."

3. The cursed is cursed from his mother's womb *(Ash-shaqiyyu man shaqa fi baini um-mihi).*

4. God does what it pleases Him; and orders what He wills *(Yef Allullahu ma yashayu wa yafhkumu ma yurid).*

5. Whomsoever God directs in the right path, thou (O Prophet) canst not direct into wrong path; and whomsoever He directs in the wrong path, thou canst not direct to the right path (*man yahi hillahu fala mudil-la lahu, wa man yuzlilhu fala hadiyalah.*

6. He gives the kingdom to whomsoever He likes; He gives honor to whom He likes and degrades whom He likes. In His hand is good *(Tuti-l mulka man tashau, wa tuizzu man tashashu wa tu zillu man tashau bi-yadi kal-khayr).*

7. If *a'yan* are the reality of *Dhãt,* then who is the cursed and the blessed?

8. If a'yan are *'adam* (nothingness); then who is the cursed and blessed—the evil-doer and good-doer.

These are the advocates of the theory of A'yni-yāt-i-Haqiqi and Ghairyat-Haqiqi—the dualists; as opposed to those who believe in A'yniyāt-i-Haqiqi (Real Identity of rabb and *'ābd*) and Ghaịryat-i-I'tibāri. (suppositional distinction).

Ishrāqin or the Realists of Plato believed in a world of ideas. God pressed His ideas (the Mahiyat) into externality. Whatever exists in this world ('Ālam-i-Mulk) has its Archetype or counterpart in 'Ālam-i-ma'ani (the world of ideas); and these two— mulk and ma'ani, are conjoined in man—Here the question arises, whether ideas are distinct from *Dhãt*.

In the knowledge of God, they are not created; but in the expressed world—the world of manifestation, they are created.

(*Māhiyat bi jali jail majul*).

Shaikh Muhiyuddin ibn al-'Arabi believed that there is only one *Dhãt* from the beginning, the *Dhãt* of 'abd is hypostatical or suppositional. Hypostatical distinction begins, as Herbert Spencer[1] has put it, in the "appearances of differences in the parts of a like substance." The *Dhãt* of God expressing or as it were crystallizing itself in forms, becomes the *Dhãt* of '*abd*. The moment, the unknown descended into its own knowledge, an aspect of its own, it showed itself to itself as '*abd*—and this was the stage of Haqiqat-i-Muhammadi. From the first to the last rung, the *Dhãt* has manifested itself in knowledge; and it is therefore the *Dhãt* that is manifest. God is thus sensed and the *'abd* is only inferred, *(Al-haqqu mahsū sun wal 'abd-u-ma'qūlun).* The Sifãt (attributes) are thus hidden and inferred, and the *Dhãt* is in the full blaze of evidence; just as the sun is in evidence and the *Dhãt* of the moon is inferred *(Ash-Shums-u-mahsū sun wal Qamaru ma'qulun.)* There are, however, others of Ibn 'Ārabi's school, who hold that Sifãt are in evidence, and the *Dhãt* is hidden. Al-Ghazzãli and Shaikh Ibrãhim Gazū r-i-Ilahi belong to this school. There are evidences in Hadith to prove this. The Prophet has said:

1. I am Ahmad without *mim (Anā Ahmadun bilā mim);* without *mim* Ahmad becomes Ahad.

2. I am Arab without *'ayn* (Anā Arabun bilā *'ayn*); without the letter *'ayn),* Arab becomes rabb. It may be observed that herein the Prophet first shows himself as *'abd,* and then says that when the letter *'ayn* disappears, he becomes rab in the state of self- annihilation.

3. He who has seen me has seen God *(man raani faqad ra-al-haqqa).*

---

1 *Essay nn Progress : its Law and Cause.*

Christ himself has also said: "He that hath seen me hath seen the Father." (St. John 14-9)

4. He who knows his Nafs knows his rabb *(Man 'arafa nafsahu faqud 'arafa rabbahu) i.e.* He who knows his own *nafs,* knows it as God.

Some, however, interpret this, as meaning that he who understands his Nafs as "ignorant," understands his rabb as "knowing." He who understands his nafs as "created" understands his rabb as "Creator" and so on. Shaikh Ibrãhim Gazūr-i-Ilahi relates a story in his "Irshādāt" (Kitāb-ut-Tasawwuf) that a certain fakir entered the cloister (Khanqāh) of Junaid, wrapped in a black blanket. Junaid asked him the reason for his mourning. He said "my God is dead." Junaid ordered the fakir to be peremptorily turned out. This was done three times. On the fourth occasion, the fakir was asked to explain himself. He said "Not knowing that my *Nafs* was a manifestation of God, I have killed it and therefore I am in mourning for it."

This Hadith about Nafs is sometimes said to be a saying of Hadrat 'Ali. It is akin to the Socratic dictum "man know thyself" which is further traceable to the Delphic Oracle.

5. Muhammad is not the father of anyone amongst you; but he is the messenger of God and the seal of the Prophets *(mā kāna Muhammadan aba ahadin mim rijālikum wa lakin rasulalla wa khātim-ul-Nabiyyin.* This is interpreted as- meaning that Muhammad (peace on him) was not of your world.

6. Among the elders of the Islamic Church, Bāyazid Bistāmi said in his ecstasy "Holy I am, how great is my glory" (*Subhāna ma azam-a-shani)* and Mar'ūf Karkhi said in the same state "I am your Rabb—Obey me" (*Anā rabbakum fabuduni)*

Thus according to Ibn 'Arabi of the Wūjudiyyah School, there is only one *Dhāt*, that has manifested itself. It is the Indian juggler's piece of pottery that being thrown up in the air comes down in the shape of a silver Rupee. This school believes in there being once *Dhãt*—but at the stage of *asma',* the *Dhãt* of 'abd differentiates itself from the *Dhãt* of rabb. In the stages above this, the *Dhãt* of 'abd is hidden in the *Dhãt* of rabb *(mundamaj),* like fire in stone or like 5,000 (say) in number one. This is *Kathrat-dar-Wahdat* (many in one). The reverse process (one in many) is *Wahdat dar hathrat,* they call *mundaraj.* There is a distinction in knowledge after the expression of asmā'i-ilahi in the form of asmā'i-kiyāni; and this distinction in knowledge is a great purdah *(Al-'ilmu hijābun ahbar);* and from this stage begin the two streams which never commingle but flow on separate forever (*maraj al-bahryni yaltaqiyan bayna huma barzakun la yab-ghiyan.*

The Shuhūdiyyahs are, however, the Realists of Plato, in-as much as they place the *a'yān* immediately below the Shuyūnāt of *Dhãt.*

Through *a'yān*. God sees himself as one. According to this school, *a'yān* are the mirrors through which God is reflected. The Dhãt of God is one—and his manifestations are many—the number of mirrors do not affect the individuality of the observer. Hence the Hadith, "He is now as He was" *(Huwal anā kamā kanā).* He was and nothing was with Him (*Al-lazi kāna wa lam yakun ma-a-hu shayun.)* Jāmi says:

Dar ayina garchi khud numai bashad
Pai vastha zi khistan judai-bashad
Khud ra bi labas-i-ghayr didan ajab ust
Kin bul ajabi kari khudhai bashad.

Although in mirror, there is constant self-expression,
And there is also separation from self;
Yet to show one's self in the garb of
another is a wonder
This wonder-doing can only be the work of God.

Shaikh Ibrāhīm Gazūr-i-Ilāhi says that the book of N*ufhatui Uns* of Jāmī contains over 600 names of Sūfis of whom 300 side with Ibn 'Arabi in maintaining that 'abd and rabb are like ice and water; or as William James[1] has put it "Each is all in God." "The finite realized as such is already the infinite in posse." Shaykh Shihābuddin Suhrawardi leads the other School of 300 savants; who maintain that the relationship between abd and 'rabb is like that of iron and fire. Temporarily iron becomes fire, but reverts to its essential condition

---

1 *The Varieties of Religious Experience,* p. 383.

Chapter V

THE THEORY OF EMANATION

Three distinct schools reigned in Greece, before the noted philosophers of that land made their appearance: the Ionic, the Doric and the Eleatic, Amongst the Ionic philosophers. Thales of Miletus pitched upon water as the first cause of all things; Anaxamines the Milesian, on air; and Diogenes of Apollonia, while accepting air as the first cause attributed to it a kind of intelligent soul. Pythagoras of the second school *viz.,* the Doric fixed on numbers as the first cause. Of the Eleatic philosophers, Xenophenes considered God—to be one and all: Parmenides considered the absolute being and absolute thought to be identical; Zeno was, however the first to proclaim the non-reality of the world and the reality of the Absolute. The question of reality *(Wujūd)* and non-reality (*'adam*) has since been taken up and discussed by Musalman philosophers. Some like Ibn 'Arabi hold after the manner of Porphryry that Existence itself is *Dhãt*. The Ash'aris, a sect founded by Abul Hasan Ash'ari hold the same view; and on this is based the belief of Ahl-i-sunna. This Existence is not derivative or limited existence. It is an entity itself. Derivative Existence is derived from this. This Existence is absolute from absolutism itself. The world is limitation *(taayyun)* of this Existence or *Dhãt* This latter has two aspects; one the aspect of *Dhãt*, in which it is present by itself and independent in itself *(As-samad);* and the other is the aspect of *asmā'* (names) in which it is united by attributes and actions (active and passive). It cannot be thus attributed except by the localization of *a'yān-i-thābita* (fixed entities, *i.e.*, entities having fixedness in knowledge); for there cannot be a knower, without a known already existing. This is the line of argument of Shaykh Muhiyyddin ibn 'Arabi (1165-1241 A. D.). Shaykh 'Abdul Karim ibn Ibrāhim al-Jili (767-81 A. D.) criticises this doctrine. The known having already existed in knowledge, the knower issued His command to it. The known has thus created the knower. This exhibits a sort of defect in Him, which is unthinkable. Reality is the non-existence of non-existence; and non reality is the non-existence of existence (*Al-wujūd 'adam-ul-'adam wal adam 'adam ul-wujūd).* Reality between two non-realities is a non-reality *(At wujūd-u-bayn-ul-adamaini adamun),* The Ash'aris hold that Existence itself is *Dhāt* and all other sects hold that existence is State (*hāl)* necessary to the essence so long as the essence abides? and that this state has no *illa* (cause). Muhammad Fudali, a savant who flourished in Egypt in the first half of the thirteenth century of the Hijra says[1] that the meaning of its being a state is that it does not attain to the degree of an entity *(mawjūd)* and does not fall to the degree of a non-entity *(ma'dūm), so* that it should be non-existence pure; but is half way between an entity and a non-entity. So the existence of Zayd, for example is a state necessary to his essence; that it cannot be separated from his essence. And when it is said that it has no cause, the meaning is that it does not originate in anything as opposed to Zayd's potentiality (Qādir, powerful), for example, which originates in his power *(qudra) so* potentiality and his existence are two states which subsist in his essence unperceived by any of his five senses: only the first has a cause in which it originates his power, and the second has no cause. According to this doctrine the essence of God is not His existence and the essences of the created things are not their existences. But Al-ash'ari holds that the existence of

1. Translated by D.B. Macdonald, *Development of Muslim Theology*

God is the self (*'ayn)* of an entity, and not an addition to it externally, and the existence of a created thing is the self of its essence. Existence and non-existence equally balance themselves and the God brought the world from non-existence into existence. It may, however, be noted that if essence is existence, it cannot be said to be "above thought, guess, imagination and fancy" as Shaykh Sa'di has put it, for existence is "that which" according to the definition of shay and can be brought within the ken of these. It is what the desirer desired *(Shaa Sha'in).* The Qur'ān, however, says that God is not like the pattern of anything *(Laysa Kamithlihi Shayun),* which may mean that he is the entity of thing itself; and shay is "a concept that could be known and of which something could be asserted, irrespective of the fact that ,it exists or not". If "that which" *(shay)* exists, it is wujūd (Entity): say London, it is "that which," and it "exists"; and so it is an entity. If this "that which" does not exist like the fabulous bird '*Unqa,* it is *'adum* (non-entity.) According to this view, existence is super-imposed on entity; and entity does not come within the ken of "thought, guess, imagination and fancy." Plotinus and Dionysius, the Areopagite, were of this opinion. This entity is, however, manifest in everything.

One day the Prophet (peace be on him) got together the leaders of the tribe of Qureish and said to them: "If you with .the sincerity of your hearts say one word, you shall become masters of Arab and 'Ajam" (*i.e.,* 'Arabistān: and 'Ajam stands for the rest of the world). Abū Jehl as the spokesman of the assembly said: "We are prepared to accept not merely one world, but tens of words from you." The Prophet said: "Say there is no god but God." The assembly was taken aback; and said:[1] "How could one God contain the world *(Kayfa zas ul khalq illahun-wahid)*;

1. From an unpublished copy of *Tannazzulati-Sittah* by Maulvi 'Abdul *Ali vids* also *Kalimatul-Haq wa Kunz-ul-Asral-ul-Qidam.*

and also said: "Has Muhammad (peace be on him) turned all Gods into one God?" This is strange *(Ajaal-al-ilakatun-ilahin wahid. Inna hadha shyun 'ujjab).*

Now the audience was purely Arab, whose language was the purest of the Arabic tongue; the language of the Qureish was considered the standard language of Arabia. They should have realized the niceties of the language; and they certainly understood that the teaching meant that everything is the manifestation of the Deity. Everything is not a Deity in itself, but it is a manifestation of it; just as every beam of light is not the Sun itself, but a manifestation of the Sun. How the *Dhãt* (in whatever sense it is taken) manifests itself and what relationship there is between the *Dhãt* and Sifãt (attributes) and finally between *rabb* and *'abd* (the Creator and created) is the theme of the Theory of Emanation (*Tannazzulãt* or descent). As explained above, the philosophers of the Ionic, Doric and Eleatic Schools had their own theories. Socrates had no definite theory. Plato had his world of Archetypes, Aristotle had two eternal principles. God and matter. It was not till the establishment of the School of Alexandria that any definite theory about the relationship of God and man was established. The Grecian, Jewish and Christian ideas were all at work. Jewish-Platonism is seen in the writings of Philo, who flourished in the first half of the first Christian century. God has revealed Himself through the world. God's first manifestation or (as they put it), the first born of God is the first Logos as in the Gospel of John; then this first Logos created the world. This is the crude form of Emanation. The world was created through the clothing of the Divine ideas in a material form. This is the first attempt at the elucidation of the doctrine of A'yãn-i-Thãbita. Dionysius, the Areopagite, wrote to accommodate Proclus to Christianity. Plotinus, the disciple of Ammonias Sacchus is the founder of the Neo-Platonic School. Zeller says that "Plotinus" system has no more right to be called a system of Emanation than a system of dynamic pantheism." His system comes nearer Shuhūdiyyah than Wujūdiyyah. "The all perfect One is ever streaming out of Himself in this way; He produced, before countless ages, another being a perfect type of Himself, the product of His own infinity.[1] This is the second principle and is called Intelligence, Reason or Logos. The theory of Emanation supposes the Universe to descend in successive, widening, circles of being from the supreme—In the highest, narrowest and most rapid orbits sing and shine the refulgent rows of Cherubims, Seraphims and Thrones[2] or as Mullā Jāmi has put it:[3]

Zan chi az kitm amada ba ay an
Safi-awwal safi malayk dan.

Whatever has come out of the recesses of nothingness
Consider the first row as the row of angels.

The theory of Immanence (Shuhūdiyyah school) declares that God is everywhere present. The. Observer is one and the mirrors are multitudinous. The multiplicity of mirrors does not affect the oneness of reflection in the numerous mirrors. He is present in His reflections in all mirrors. God is as near His *'abd* here as on the other side of the grave.[4] *Wa huwa ma'kum ayna ma kuntum.* (He is with you wherever you are). The theory of Emanation is compared to a pyramid which extends from a point on the top downwards to the base in expanding gradations. The symbol of Immanence is a point in the centre, which expands all round towards the sphere. The first theory held its ground in the West from the days of Dionysius the Areopagite, (middle of the sixth century) down to the fourteenth century. Eckhart the mystic of

---

1 Morell's *History of Philosophy,* p. 115.
2 R.A. Vanghan's *Hours with ths Mystics,* pp. 278, 280.
3 *'Aqāyd-i-jāmi.*
4 Sūra Hadid (lvii-3).

Rhine-land (middle of the 14th century) substituted the idea of Immanence for that of Emanation. So also Shaykh Akbar (twelve century) perfected the idea of Wajūdiyyah; and 'Alā'ud-Dawlah Samnāni (beginning of the 14th) and his disciple, 'Abdul Karim al-jili replaced it by the idea of Shuhūdiyyah. The atmosphere of the Middle Ages was surcharged with Spiritual Electricity. There was no tangible communication between the West and the East; and it cannot therefore be said that currents flowed, from the East to the West or *vice versa.* The third principle is the soul. The fourth is Nature (Tab'iyāt-i-kul). The theory of 'Ālam-i-Mithāl had just then put forth its nebulous adumbrations in the "daemon theory". It did not as yet form a world by itself. But a daemon attached himself to each individual, like the Socrates' daemon who could tell him when a flock of sheep was coming from an opposite direction, and thus warn him to enter a side lane. Last comes the manifestation of the Universe. The links of the chain were thus forged by Neo-Platonists. They were burnished and set in concatenation by Muslim Philosophers who based their teaching on the Qur'ān and Hadith.

The Theory of Emanation is a discussion of the origin of things. It forms the province of Haqāyiq (Greater Mysteries); the other province called Daqāyiq (Lesser Mysteries) is related to the mystical side of sufism The material superstructure of sūfism has a Neo-Platonic basis; the mystical side, the Daqāyiq, is an original attempt at the elucidation of the mysteries of life and is purely Islamic in origin.

Mr. E. G Browne says that "Ibnul-Farid,[1] like Muhiyyuddin ibn 'Arabi had no connection with Persia and so Dhun-nūn Misri; and hence sūfism is not a manifestation of Persian or Aryan thought, etc. Too many of those who have written on sūfism have treated it as an essentially Aryan movement, and for this reason, it is

1. Born at Cairo. 355 A.H.

particularly necessary to emphasize the fact that two of the greatest mystics of Islam and perhaps a third, Dhun-nūn Misri, were of non-Aryan origin."[1]

The Daqāyiq are really the theories of ascent (*Taraqqiyāt);* and these are purely of Islamic origin. The theories are several and varied; for as the saying goes, "there are as many ways to God as there are souls of men" (*al-turuqu 'ilallahi ka nufusi bani adama)*. Existence has descents, *i.e.,* manifestations according to limitation. These are the potentialities *(Shuyunāt)* of Existence like the potentialities of a tree in a seed. No attributes or asmā' (names) are to be found in this stage; the *Dhāt* is called Munqatui Ishārāt (Dropping of all indications), *Dhāt*-i-sadhaj (uncoloured *Dhāt*), Majhūl-ul Nāth (undefined by attributes), Ghayb-ul-Ghūyub (the unseen even in thought). La Taiyun (the unlimited), Ghayb-i-Mutluq (the absolute unseen), Wujūd-i-bahat (Pure Existence), 'Ayn-ul-Kāfūr (Reality of Camphor, *i.e.,* that which falls in Camphor becomes Camphor itself). Every descent has a world of its own for its manifestation. The second stage is called Wāhidiyyat. Between these there is the borderland called Wahdat; just as the present is the borderland between the past and the future. This is called *barzakh* (and the *barzakh* in the present instance is Wahdāt). It is also called Haqiqat-i-Muhammadi (the Reality of Muhammad). It is the mirror through which God sees His attributes and asmā'. Unless the glass is coated with mercury, the seer cannot see his face in it; (*i.e*, without the coating, there can be no reflection of one's face.) Without the *barzakh,* the manifestation of attributes is unthinkable. The third is the world of souls, (it is also called *'Ālam-i-Jabrūt)* the fourth is *Mithāl* (it is also called *Malakūt},* the fifth is Shahādat (the external world) and the sixth is Insān-ul-Kāmil (the perfect man), which includes all the attributes and asmā'. The Reality Muhammad

1 *The Literary History of Persia,* Vol. II, pp. 501-505.

has thus fully manifested itself in Ādam. There are thus *six* stages and five manifestations and these latter are called Hadrat Khamsa (the five Presences).

In the psychology of forty years ago, only Mind and Matter found a place; there was no corner for God. Mind was "no-matter," and matter was "never-mind"; if mind was not reduced to an effulgence of matter very much like bile, as the product of liver or if matter was not reduced to a Mind dormant as in the case of Schelling. Mind was only a series of the states of consciousness. How these fleeting states were linked together was no more known than the missing link in the biology of Darwin. This theory has now given place to a field of consciousness or awareness, which cannot be brought within the four corners of a definition. There is a field of consciousness, *plus* its object as felt or thought of, *plus* its attitude towards that object, *plus* the sense of self to whom the attribute belongs.[1]

A point first appears on the unlimited disc of consciousness. This point is an imaginary limitation; an attitude is then created between this point and consciousness; and then again the idea of consciousness acting on that point, comes into play.

That point according to Sūfis, (which is neither essence nor extension as defined by the Megarian Euclid), is the limitation of *Dhãt* in its own knowledge. Thus the *i'tibar* (imaginary limitation) of *'ilm* (knowledge) is realized. The *Dhãt* as it were descends into its own knowledge. The limitation of the *Dhãt* in knowledge involves the idea of Existence. Its realization of itself is "I" *(Nūr)*. Dawning on itself, it becomes aware of its potentialities *(Shuyūnāt)*; this is shuhud. In other words, when the Dhãt dawned on itself it found itself possessing attributes *(ergo* names.) Existence is thus a statement of possession of relationship. The dictum of 'Abdul Karim Jili was *Laysal wujudu siwal khayali inda mon udri ul*

1 James: *The Varieties of Religious Experience,* p. 499.

khayal. (Existence is nothing else than thought itself). When the *Dhãt* knew its own attributes and names, knowledge was found; when it discovered beauty, Nūr was found. When it knew itself, it was its *shuhūd.* Or as some others say; dawning on itself was Nūr; discovering itself. Existence; being by itself shuhūd; and knowing all these knowledge. Others again say that the totality of *a 'yān* is the 'Aql-i-kul (Absolute Reason). The relationship between the *Dhãt* and this totality is an attribute. Originally this totality was in annihilation, much as sparks are, in the *Dhãt* of stone; or were merged therein. The first attribute was 'Ilm (knowledge); when the totality of *a 'yān* appeared, the *Dhãt* gave prominence to *a 'yān* over 'adam (nothingness). This was *irāda* (will) of the *Dhãt*. When it worked on *a 'yān*, power came into prominence. When the *Dhãt* beheld them, before their manifestation, it was sight; when the aptitudes of *a 'yan* became prominent, they as it were proclaimed their individuality, the *Dhãt* heard this. It thus had Hearing.

In the first stage, which is called *Ahdiyyut,* there is the unlimited. In the second, which is Wahdat, four potentialities *(shuyūnat)* are found. Plato found his God above being, Plotinus gave Him being, thought and power and called Him Dimiurgus. The *i'tibarat* of the *Dhãt* were the hypostases in the Divine Nature as propounded by Plotinus. In this second stage, there is no differentiation of one from the other or from the *Dhãt.* The potentialities of the *Dhãt* were thus first manifest in knowledge. In the third stage (or second limitation) the knowledge of self became cognizance of *Shuyūnāt (Ann-Allaha kad ahāta bi kulli shayin 'ilma)*[1] God's knowledge surrounds all things. Existence becomes Life *(Allahu la ilaha illā hual hayyul qayyum).*[2] There is no god, but God; He is ever living and supporting. Nūr becomes Ego

1 Sūra Talaq (Ixv. 12).

2 Sūra Baqara (ii. 255).

(La tudri-kuhul-absar). Eyes do not see His *Dhāt*; and Power becomes will *(fa'alūn limā yurid).*[1] He does what He wills. When before their external manifestations, the *Dhāt* realized. Its potentialities, Its sight (Basr) was in evidence (*Wa huwa Samiun basir),* He is the hearer and the seer. When the requirements of these potentialities according to their aptitudes were realized. Hearing was in evidence *Alam ya'lam-bi-ann-allaha yarā.*[2] Do they not know that God sees. When in the same state, the *Dhāt* attended to these requirements, it became speech, *Kallimallahu Musa taklima* (God spake unto Moses). Thus there was first the *Dhāt*, the unknown and unknowable of Herbert Spencer about which Hadith has said *la tafakkuru fi Dhatihi-wa-illa-tafakhakuru fi sifati* (Do not contemplate on *Dhāt*, but contemplate on Sifāt). This is the stage of Ahdiyat. Then four i'tibārats (imaginary relations or hypostases) are found, knowledge of self, existence, light, power. This is the stage of Wahdat.

The third stage is then reached, called Wāhidiyat in which knowledge of self becomes knowledge of Shuyūnāt; Existence becomes Life; Light becomes Ego; Power becomes Irāda *(*Will*)'* and to these Sight, Hearing, and Speech are added as explained above. As six out of these attributes are dependent on existence; existence is shown first in calculation. Without existence, there could be no knowledge. Some others give *knowledge,* the premier place in the *i'libārāt* and call it Imām-ul-Āyimma; for without a cognizance of existence, existence is not realized— (Descartes' dictum of *cogito ergo sum).* Shaykh Muhiyyuddin ibn 'Arabi and his followers belong to this school of thought. They say knowledge is realized only after the potentialities (*shuyūnāt)*have been realized; thus the *Dhāt* is dependent on shuyunat for its own realization. Shaykh 'Abdul Karim Jili in his *Insān-ul-Kāmil* is,

1 Sūra Hūd (xi. 107).

2 Sūra Alaq (xlvi. 14).

however, of another mind. God is spoken of in the Qur'ãn as *as-Samad* and *ghani* both meaning "Independent". This view of Ibn 'Arabi, he thinks, militates against His Independence. He says that God has Personal knowledge; as He is aware of his *shuyunāt* without the relationship of the knower, the known and knowledge. These *shuyūnāt* in knowledge have their own peculiarities. Their peculiarities were their own, and God commanded them "to be" and they "became". Before their manifestation. God was aware of them. This school gives the premier place to Irāda in the seven *i'tibārāt.* They believe in the doctrine of *volo-ergo sum.* There is thus *Dhãt* corresponding to Universal Consciousness (Ahdiyyat), a point appears in its disc (so to speak) and four *i'tibārāt* appear.

This is Wahdat called also the Reality of Muhammad *(Haqiqat-i-Muhammadi).* These i'tibārāts were differentiated and became more pronounced; and seven *sifāt* (attributes) are in evidence. David asked of God, "O Lord, where wert Thou, before Creation? "I was a hidden treasure, I loved to be known and created the world to be known." This is a Hadith-i-Sahih, though coming under the category of Da'if. The Prophet was asked by one Abi Zarara, "where was God before creation?" *(Ayna kana rabbuna qabla an khalaq-al-khalqa).* The answer was: "He was in a cloud *(ama);* above which, there was no air and below which, there was no air." Man can contemplate as far as I'tibārāt (Wahdat) but cannot pierce further. A screen always hides his view. Shaykh Muhiyyuddin ibn 'Arabi connected the *ama* with Ahdiyat, but other thinkers connect it with Wahidiyat *i.e.,* the *Dhãt* in these stages is covered by the *ama* (cloud of attributes or *asmā'*) and thus is indiscernible. Between Ahdiyat and Wāhidiyat is the line of demarcation (*Barzakh);* much as the present is a line of demarcation between the past and the future, or the imaginary line between the different hues of a rainbow. Wahdat is the dawning of self on self. Wahidiyyat is the dawning of self on its potentialities.

Wāhdat is the reality of Muhammad; and the world is a manifestation of that reality. It is said that the *realities* of the souls and bodies of the world are the details of the reality of the soul and body of Muhammad.[1] A doctrine like this regarding Christ amongst the Christians might have given rise to the idea of transubstantiation, which however is traced to the festival of 'the Lord's supper.'

The reality of Muhammad finally became the figure of Adam. According to Imām Qistalāni, Tahir ibn 'Abdulla Ansāri said that Muhammad (peace be on him) said, "the first thing which was created was the light of your Prophet, which was created from God." Another Hadith says : "O Jabir, the first thing created was the soul of thy Prophet." A third: "I have a special time with God, in which is not contained the nearest angel or a sent Prophet." "I was a Nabi, while ādam was between water and mud." The Qur'ãnic text: "Muhammad is not the father of any of you, but he is a Messenger of God and the Seal of the Prophets"[2] is explained by Najmuddin-i-Kubra[3] to mean that he is not of your world.

The Wahābis who are the Puritans and literalists of Islam do not believe in the doctrine of the Reality of Muhammad.

The four *i'tibārāt* of the first limitation, Wahdat, multiplied by the seven sifat of the second limitation Wahidiyyat (called also *Ummahat-us-sifāt,* mothers of attributes) give 28 sifāt *ergo* 28 names, of which the world is a manifestation. The following diagram gives an idea of the twenty-eight names both manifest and unmanifest.

---

1 *Haqāyiq Nāma,* commentary on *Jam-i-Jahan Numa* by Ibrāhim Shuttari of Ahmedabad. p. 191.

2 Sūra Ahzab (xxxiii. 40).

3 *Murṣad-ul-Ibad,* p. 90.

Diagram showing descent from Ahdiyat to Perfect Man. The left hand arc shows Asma'-i-Ilāhi (Divine names); and the right hand arc shows Asmā'-i-Kiyāni (Worldly names); and the middle line is the Barzakh between the two sets of names.

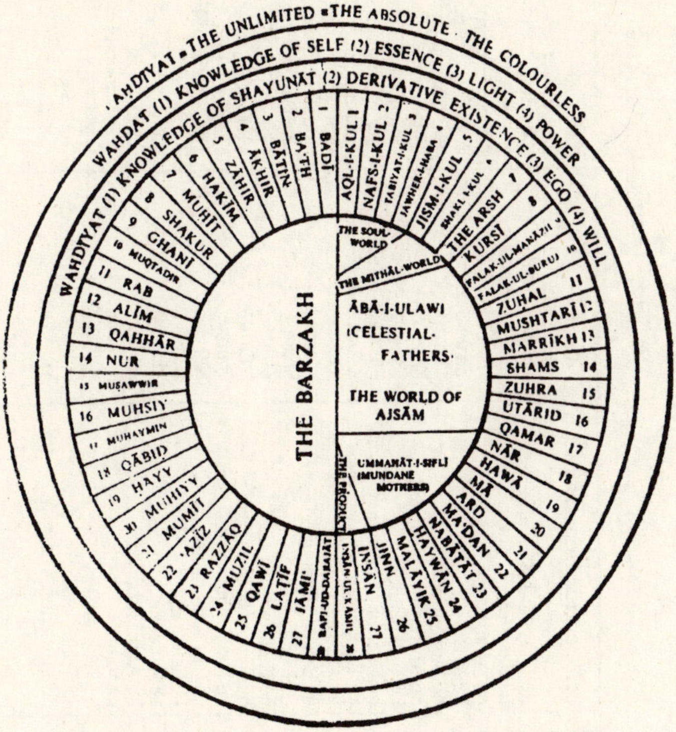

Translation of the Names and their Significance

S. No.	The Creator's Names	Translation	The Created Forms	Translation	The Arabic Letter correspondings to each
1	Badi	The Wonderful Originator	Aql-i-kul	Absolute Reason	Hamza
2	Bāidh	The Cause	Nafs-i-kul	The Preserved Tablet	Ha
3	Bātin	The Unmanifest	Tahiyāt-i-kul	Absolute Nature	Aiyn
4	Ākhir	The Exterior	Jauher-i-Haba	Essence of Matter	Hai
5	Zahir	The Manifest	Jism-i-kul	Absolute Corporeality	Ghain
6	Hakim	The Wise	Shakl-i-kul	Absolute Form	Khay
7	Muhit	The Surrounder	Tha Arsh	The Throne (of God)	Khaf
8	Shakūr	The Multiplier of rewards	Kursi	The Seat	Qaf
9	Ghani	The Independent	Falak-ul-Manāzil	Crystalline Sphere	Gim
10	Muqtadir	The Exertor of influence	Falak-ul-Burūj	Sky of Zodiacs	Sheen
11	Rabb	The Supporter	Zuhal	Saturn	Ya
12	Alim	The Knower	Mushtari	Jupiter	Zad
13	Qāhir	The Overwhelming	Marrikh	Mars	Lam
14	Nūr	The Light	Shams	The Sun	Nun
15	Musawwir	The Painter	Zubra	Venus	Ray
16	Mūhsiy	The Recorder	Utārid	Mercury	Toe
17	Muhaymin	The Guardian	Qamar	Moon	Dal
18	Qābid	The Curtailer of life	Nār	The Sphere of Fire	Tay
19	Havy	The Life	Hawā	Air	Zay
20	Muhiyy	The Quickener	Mā	Water	Sin
21	Mumit	The Annihilator	Ard	Earth	Sad
22	'Aziz	The Valued	Ma'dan	The Minerals	Zoe
23	Razzāq	The Providence	Nabātāt	Vegetables	Tay
24	Muzil	Teh Degrader	Haywān	Animals	Zal
25	Qawi	The Powerful	Malāyak	Angels	Fay
26	Latif	The Minute Observer	Jinn	Jinn	Bay
27	Jāmi'	The Gatherery of all	Insān	Man	Meem
28	Rafi'ud-Darajāt	The Elevator of Rank	Insān-ul-Kāmil	The Perfect Man	Wau

"We have issued two oceans that never mingle together; between them is a Barzakh, that is never removed." (Sūra Rahmān, Iv : 19-20).

"I swear by the Lord of the Easts and Wests; that We are able to destroy them and substitute better than them in their places." (Sūra Ma'ārif, lxx: 39). The left hand names are the Easts and the right hand names are the Wests referred to.

The first three stages or two limitations are called Zuhūr'i-'Ilmi (manifestation in knowledge) or Marātibi-Ilāhi (Divine Ranks); and the succeeding three stages (Arwāh, Mithāl, Ajsām), which are manifestation of names are called Maratib-i-Kouni (worldly ranks). Each succeeding stage is a covering over the next higher one, *i.e.,* the higher stage is obscured by its lower manifestation, while at the same time, the latter is the form of the higher one. The twenty-eight names have multiplied themselves by permutation and combination into innumerable names, in fact into as many names as there are drops in the Ocean. God has hidden Himself behind 70,000 screens of light and darkness (*i e.,* names of beauty and glory.) *(Inn-allahi taala sab'ina alfa hijabun min nurin wa zulumatin.)* These are *taiyunāts* (limitations). But what is a limitation ? It is so far as Existence is concerned, nothing else than Existence itself; while Existence in respect of limitation is not the reality of limitation, *e.g.,* the form of a jug in respect of clay is nothing else than clay itself, while clay in respect of this form is not the Reality of the form. So also the simile of letters and ink. They call this doctrine, 'Ayniyat-i-haqiqi and Ghariyāt-i-I'tibāri. (The reality of sameness and differentiation in fancy) External figures are, therefore, the shapes of Existence. A Deccani poet, Maulānā Bhari has sung:

Yih rup tira rati ratti hay
Parbat parbat patti hay
Parbat men adiq na kam patti men
Yaksan rahayi ras aur ratti men

O Thou, Thy form is in each atom.
In mountains, so in leaves
Not big in mountains nor small in leaves
It is same in heaps as in atoms.

THE A'YAN-I-THABITA

Ghariyat'i-I'tibari. The twenty-eight attributes became twenty-eight names *(asmā')*. His first *ism* (name) was Badi (Creator), called also Qalm-i-A'lā (the Pen). This name is the repository of all other names that ever manifest themselves. It has two sights, or to put it in modern phraseology, two angles of vision; one on its own entity or *Dhãt*, and the other on its attributes. From the first point of view, Bāith came into being; and from its second, 'Aql-i-kul. Similarly from the personal view of Bāith, the name Bātin came into being; from its attribute-aspect Nafs-i-kul; and so on till the last Divine name and its worldly counter part (as in the diagram). Thus each name has its view on each succeeding name and through it on the one that succeeds it till the very last. It is therefore said that the soul world has its sight on the material world. So long as Soul has its sight on Rafi'-ud-darajat, its counter part "Perfect man" is in evidence. When it shifts its sight to Al-Mumit, its body dies and he lives in the *mithāl* world. This being in descent, the upper-most reality is manifest in man Shaykh Muhibulla of Allāhabād, a commentator of *Fusus-ul-Hikum* has said: *Arawhina ajsadina ajsadina arwahina* (our bodies are our souls, and our souls are our bodies). The first series of names are called āsmā -i-ilāhi (Divine names) or necessary names and their "counterpatts are called asmā -i-kiyāni. Each *ism* in the first set taking a form *('ayn)* bacame an ism-i-kiyāni just as Ahdiyat taking a form became Haqiqat-i-Muhammadi. The influence that each *ism* (name) exerts on its counter-part is called the Divine

Breath or inflatus (Nafs-i-Rahmāni). "There is no creeping creature on the earth, whose forelock is not in the hand of its rabb. That rabb is on the right path"[1] (*Wu ma min dabbatin fil arvi illa hua akhizum bi nasiyath-i-ha. Haza rabbi ala siratin musta im.* Each ism-i-Ilāhi comprises all other asmā' but goes by the particular name of that *ism,* owing to the predominence of its particular attribute:

Gulshan-i-Rāz says:
Agar ek katra ra dil bar shigafi
Berun-ayad azo sad bahri safi

If you cleave the heart of one drop of water
A hundred pure oceans emerge from it.
This is known as the doctrine of Indiraj-i-kul fil kul.
(Pervasion or immanence of all in all).

Ghariyāt-i-Haqiqi. The doctrine of *a 'yan* approaches very near to the aeons of the Christian gnostics; but the idea is centuries older than the Christian mysticism. It is the "Eternal Idea" of Plato (Archetypes), to which his immediate disciple,[2] Aristotle had given the name of *entelecheia.* An "eternal idea" contains all that is to become manifest. The idea of Zayd in God's knowledge is the general idea of the man from his conception in the womb till his dust returneth unto dust, or still further till he journeys back through *mithāl, arwāh* and reaches the point from which he started.

Gulshan-i-Rāz again:
Kaz andar amad awwal ham bi dar shud
Agar cheh dar maad az dar bi dar shud

Man returneth to the door from which he started
Although in his search, he went from door to door.

---

1 Neander's *Church History* quoted by Dr. Canon Sell in his *Essays on Islam,* p. 10.

2 *Outlines of the History of Philosophy,* p. 145.

The changes that take place are merely the unfolding of that idea ; or as Zeller has put it, "though ideas are eternal and unchangeable, things are regarded as derivative, perishable and in constant change."[1]

In the first named theory, the descent is gradual from Ahdiyat, Wahdat, Wāhidiyat, Sifāt, Asmā, .and A'yan. At the last named stage, the differentiation between *rabb* and *'abd* appears. In the second named, theory, there is God and his *shuyūnāt.* The *shuyūnāt* are both co-eternal with and disappearing in *Dhāt* like billows and the ocean.

According to the second theory, the manifestation of Badi was 'Aql-i-kul. When the latter realized its potentialities of manifesting a world, it prayed to Badi for a Companion, then Bāith the interior of Badi came into play, and manifested Nafs-i-kul. By the conjunction of 'Aql-i-kul and Nafs-i-kul, Tabiyāt-i-kul came into existence. Paracelsus has said, that this was a marriage between heavenly influences and terrestial objects to which the Grecian Theosophist gave the name of Gamabea (which the Sūfis call Izdawaj).[2] Then the product is a third *ism*. This, however, is liable to the objection that when a thing comes out of another thing, it must leave a blank in the latter.

According to the first theory, the *a'yān* are fixed forms in the knowledge of God, they never come out leaving a blank there.

Al ayan-i-thabitalum ma shummul rahiya tul-wujud. (The *a'yān* have not smelt the smell of Existence), as remarked by Shaykh Akbar.[3] The difference between Plotinus of Alexandria and the Shaykh is this that while the former "refused to ideas any existence externel to our own minds" a sort of Berkelianism, the latter refused to Ideas any existence outside God's mind." The

1 Zeller's *Outlines of the History of Philosophy,* p. 145.
2 R.A. Vaughan's *Hours with the Mystics,* p. 75.
3 *Fusūs-ul-Hikam*—Fusi-Idrisi.

Grecian philosophers believed that aeons had come out of God's knowledge, and had an external existence,

As regards the mutability or immutability of *a'yān*, the same Muslim authority on *Ghairyat-i-I'tibāri* thinks that they are immutable, even in manifestation; for if they were mutable, they would indicate a change in the eternal knowledge of God—a hiatus of ignorance in Divine knowledge, which is unthinkable. Some hold that *a'yān* are immutable; but their peculiarities and effects are extension, and *a'yān* are essence. There can be no change in extension, without a change in essence. Shaykh Abū Sa'id Abul Khayr is of opinion that both *a'yān* and their effects are liable to change in the stage in which the lover himself becomes the beloved; Shuyūnāt disappear in *Dhāt*.

Ishq-o-ashaq mahu gardad zin muqam
Kud hamo mashuq manad wussalam.

Shaykh' Alā'ud-Dawlah Samnāni (the philosopher-governor of Samnān in Persia), the real founder of the Shuhūdiyyah School, and prototype of 'Abdul Karim Jili is of the same opinion with the exception that though the distinction of "I" and "thou" disappears, duality still remains; the shadow (the world) cannot become the substance (God). The difference between the two schools is really owing to the point of view that each takes regarding the stage at which *a'yān* make their appearance.

From Falak-ul-Manāzil to Qamar in the diagram are the Planets, which work on the Inferior Material world, which is from the sphere of fire to Insān. The net result of this working is the production of Insān-ul-Kāmil (the Perfect Man). This no doubt leads to a belief in astrology and theurgy.

In astrology, the influence of heavenly bodies on the destiny of man is calculated. Man is a conglomeration of all the asmā', each heavenly body is a manifestation of a particular *ism* (name) and so the position or as it is called the sight, of a particular heavenly body has an influence on the destiny of a particular individual at a particular time. In theurgy *('Ilm-i-faksir)* again, the influence of each of the 28 Arabic letters has an effect at a particular time. In the statement subjoined to the diagram, it will be seen that each *ism* is represented by a particular letter. When the Divine One emerged from self-absorption, He became aware of Himself—this is the stage of Self-Love. *(Fa ahbubtu-an-urifa.*—He loved to be known. Vibrations brought about by Love gave rise to sounds which were the sounds of letters, and these sounds manifested themselves as asmā '-i-Ilāhi. Like in the case of heavenly bodies in astrology, each sound, *ergo,* each letter of the Arabic alphabet represents an *ism.* If, therefore, an amulet is prepared, consisting of particular letters, the asmā ' represented by these letters must find their manifestation. The idea therefore is that a theurgist or *Mashshāyikh* who has selflessly practised in this art, can bring about a particular desired effect, by the manipulation of the Arabic letters. He is supposed to have permission from his Pir who grants him the same, after he is fully satisfied about the moral character or selflessness of his *murid;* the same precaution as is taken in the case of teaching Hypnotism or Mesmerism.

Thus in the manifest world, there is the soul-world and the material world and the barzakh (the intermediate stage), which is also called 'ālam-i-mithāl.

ALAM-I-ARWAH (THE SOUL-WORLD)

The first four *Asmā '-i-Kiyāni* form the soul world. 'Aql-i-kul is the form of Existence of God's knowledge. It is called *Qalam-i-A 'ālā*, (The Exalted Pen) in the language of *shara.* All individual souls are contained in this; and are, as an embodiment of one soul, called Rūh-i-A'zam (the Great Soul); and out of this, individual souls manifest themselves. Maulānā, Rūmi says: "There is differentiation in the Animal Spirit; the Soul of Humanity is one."

Tafriqa dar ruhi haywant buwad
Nafsi wahid ruhi insani buwad.

This doctrine is known in the West as Averroism, the doctrine of the Muslim philosopher of Spain, Averroes (Ibn-Rushd, 1126-1198) who maintained.[1] "that the spirit or the rational part of the Soul is one in all. Individual Souls are the manifestation of this one Soul." Nafs-i-Kul is the breath of the *Dhāt* and the embodiment of God's knowledge of Creation. All forms of Existence are impressed on it. It is also called Lawh-i-Mahfūz (the Preserved Tablet). Whatever was or is to happen is, as it were, written down by the Exalted Pen on this Tablet. In the first. God's knowledge finds a habitation; and in the second, it takes a shape. The second is also called *Ummul-Kitāb* (Mother of Book). There are also called Exalted angels as they work out God's decrees automatically. Under them are minor pens and tablets (both minor angels). The decrees in these are liable to change, but not of the Preserved Tablet. The third is *Tabiyāt-i-kul,* (absolute nature); this too consists of angels and they mould Nature which is the nature of God according to which the nature of man is manifest. *Fit-ratulla hil-lati fataran nasa alayhai. Jawhar-i-Haba* is the Essence of Matter (Prima matrix), the fourth angel, it is the nebula of which the creation is a manifestation as subsequently postulated by Kant and Laplace. It is the mercurial covering at the back of a mirror, which enables the mirror to reflect forms. *Jism-i-kul is* absolute corporeality. The first set of angels are called *malā -i-a'alā* (the highest angels); and they were not commanded to worship Adam.

The pre-natal existence of individual souls is acknowledged in the Qur'ãn, (Sūra vii; 71). "The Lord drew forth their posterity

---

1 De Boer's *History of Muslim Philosophy,* P. 179.

from the loins of the sons of Adam." As the souls came out, they arranged themselves in four rows: the first row was of Prophets; the second, of saints, the third of believers, and the fourth of non-believers. It was asked : "Am I not your Lord?" they all said : "Yes"—.Again in (Sūra xxiv: 35) ; "the body is compared to a lantern; the vegetable spirit, to the lamp: the instinctive spirit, to the oil; and the spirit of humanity to the fire that kindles. The Proverb (xx: 27) expresses the same idea. "The life of man is the lamp of the Lord." A Hadith related by 'Ā'yisha says: *"Al-arwah-u junudun-mujunidum, fama taarafa minha italafa-wa-ma-man tanakara minha ikhtalifa.* "Souls are a collected army. Those in it who recognised each other, began to love each other, and those who did not recognize each other, were repugnant towards each other." Such was also the theory of Love, propounded by Plato. At the instigation of the Jews, says Ibn Khaldūn, Nāsir ibnul Hūrris and 'Utba proposed three questions to the Prophet: (peace be upon him) one of which was; What is the soul? To this, the Qur'ān says, "They ask thee about the Soul, says: "Soul is the command *(amr)* of the Lord thy God." *(Ar-Rūhu min amr-i-rabbi);* soul thus belongs to the world of command and comes after the first three stages (Ahdiyyat, Wahdat and Wāhidlyyat) and is in limitation. But the Qur'ān also says: *Nafaktūfi hi min rūhi.* We breathed unto him (Ādam) out of Our own Rūh. This soul is the Ruh-i-A'zam (Haqiqat-i-Muhammadi) which is the stage of Wahdat itself and is not under limitation. Though the individual soul is a limitation; it is free from matter and extension, and from colour and form. It is cognizant of self and not-self, but not liable to be sensed by any of the senses. The limitations of Rūh-i-A'zam are the souls of men, and when such limitation is manifest in body, it becomes animal-spirit. It is subtle in nature, and each particle of it is connected with each particle of the body. This soul is liable to reward and punishment; as it alone tasted of the pleasures of the body. It is immortal in nature, and after the decay of the body assumes a thought-shape. In the theory of gradations (*tanazzulāt),* it has been said that each gradation is the form of the next higher grade, and the lowest grade is the form of all the higher grades up to the highest. It has been shown previously that as each *ism-i-Ilāhi* takes a form, it becomes an *ism-i-kiyāni* ia the manifest world. *Dhãt* with a relationship (attribute) becomes an *ism, i.e.*, it is infinite and *ism* is finite. If the *ism* is inclined towards absolutism (Nirguna) it is *ism-i-Ilāhi,* if it sees form and is inclined towards finitism, (Sarguna) it is ism-i-kiyāni and becomes an *'ayn* which is a shadow of *ism-i-Ilāhi.*[1] The first i*sma-i-Ilahi* directly influences its *isma-i-kiyani* and indirectly all the lower ism-i kiyāni down to the lowest one. No sight reaches Him; He reaches the sight, the Subtle and Knowing; *(Latudri kal absar, wa hua yudrikal absar wa hua latee-fun khabir)*.[2] Thus it is said that it has its sight or vision on its corresponding and lower *āsma'*.

In the "Book of Apples" attributed to Aristotle, the Essence of Soul is said to consist of knowing; and the punishment for not knowing is going down into still deeper ignorance. The spirit is described by Bergson as memory; and matter as succession of images. The Sūfis, however, characterise Nafs with desire, Qalb with knowing, *soul* with sight, and *ser* with contemplating, and *Dhãt* with appearing. Since the *Dhãt* appeared, we appear, all images are of this appearance. Since the *Dhãt* contemplated we contemplate; since the *Dhãt* saw, we see (Light is the stage of soul); since the *Dhãt* knew, we know (stage of qalb); since the *Dhãt* desired, we desire (stage of Nafs); sight and not knowledge is thus the faculty of the soul. He who is blind here (in this world) will be blind in the next world and still worse *(Man, kāna fi hazi-hil a'ma fa-huwa fil akhirati a'ma wa azzallu sabila.*[3] The

---

1. Vide the marginal note to p. 140 *of Jawāhir-us-Sulūh.*
2. Sūra Rūm (xxx. 32).
3. Sūra Bani Isrā'il (xvii. 72).

author of "Shar-i-Muwāfik" (p. 583) commenting on this, says that "the spirit will either be in ignorance or it will be in enlightenment. Those in ignorance will go from bad to worse. Those in enlightenment will suffer till they improve." The faculty of sight being the characteristic of the soul; the soul is said to be neither in the body, nor without it. The sun illuminates a house, the illumination is neither within the house nor without it. The soul has three sights; when its sight is on *Dhāt* it is called Amin Rūh (the trusted soul), its sight is called Amin Nūr. When its sight is on Mumkin-ul-Wujūd (thought-world), it is called Rūh-i-Muqim (stationary soul); and its sight is called Anā -Nūr (Ego-sight). When the soul's sight is on Wājib-ul-Wujūd (Causal Existence), it is called Rūh-i-Jari (the travelling soul), which leaves the body in sleep, and wanders about in the spirit world ; and its sight is called Min-Nūr. Rūh has a more influential sight on the body in wakefulness than in sleep. In sleep it has a more influential sight on mithāl.

ALAM-I-MITHAL (THE WORLD OF SIMILITUDES)

This is the fifth limitation. It is the world of archetypes of Plato or the world of Correspondence of Emanuel Swedenborg. It is the borderland, between the soul world and the causal world. It does not consist of matter, yet it is dimensional, characterized by colour like the world of dreams.

It is also called *'Ālam-i-Ghayb,* a world that is outside our sight.

Ghayb ra abri wa abi digar ust
Asman wu aftab-i-digar ust
Nayad an illa ki bar pakan pidid
Baqiyan fi labs min khalikin jadid

(Mathnuwi)

The mithāl world has clouds and rain of its own

Has a different sky and sun
This is not open to the eye of the ordinary man
Who is deceived by the phantasma goria of the World.

Sir Sayid Ahmad Khān thought that whatever is outside our sight is *Ghayb*—like the force of gravitation; but this *'Ālam-i-Ghayb is* a real world corresponding to our World. There is pre-established harmony between the two, like the harmony of two clocks correctly set, or of the hand and the key which it turns. The very term material world." say Balfour Stewart and Tait[1] "is a misnomer, the world is a spiritual world merely employing matter for its manifestation. We are led by scientific logic to an unseen and by scientific analogy to the spirituality of the unseen. In fine, our conclusion is that the visible Universe has been developed by an intelligence resident in the Unseen."

It is not the world that comes after death which is also called *mithāl* or barzakh.[2] To the latter,[3] the individual souls carry away the traits of character peculiar to them. Each individual reaps the fruits of his actions; and lives till the day of judgement, in what 'Abdul Karim Jili call Hayakal-i-Khayāli (Thought-circles) or what Shaykh Shihābuddin Maqtūl, known also as Shaykh-ul-Ishrāq, the exponent of Plato's Realism, called 'Ālam-i-Asbab (the world of objects); or what Shāh Waliūllah Sahib of Delhi has called Nusma. Those who thus live in *mithāl* and are blessed souls have been described in the Qur'ān as linving in "crops of green birds." Thought is of two kinds, the thought that works through the brain called *Khayāl-i-Muttasil* (attached thought); and the thought that does not work through the same is called *khayāl-i-Munfasil* (separated-thought). The one is called Falsidical and the other Verdical in Mr. Meyer's "Survival of Human Personality."

---

1 The *Unseen Universe,* p. 221.
2 *Al-Tukashshuf.* Part II, p. 5.
3 *Ibid.*, Part III .p.4.

This latter work and Sir Oliver Lodges "Survival of Man," are replete with examples of recorded manifestations of veridical thought. *Mithāl* is therefore a veridical thought world; which is as real as, if not more real than this world; for what occurs in this world, first takes its shape there.

With the shapes of thought-world, angels descend on the Earth. Gabriel used to appear before the Prophet (peace be on him) in the form of Dihya Kalbi;

Khizar also appears in the thought-body. 'Umar could appear before the army of Sāriah ibn Rustam; and direct Sāriah towards a certain mountain; while he himself was preaching from his *minbar* In the Mosque at Madinah. Call it clairvoyance and clair-audience as you may. Munkir and Nakir, the two angels that appear before the dead body in the grave, appear in thought-bodies. Actions are extensions in this world; their realities are *Jawāhir* (Essence), that remain after extensions disappear. These *Jawāhir* appear in the shape of 'behisht', etc., in the case of good actions and in the shape of fire in the case of evil actions, for the origin of evil is fire.

ALAM-I-AJSAM (THE CAUSAL WORLD)

From the diagram, it may be noted that asmā'-i- kiyani from 1 to 4 from the soul-world; these higher asmā' are the same as the Malā -i-A'alā' (which are unconsciously absorbed in the contemplation of God). They are the counter-parts of *Badi, Bāith, Bātin, Ākhas* which having taken forms *(a'yan-i-thābita)* have manifested their counter-parts *viz..* Absolute Reason, Absolute Breath, Absolute Nature, Essence of Matter. From the fifth to the eighth in the diagram are *mithāl* manifestations; and from nine to twenty-seventh are corporeal manifestations. Again from 8th to 17th are superior Fathers (*Ābā -i- 'Ulawi*): and from 18 to 27 are Inferior Mothers *(Ummahat-i-sifli).* The first set working on the second set produce the Perfect man *(Insān-ul-Kāmil).* Just as Badi contains in itself all the succeeding names; so does Insān-ul-Kāmil contain in itself all the proceeding *asma-i-kiyāni* and is the representative of them all. Hence Insān-ul-Kāmil is the Vicegerent of God on the earth. Thus has God made man in His own image. (*Khalaq-al-Insana ala suratihi).* Some commentators take *He (His)* to mean "Man's image," *i.e.,* God created man, in man's own image; since every asmā '-i-kiyāni and is a figure of every ism-ilāhi, no superiority of man is made out by such an explanation. Man therefore is the representation of all names. St. Anthony, a Christian Mystic Father[1] is said to have observed 20,000 angels dancing a saraband on the point of a needle, *i.e.,* on the *dhāf* of man, there is a display of manifold *sifāt* and *asmā'.* The angels in the *Malā -i-A 'alā* were not commanded to worship Ādam; for when Iblis refused to prostrate himself before Ādam saying: "Thou hast created me out of fire and him out of earth" (*Khalaq-tana min nari-w-khalaq-tahu min teen)."* God said : "What has prevented thee from prostrating before him.whom I have created with both my hands. What ! You showed pride or went thou of the Malā-i-A'ala' (*Ma, man'aka an tasjuda limā khalaq-tū bi yadia astakbarata ain kunta minal 'alimin).*[2] Excepting the *mala-i-A 'alā,* all angels worshipped Ādam, *i.e.,* all other Kiyāni names are sub-servient to Ādam, who is the embodiment to all Kiyāni names. Hence man has not to worship any particular Kiyāni name or names; he is not to worship the god or angel of fire, or of air, or of earth, though he knows that these are incessantly working out their allotted task. Besides each name is a "limitation". Without keeping the "named" in view, a particular aspect of it cannot be worshipped. If the "unlimited" and "unnamed" is in view, the

---

1 Clodd's The Pioneers of Evolution, p. 17

2 Sūra Sād. xxxviii, 75.

worship of it through a particular name will be justifiable. But this is impossible in the nature of things. The author of *Gulshan-i-Rāz* says:[1]

Musalman gar bi danisti ki buth chist
Bi danisti ki-din dar buth paras thist
Agar mushrik zi din agah gushti
Kuja dar din-i-khud gumrah gushli
Na dyd wu dar buth illa khulqi zahir
Badan illal shud undar shara Kafir.

If the Musulman but knew what is faith,
He would see that faith is idol-worship.
If the polytheist only knew what idols are,
How would he be wrong in his religion;
He sees in idols naught but the visible creature ;
And that is the reason that he is legally a heathen.

After Jawhar-i-Haba, is the 'Arsh or the throne of God, which encircles the Universe : there are four angels bearing this throne. Within the cavity of the *'arsh,* there is the *kursi* (seat) in the form of a square. On this seat, there are the two feet of God (glory and grace). From this seat, shine forth on the earth, the glory and grace of God; the latter over-shadowing the former. Then the crystalline sphere which is subject to constant changes, hence constant changes in the Universe, brought about by this firmament. The succeeding names all culminate in Insān-ul-Kāmil; the developed tree finally ending in the seed from which it sprang.

To put the whole theory in a nutshell, the *Dhāt* saw itself in *sifāt;* this was a *tajalli* (illumination). The *sifāt* are like the mercurial coating of the mirror. This coming into being of illumination, gave rise to duality. This illumination manifests itself

1 *Whinfield.* p. 84.

as soul,—when soul saw itself, it was *mithāl,* the coating of the mirror of soul was body—for there can be no reflection, without a coating. When the coating of the body and the gaze of the seer disappear, the seer (the soul) itself remains. So also, finally when the *Dhai's* gaze disappears, the soul disappears, and absolutism alone remains.

Chapter VI

INSAN-UL-KAMIL

In the diagram in the "Theory of Emanation," after the first three stages, Ahdiyyat, Wāhdat and Wāhidiyat, twenty-eight asmā'-i-ilāhi with their tewenty-eight asmā'-i-kiyāni are shown in the downward arc of descent, the last *ism* reached is Insān-ul-Kāmil, corresponding to the name Allāh, the top-most point in the arc. Thus man embraces the spiritual, the mithāl and the physical worlds, The Qur'ãn says, *Sanurihim ayātina fil āfaqi, wa fi anfusihim hatta yatabayyana lahum annahul haqq.*[1] "We shall show them our signs both in the horizons and in their individualities, so that it may be made clear to them that this is the truth."

SPIRITUAL ASPECT

The first four asmā '-i-ilā hi viz., Badi, Bātin, andĀkhar, with their corresponding asmā '-i-kiyāni, the Absolute Reason, Absolute Breath, Absolute Nature and the Essence of Matter form the Soul-world. The next three asmā,' Zāhir, Hakim and Muhit with their corresponding asmā'-i-kiyāni. Absolute Corporeality. Absolute Form, and the Throne from the mithāl world. In the first stage of Ahdiya, the name Allāh is really the named. The soul-world is the soul of the name Allāh, and the mithāl-world is the heart of the same name. Of the remaining twenty-one asmā' ten form the celestial fathers and ten the mundane mothers, the result of these being Insān-ul-Kāmil, the 28th name.

---

1 Sūra xii : 53.

Haq jani jahan ast wa jahan jumla badan
Arwah wa malayk chu havasi ein twn
Aflak wa muwalid wa anasir aza
Tawhid hamin ast digar shewa wa-fan

All are parts of one stupendous whole
Whoes body Nature is, and God the Soul.

When the *Dhãt* inclines itself towards Itself, it is named Wãjib-ul-Wujũd, (Necessary Existence); and when It inclines towards Its Sifãt, it is named, Mumkin-ul-Wujũd (Contingent Existence). Mumtani-ul-Wujũd (Negative Existence) is like the fabulous bird 'Unqã which has a name, but no existence. In Ahdiyyat again, the *i'tibãrãt* are suppressed: in Wahdat, they are in evidence, and in Wãhidiyyat, they become manifest and show themselves as sifãt. These three form the stage of La Bi Shart-i-Shay. In the soul-world, the i'tabãr of knowledge becomes the knowledge of sifãt. When His knowledge is that He is active, the *ism* becomes 'Aql-i-kul; when knowledge is that He is passive, the *ism* becomes Nafs-i-kul. When the *Dhãt* finds itself immanent everywhere in the seen world, the *ism* becomes Tabiyat-i-kul; when it finds itself manifested everywhere, it is Shakl-i-kul; and when it finds itself as thingness of things (*Ding an sick* of the Germans), it becomes Jism-i-kul and so on in the soul and *mithãl* worlds. These two latter worlds form the stage of Bi Shart-i-La Shay, The four i'tibãrãt in Wahdat and the seven sifãt in Wũhdiyat have no opposites; they are personal. The seven asmã' in the soul and mithãl worlds have no opposites. After Al-'Arsh, materiality begins (Bi Shart-i-Shay) and asmã' appear in opposite, *e.g,* Hãdi (one leading might) as opposed to Mudhil (one leading astray); Muhiyy (the quickener) as opposed to Mumit (the Killer). The Qur'ãn says, *Khalaqallahu saaba samawatin thumma stawa alal arsh*[1] "God created the seven heavens and took his stand on the 'Arsh," *i.e.,* after Al-'Arsh His opposite and contrary asmā' (Jalāli and Jamāli) make their manifestation; and variety and diversity begin the world. These manifestations of names in the material world culminate in Insān-ul-Kāmil. Just as the name God 'is conglomerate of all asmā'-i-ilāhi, the name Insān is conglomerate of all asmā'-i-kiyāni. Man is thus 'abd, the opposite of rabb, and appears at the lowest point in the arc of Tanazzulāt, opposite the name Allāh, which is at the highest point. He is composite of both Jalāli (glorious) and Jamāli (beautiful) names; for God made man with both His hands. He is a manifestation of all names that come under this category. In fact everything is a Mazhar-i-Atamm, that is, it contains all asmā' in itself,

Agar yak qatra ra dil bar shigafi
Burun ayad azu sad bahr-i-safi

(Gulshan-i-Raz)

If you cleave the heart of one drop of water.
A hundred pure oceans emerge from it.

but it has the potentiality of manifesting one *ism* or a few asmā' while man has the potentiality of manifesting all the known asmā'. The form of the Prophet (peace be upon him) in God's knowledge is that of the *ism* Hādi (one who rightly guides); but in manifestation, the name sometimes assumes the aspect of Mudil. The Qur'ān has been the same from the very first; not a jot or title of it has changed; yet there are as many as 72 sects (and innumerable sub-sects) in Islam brought about by its interpretations. One interpretation alone can be true and the rest false. The form of the Prophet in 'ālam-i-arwāh is that of the name hādi; but in the causal world, his teaching has been misappreciated by some people; and to these latter, he stands in the name of Mudil. Each man's

---

1 Sūra xvii ; 54 ; x : 3.

form in the mithāl world is that of hādi, and he must work up to that name; but owing to different influences of the world, he becomes the manifestation of Mudil, which is the dross that is to be burnt up, for the alloyed gold to become pure. "Thus was man created in the best form and sent down to the worst plane"—*Khalaqul-insāna fi ahsani taqwim thumma radadnahu asfala safilin.*[1] Iblis also is a part manifestation of the name Insān-ul-kamil in the material world. He is a form of the name Mudil (one leading astray) in the Spiritual World.

Khalaqar-Rahmānu ala sūralihi, "God made man in His own image." God has the attributes of Living, Knowing, Powerful, Willing, Hearing, Seeing, and Speaking; so also Man has these attributes, but in limitation. God is *Dhãt* unlimited; man is *Dhãt* limited. God has Sifāt and asmā; all known to Himself, man has knowledge of some sifāt and asmā'; for there are sifāt and asmā' of His, which are known only to Himself and to no created being. God is eternal by Himself, man is eternal so far as God's knowledge is concerned; and God's knowledge is eternal. Thus man is an image of God; but not in the sense, in which a clay-idol is a model of a real person. Kabir Dās has put this idea in his own blunt way:

Har ko kya puchhat ho,
Kaya bataun har kaysa hai
Kaya khunti say bandhun bhainsa hai
Ya hath men de dun paisa hai
Tu jaysa hai har waisa hai

What do you ask about God ?
How can I show what He is like.
Is It a buffalo to be tied to a peg,
Or a coin to be passed over to you ?
He is like what you are

---

1 Sūra xiv I,

Three persons are said to have been interrogated by Imām Jāfar-i-Sādiq regarding God. One said, "I worship a God, who possesses all the attributes." The Imām said he worshipped a man-god or an idol; since eating, drinking, dying are all the attributes of a created being. These are the pantheists. Another said he worshipped a God who had no attributes. The Imām said he worshipped a nothingness (Philosophical nihilism like that of Buddha). And the third said he worshipped a God who had the attributes of perfection, and was devoid of the attributes of imperfection and decay, which are attributes in limitation that are manifest from the side of *Ādam.* The Imām said, he worshipped the true God of the heaven and the earth.

The word Insān is variously derived—some derive it from *uns,* love; some derive it from *nas* forgetfulness, because life on earth begins in forgetfulness and ends in forgetfulness. Some say the word comes from *'ayn san,* "Like the eye." Man is the eye with which God beholds His sifāt and asmā' in limitation; Insān-ul-Kāmil is thus the mirror in which God's sifāt and asmā' are fully reflected. *Gulshan-i-Rāz* says:

Adam ayina alam aks wa insan
Chu chashm-i-aks dar way shakhs pinhan
Tu chashm-i-aks-i-wa wa nur-i-did ast
Bi dida dida-i-ra dida did ast

Not being is the mirror, the world the reflection and man
Is as the reflected eye of the Unseen Person
You are that reflected eye and He the light of the eye,
In that eye His eye sees His own eye.

To Insān-ul-Kāmil, God is not a screen from His creation, and creation is not a screen from the Creator. He becomes equipoised in both directions. *(Māsāwiy-ut-tarfayn).* He is one who has performed his sulūk (pilgrimage) *in* God (Sayr-fillah) and *with* God (Sayr)-ma Allāh), and reached the point of

Haqiqat-i-Muhammadi, which is *Qaba-Qawsayn awa adna,*[1] the point at which the two arches of the bow meet and still nearer than that." He becomes the axis around which the whole existence turns and sheds light on the heart of other created beings. In fact, he is the direct pattern of Haqiqat-i-Muhammadi and the rest of mankind are indirect patterns or copies of his individuality. This is what Shaykh Ibn 'Arabi calls "the wisdom of individuality" in his chapter on Fus-i-Muhammadi. Creation began with Muhammad (peace be upon him) *i.e.,* with Haqiqat-i-Muhammadi; and the wisdom of existence completely manifested itself in his individuality. "I was a Nabi" he said, "when Ādam was yet between water and mud." *Ana nabiy-yun wa Adamu baynul mai wat-tin, i.e ,* I was Nabi, while Ādam was yet in the knowledge of God, and had not taken his earthly form.

The name God is also conglomerate of the names, Awwal (the First), Bātin (the internal), Zāhir (the external), and Ākhir (the last). To the first name, corresponds the world of a'yān-i-thābitah (or the soul world—names 1 to 4); to the second, alam-i-mithāl (names 5 to 7), to the third, 'ālam-i-shahādat (the causal world—the rest of the 21 names), and to the fourth, 'ālam-i-ākhirat (the future world) (names partly revealed and partly not revealed). Thus the name *'abd* is a conglomerate of all these asmā'; it comprises all the asmā'-i-kiyāni, which is *Dhāt* with attributes in limitation, just as God comprises all the asmā'-i-ilāhi which is *Dhāt* with infinite and unlimited attributes. *'Abd* does not merely mean a servant, it conveys the idea that it comprises all the asmā' acted upon, subservient (murbub), in opposition to all the asmā' that act and that are masters (rabb).

The perfect *'abd* could not fully and completely manifest himself in all his perfections all at once, as the world was not

1 Sūra liii. 9.

prepared to receive him; and so each item of his perfection manifested itself from time to time according to the requirements of the world. The Mathnawi puts the idea thus:

> *Nam-i-Ahmad nam-i-jumla anbiyast*
> *Chun ki sad amad nawad ham peishi mast*
>
> The names Ahmad is conglomerate of the names
> of all Prophet is
> When you have one hundred, ninety also in with you.

Hence the Qur'ān says: "Do not differentiate between any of God's Prophets" *(La nufarriqu bayna ahadin min rusulihi).*[1] The perfect '*abd* appeared in the fullness of time in "the Seal of the Prophets." The line of Prophets here ends; but the line of Walis, the interior aspect of Prophetship still continues. Sri Krishnā is reported to have said:

> *Chu ahwali dunya bi gardad khasai*
> *Numayim khud ra bi shakli kasai*
>
> When the affairs of the world get rotten
> I show myself in the form of somebody.

A wali ascends to the highest point of the arc, and loses himself; so whatever emanates from him is the work of God. He becomes the instrument of God (Qurb-i-Farāyid); a Prophet descends (in his Satar-ma-Alla) after reaching the very same point, with Divine attributes, to the lowest point of the arc for the benefit of humanity; and God becomes his instrument (Qurb-i-Nawāfil). A Prophet has to coordinate and harmonize the affairs of the world. *Ya Dandu inna ja'alnaka khalifatan fil-ardi fahkum bainun-nāsi bil haqqi wa lā tattabi' ul-hawa.*"[2] "O David, We have made thee our vicegerent on the earth, so that you rule over the people with justice."

---

1. Sūrạ ii. 275
2. Sūra xxviii 26.

The *ism* Zāhir requires diversity of asmā'. When the asmā'. are manifest, they become a'yān-i-khārija (the manifest a'yān); and there is conflict of interest among them. The rabb is satisfied and pleased with its own murbūb. The *ism* hādi (one who guides aright) is pleased with its own *murbūb*—those rightly guided, *i.e.,* those who say their prayers, the charitable, the kind, etc. And the rabb-i-mudil (one who leads astray) is pleased with its own *murbūb*—the profligate, the cruel, etc. Hence Jesus Christ's prayer to the Lord: "Lead us not into temptation but deliver us from evil." (Luke II—*4), i.e..* God in His name Mudil leads us astray, and in His name Hādi guides us into the right path. The Qur'ān says; *Mā min dābbatin illā hua akhizun bi nāsiyatha inna rabbi 'ala sirātin mustaqim.*[1] "Of the creatures that creep on the earth, the forelock of each one of them, is in the hand of its rabb and that rabb is on the right path." This is like each member of the Parliament thinking himself on the right path, or each party of the Parliament indulging in its own justification. To keep these jarring elements, in order, a speaker is required. And so to keep the jarring and antagonistic asmā,' in order, a manifestation of the name Hādi is required; and this manifestation is a Prophet who distributes justice according to everyone's due and according to everyone's *'ayn.* One lakh and forty-four thousand Prophets, and more, have appeared, till the full manifestation of Haqiqat-i-Muhammadi appeared in 'Muhammad (peace be upon him). Whatever is manifest in the world is immanent *(mundarij)* is Haqiqat-i-Muhammadi ; and the latter is immanent in the Absolute God *(Dhāt-i-Mutlaq).* Hence there is no "and" in the Muslim Kalima which says "there is no Allāh, but God, Muhammad is the Prophet of God" ; although the two parts of the Kalima are taken out of different places in the Qur'ān.

---

1. Sūra xi 56.

PHYSICAL ASPECT

The Physical world is the manifestation of the name—Az-Zāhir. Just as the soul-world and the *mithāl*-world as found in man, the Physical Universe is also found in him in miniature. The twenty names from Al-'Arsh, (the Throne or Empyrean) to Insan (man) are found in him thus,

8. Kursi (the seat)—Primum Mobile—Skull.
9. Crystalline Sphere (Firmament of no stars)—Membrane in the skull.
10. Zodiacs—(Firmament of fixed stars)—vide 'X' below
11. Sature—Spleen.
12. Jupiter—Liver.
13. Mars—Kidneys.
14. The Sun—The black spots in the heart.
15. Venus—Gall-bladder.
16. Mercury—the brain.
17. The moon—Lungs.
18 Sphere of Fire—Bile.
19. Water—Phlegm.
20. Sphere of Air—Blood.
21. Sphere of Earth—Black Bile.
22. Minerals—The Teeth.
23. Vegetables—Hairs and nails.
24. Animal—Lust.
25. Angels—Good Khatras (or affections of the mind)
26. Jin—Suspicions of the mind.
27. Man—The mind.
28. The Perfect Man—the conglomerate of all above.

(X) the Zodiacs are represented thus in the body:

1. Head—Ram (Aries).
2. Neck—Bull (Taurus).

3. Hands—Twins (Gemini).
4. Nipples—Cancer.
5. Breast—Lion (Leo).
6. Heart—Ear of Corn (Virgo).
7. Navel—Balance (Libra).
8. The private part—the Scorpion.
9. Thighs—arches (Sagittarius).
10. Buttocks—He-goat (Capricorn).
11. Legs—Watering-Pot (Aquarius).
12. Soles—Fishes (Pisces).

The twelve gate-ways in the human body also represent the twelve constellations of the Zodiacs In man, there are said to be 360 bones, which represent mountains; 360 arteries and veins which represent rivers and streams. The stomach is the ocean replete with reptiles. Hairs on the skin are the trees; the teeth are carnivora ; birds represent Spirituality. Face is the populated area; and back, the barren land. Infancy is spring; youth, summer; old age, winter; dotage, autumn. Health and wealth—represent Paradise; poverty, hell. The tongue represents Gabriel; and nose, Isrāfil; body, Michāil; ears, Izrāil. Insān (man was from eternity in the original knowledge of God, and he is there, even now as he then was (*Al-ana kama kana);* and he will be there forever; for God's knowledge is eternal; and a hiatus in it is unthinkable, which will be the case if he disappears from there. Death in his case is merely disappearing from the *ism* Az-Zāhir, into the *ism* Al-Bātin. Sleep and forgetfulness are reversion to the first stage of Ahadiyyat, in which the *Dhāt* was self-absorbed. God, one of whose names is Al-Ghani (the independent) created man by His wish, *i.e.*, will. The same wish appeared in man in the shape of Helplessness, Fear and Sorrow. God thus is all powerful; and man, all powerless; the one has the consciousness of fulness and the other of emptiness.

SYMBOLICAL ASPECT

Once Hadrat 'Ali was delivering a sermon, and was so absorbed in himself that he gave out *Ana nuqiu bai Bismillah; anā Qalamun wa anā Lawhun mahfuzun, ana 'Arshun wa anā Kursiyun wa anā Samawāt* (I am the point of *ba* of Bismillah, I am the Pen, I am the Preserved Tablet, I am 'Arsh, etc.) Now that the *Dhāt* is undefinable; its definition like that of the Euclidian point is negative. It is more possible to say what it is not than what it is. When the *Dhāt* threw out its shadow, it became cognizable. *Alam tara ila rabbika kayfa maddaz-zilla.*[1] "Do you not see how your rabb has lengthened His shadow?" When this point lengthened itself into seven points, it became cognizant of itself. Arabic calligraphists make an *alif,* of the length of seven points. When these seven points appeared, Ahdiyyat became Wāhidiyyat. These are the seven sifāt, 'Ilm, Nūr Wujūd, Shuhūd, Samā, Basar, Kalam (Knowledge, Light, Existence, Observance, Hearing, Sight and Speech). With the appearance of these sifāt, and with still further devolution, Wājib-ul-Wujūd (Necessary Existence) became Mumkin-ul-Wujūd (Contingent Existence). The *alif* tilted from perpendicularity to borizontality, and became *bay* which is really an *alif* with a dot below. Now this *alif* is found in all the twenty-eight letters of the Arabic Alphabet, either straight or curved, *i.e.,* the Necessary Existence pervades all forms of existence in the manifest and unmanifest worlds.

The word "Allāh" in Arabic is really Al-Ilah (abridged by usage into Allāh) composed of four perpendicular lines (*alifs)* and a line, which is a part of *ha* and a half circle which is a part of the same letter. The mineral world consists of lines—one stright *alif* (the trunk) with some horizontal *alifs* as branches, and a root below *(ha)*

---

1 Qur'ān, xxv : 45.

Her giya hi ki az zamin ruyad
Wahdahu lā sharika lah guyad
Every blade of grass that sprouts out
Proclaims 'He is one without a partner.'

A bird consists of one horizrontal *alif* (the body) with two *three* below (legs), and two above (wings) and a hay (head) in a horizontal position. A quadruped, consists of one *alif* horizontal (body), four *alifs* below *(legs)* and a hay (head) in horizontal position. In man, the body forms one *alif,* hands and legs form four *alifs* and the *hay* the head. Here the tree gets bodily upside down, the root is thrown up in the air, and the branches are planted on the ground. The name Allāh is found inscribed on the face of man; the first *alif* begins from top of one ear and goes downwards; the four *alifs* are, two on each cheek and two beside the nose, on each side, the *ha* is the other ear, *vide* diagram No. 1 (p. 77). The Hand of the man with its four fingers and a thumb form the same name and the body of man is modelled after the Arabic name Al-Ilah. When a wild beast stares a man in the face, it is overcome with fear, owing to the delineation of this word on his face. Similarly, the name Muhammad (peace he upon him) is delineated on the face of man, *vide* dragram No. 2 (p. 77) and also on each perpendicular half of his body. The head forms the *mim,* the hand *ha,* the waist and the thigh another *mim* and the foot, *dāl.* Devout Muslims wish to be laid in their death-bed in such a posture that half or upper side of their body (in horizontal position) gives rise to a curvature which forms the delineation of the letters of the word, Muhammad in Arabic, *i.e.,* they wish to lie in Barzakh-i-Muhammadi or the Barzakh of Insān ul-Kāmil.[1]

---

1. Vide *Risāla-i-lsm-i-Dhāt* (unpublished) by Hadrat Makhdūm ibn Abdul Nabi Savi; and *Tajalliyāt-i-Rahmāni* by Saiyid'Ali Muhammad Husayni, pp. 144-145,

DIAG. No. 1.

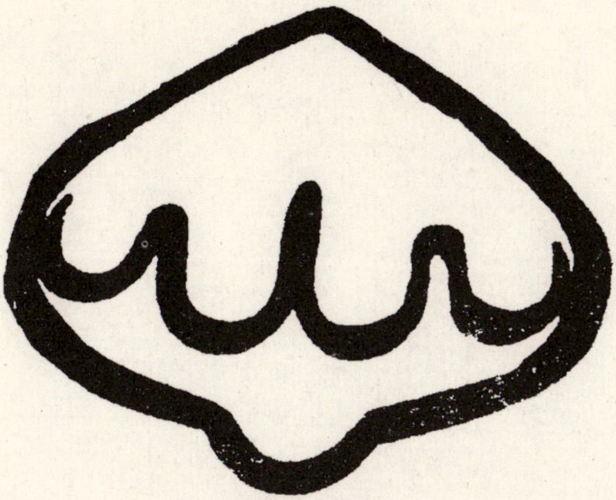

DIAG. No. 2.

Chapter VII

FANĀ AND BAQĀ

Fanā in its literal sense is the state of a *shay* (thing), that does not last, *i.e.,* when permanence of the state comes to an end, it is said to have attained Fanā. The world will attain the state of Fanā; and the Futurity will remain .in Bāqā *(Wal akiralu khiarun wa abqa).* Fanā is not considered to be an attribute; it is not like a dissolution, as of sugar in water. The author of "Kashful-Mahjūb"[1] thinks that it is not the disappearance of essence. Baqā is that which was not, and became; and will not subsequently become Fanā, like heaven and hell. It is also that which was not non-existent before, and will not be non-existent afterwards like the Essence of God. The Muṭakallimin (the Muslim Scholastic Theologians) consider that Fana is the process of thc becoming *nought* of the attributes of a *shay;* and Baqā is the everlastingness of the same attributes. With the Sūfi, Fanā is the non-cognizance of one's attributes as one's own; and Baqā, is the recognition of the same as the attribute of God. In Fanā, the *'abd* has no consciousness of his self, *i.e.,* his self does not exist for him; but he is conscious "only of the manifester, the manifested and the manifestation." So long as you are present in your own sight. God disappears, and when He is present in your sight, you disappear. Take an example, when you are concentrated on words, you lose sight of ink, and when you are concentrated on ink, you lose sight of words. Shāh Kamāl, a Sūfi poet of Gurrumkondah in

1 P. 262.

Cuddapah has said:

Dhãt-o-sifãt mere Dhãt-o-sifãt unke
Bande mein aur Khuda mein nisbet isay kayhte hain.

My attributes and my essence are His attributes and His Essence,
This is what forms relationship between *'abd* and God.

In Fanā, the significance of the *possible* disappears in the consciousness of the *'āriff;* the material body of him, of course, does not. Some consider that Fanā is the disappearance of a *shay* in knowledge, and not the actual disappearance of corporeality. Others consider that it is disappearance *in sight.*

Some others, again, consider that it is the disappearance of the "I" ness (Ego) of *'abd* in the "I" ness of God. In Fanā, the 'abd finds these limitations *(tai'yunāt* as the limitation of God and spreads his "Iness" everywhere. In Baqā, he finds everything as his own manifestation. The limited consciousness of *'abd* is lost in the unlimited consciousness of God. In Baqā, the consciousness of God underlies the consciousness of *'abd.* Jalāluddin Rūmi says:

'Ilm-i-Haq dar 'ilm-i-sūfi gum shawad
Aein sakhun kai bawari mardum shawad
'Ilm-i-Haq nuqi ast wa 'ilm-i-sūfi khat
Az wujud nuqt bashad bud-i-kha,

The consciousness of God is lost in the consciousness of sūfi
How can common people believe in this,
Sūfis knowledge is line and God's knowledge, point.
The existence of a line depends on the existence of point.

The Sūfi thus finds his self annihilated; and also himself

without the self everlasting. This is cosmic consciousness, which the Qur'ãn has called Muqām-i Mahmūd (the Praised Station), which is reserved for the Prophet (peace be upon him); and from which he will plead for intercession on the Day of Judgment.

St. Bernard, the mystic of Rhineland, of the 14th century, identified his own thoughts with the mind of God. With the Christian Mystics of Germany, annihilation was not making nought of the reality of *'abd,* but it was making nought of the aspect of humanity in Divinity. It is said that the question of Khilāfat was, in the first instance, determined by the answer given to the question of Fanā, and Baqā.

When it was announced that the Prophet (peace be on him) had departed this life, the people gathered together at Thaqifa Bani Sā'ida, and went up to 'All his cousin and son-in-law (husband of his beloved daughter Fātima), and said: "What is your vision of God?" He said: "I do not see *shay,* but I see only God." *(Ma raylu shayan illa raytullah).* Then they went to 'Othmān, another son-in-law and put the same question to him. He said: "I do not see shay, but I see God after it" *(Ma raytu shayan illa raytullah ha badabu).* Then to 'Umar. He said: "I do not see shay, I see God before it" *(Ma raytu shayan illa raytullah ha qublahu).* Then they went to Abū Bakr, He said: "I do not see shay but I see God along with it" (*Ma raytu shayan illa raytullah ha ma a hu).* Now about the time of the demise of the Prophet, there were 144,000 companions, (according to the article on "Ashāb" in Hughes' "Dictionary of Islam"). The electorate thought that although the "vision of God" of Ali was the most perfect, yet it was too impracticable to steer the ship of the state, and so they elected Abū Bakr, who had both the rabb and *'abd* in view at the same time, to be the first Caliph of Islam,

In Fanā, the essence, attribute and action of *'abd* become the essence, attribute and action of God, and not that those of *'abd* are dissolved like sugar in water, in the essence, attributes and actions of God. The *'abd* has no consciousness of "Other than God" (masiwālla). God becomes actor, and *'abd* becomes His instrumentality (Qurb-i-Farā'yid). Jalāluddin Rūmi has expressed this in the form of an allegory:

Nuh guft ay sar kashan man man nayam
Man zi jan mardum zi janna mi ziyann
Chun bi murdam az hawas-i-bul bashar
Haq mara shud sam-o-idrak-o-basar
Chun ki man man nis lam, aein dam zi oust
Peish i aein dam har ki dam zad kaffir oust

Said Noah to his nation, "I am not I"
I am not. It is God that lives.
When the "I" ness disappears from the sense of man,
It is God that talks, hears and understands
When the "I" is not I, the "I" is the breath of God
It is a sin to assert one's "I" with Him.

The reverse process in which 'abd becomes actor; and God his instrumentality is called Qurb-i-Nawāfil *(wabi yasmau wa bi yabsuru)*—Through Me, he hears and through Me, he sees. Those who see the world in evidence, and the Truth hidden are called the men of reason *(zawil-'aql)*; and those who see the Truth in evidence and the world hidden are called the men of sight *(Zawilayn).* The Fanā, is said to be of two kinds, the Fanā in essence like ice or hail disappearing in water, and the Fanā in attributes, like iron disappearing in fire, *protem.* In the first instance, the *'ābd* becomes Him *(Hu-Hu);* in the second, he becomes like Him *(Ka anna hu-hu).* The first Fanā, which is in *Dhāt* is the privilege of the Prophet (peace be on him), and none else; since the Reality of Muhammad was the first cognition of,God as Himself. This is not the name of a mere state of consciousness.

Bāyazid-Bistāmi has said that everybody has his state (*hāl).* Hāl is the result of thought—the Perfect man is not subject to thought, he has the reality of illumination; his mind's eye (oculus cordis as the Latin mystics called it) is opened, and he is illumined; and Baqā is not therefore the mere result of ecstacy *(wajd).* Fanā is attained in various ways. In the first instance, there is the attraction from God. The Qur'ãn says that "An attraction from God is equal in effect to the virtues practised in both the worlds *(jaz batun min jazbat ilahi mutawazi min amalith thaqalayn.*[1] A Hadith says: "There is a time for me with God, in which neither the nearest angels, nor the sent prophets can be contained *("Li mallahu waktum la yas ani fi hil malikkil muqarabun wa la nabiyyil mursalun.* The term Fanā was made use of to express the sense of the result of attraction and absorption by Abū Sa'id Ahrār. In the second instance, it is realised by the observance of *ahkām-i-Shari 'at* (the Ordinances of *Shari 'at*), an account of the spiritual significance of which, will be given in the Chapter on the "Five Pillars of Islam". The esotericism of the *Shari 'at* is the establishment of connexion between rabb and *'abd.* The exotericism of the same—is the maintenance and practice of certain bodily actions, *(i.e.,)* certain bodily actions must be performed to keep up this connexion. Loyalty to the King is the Summun bonum of life, corporal life of an individual or the corporate life of a community. When once loyalty is established, it must be kept up. Otherwise, with disuse, it might lose its strength and vitality. Use and disuse have played a most important part in the formation of the organised world. By the process of use and disuse, Charles Darwin thought, new species evolved and old species disappeared. Similarly use and disuse play an important part in preserving, strengthening, and perfecting a feeling. The sense of oneness with God can be maintained by the performance of certain acts. These

---

1 Qūr'ãn, xxii : 46.

acts are the ordinances of Islam, which are compulsory on all Muslims. The acts can never be dispensed with, seeing that human nature is what it is. Adepts have, however, devised short-cuts to the attainment of a knowledge of God. There are as many ways to God, as there are souls of men *(Al-turqu ilallahi ka nufus 'i-bani adama.)*

Excepting the*Āzad-mashrab*-Sūfis who have discarded outward demonstration, all are agreed in keeping up the law and the Prophets. A Pir-i-Kāmil is therefore one who strictly observes the outward law, while, he adopts his own short method. This method consists in what is called sulūk (pilgrimage). The course on the downward arc is the Tanazulāt-i-sitta (the six downward stages) *vide* the "theory of emanation." It is the Journey of God towards *'abd,* the journey of the ocean towards the drop. The course of the *'abd* in the corresponding upward arc is his own sulūk, it is the journey of 'abd towards God; the journey of the drop towards the ocean ; it consists of four stages according to Shaykh 'Abdul Karim al-Jili.

1st Safar-ullah[1]—This journey of *'abd* towards knowledge journey from sinfulness towards submission to ceremonial institutions.

Second Safar-ilallah.—Journey from neglectfulness towards the repetitions of God's name or of the *ism* of which the *'abd* is a manifestation (according to Kaisari).

Third Safar-fillah, i e., journey back on the lines of God's names and attributes.

Fourth Safar-billah.—When the sālik (pilgrim) reaches the summit, he comes down again to the lowest point with the attributes of God for the reformation and enlightenment of the world. 'Gulshan-i-Rāz" says:

---

1. *Jawāhir-us-Sulūk, P.* 10.

Kasi mardi-tamam asi az tawammi
Kounad ba khwaja ji karey ghulami,
He is the perfect man who with his perfection,
And in spite of his mastery, does the work of a slave.

In the *safar-ilallah,* the *'abd* attains Fanā, and in the *safar-fulah,* he attains Baqā. In the first, he merges into the *ism,* of which he is a Manifestation. In the second, he obtains permanence (permanent hold) in that *ism.* The Prophet, however, reverted to the shan from which he was directly manifest.

In *safar-ilallah,* the sālik is still in limitation, *i.e.,* he is still a salik, only that he has acknowledged that there is no existence save that of God. In *safar-fillah,* the mysteries of Nature clear off before him, he becomes majdhūb (the attracted). Fanā is the termination of *safar-ilallah;* and Baqā is the commencement of *safar-fillah.* With the sect of Shuttaris, the sālik descends, of himself, in his own knowledge—there is no annihilation of self with them. *Faqr* is another word for Fanā. The Prophet has said; *'Faqr* is my pride, and it is from me *(Al-Faqr-u-faqri walf aqru minni).* He also said that *faqr* is the blackening of the face in both the worlds *(Al-faqru swadul wajh fid darain), i.e.,* when the face is blackened, it disappears. A *faqir is* therefore synonymous with *fani* (one who has attained Fanā). Some, however, omit the first *safar;* Kaisari in his commentary on Fusūs-ul-Hikam (Fasi-Adami) refers only to the last three stages, of which the first two are in the ascending scale; and the last, in the descending.

In performing these journeys, some sāliks have sudden elevation and transport, like in the case of Jacob Behmen, the Cobbler-mystic of Gorlitz in Germany; and St. Paul who suddenly got into a state of ecstacy. The mysticism of the Middle Ages was united with the dialectics *(Kalām)* of the Schoolmen, by Hugo of the School of St. Victor in Paris; as the Sūfism of Islam was united with 'Ilm-i-Kalām by the Imām Hujjatul-Islam (Ghazzāli). Hugo made a three-fold division of human faculties, *cogitatio* (Mujāhada) *Meditatio* (Murāqaba) and *contemplatio* (Mushahada). In his loftiest elevation, man beholds all things in God. Richard of the School of St. Victor had six stages of contemplation, two visible, two invisible, and two divine. The Sūfi has four stages in his upward course. First, he observes that all objects are the manifestion of God's names and attributes. These are the multitudinous objects in which He is reflected. Here he performs a *jihād* against his *Nafs,* which considers objects as having independent existence—this is mujāhada. Then he observes that the world, as a whole, is a mirror and manifestation of God's names and attributes. This is mukāshafa. Then he sees that his own knowledge surrounds all things. He is thus the mirror in which the world is reflected. Before, the non-ego was the mirror; now his own ego is the mirror. This is murāqaba. Then be removes all objects including his self (*i.e.,* both ego and non-ego) from view as non-existent and finds the seer and perceiver is God Himself. This is mashāhada. *Kullu man alaiha fan wa yabqa wujhu rabba ka zul jalali wal ikram.* (All objects are to be annihilated; and there will remain the face of the Lord thy God—-with His glory and beauty). Maulānā Rūmi has put the same idea in a terse manner:

Gar tu bar khizi zi ma wu man dami
Har du alam pur zi khud bini hami
Aein ta'ayyun shud hijabi ru-i-dost
Chun ki bar khizad ta'ayyun jumla ust.

If, for a while, you rise higher than I and Thou,
You will find both the worlds full of yourself
This ta'ayyun is the veil on the face of thy friend,
When the ta'ayyun disappears all is Him.

The doctrine of 'Hama-oust' is not therefore that all things taken together are God—as the pantheists affirm; but it is the disappearance of all ta'ayyunāt in the knowledge or sight or both of the *Salik;* in whose view, the worlds are limitation of appearances—and the reality is the essence of God.

In this, the final stage, the *'abd* may be said to be re-incarnated. He has died to himself, and lives in the life of God. There is no re-incarnation with the Sūfi, in the sense of God taking on flesh and appearing among mankind for their reformation, like in the case of Sri Krishna, who is reported to have said:

Chu ahwāl-i-dunyā bi gardad khasay
Numāyim khud ra hi shakli kasay.

When the affairs of the world become rotten,
I shew myself in the semblance of somebody.

Here, it is the sālik that transforms himself mentally, morally and spiritually into another character; so much so, that his essence, attributes and action become the essence, attributes, and actions of God.[1] He "is born again, not of corruptible seed, but of uncorruptible, by the word of God, which liveth and abideth for ever." *Gulshan-i-Rāz* says : (lines 348-49).

Baqa-i-yabad wu bad az fana baz
Rawad anjami wu digar hi aghas
Shariat ra shaari khish sazad
Tariqat ra wi sari khish sazad.

He finds life after dying to self and again
He runs another course, from his end to his beginning.
He makes the law his upper garment
But know very truth is the station of his nature.

In the journeys on the upward arc, (safar-il-allah and safar-fillah). God is the mirror of sālik. The mirror, in the intensification

1. I Peter. chap. 1-23.

of gazing, vanishes from view *(i.e.)* gets hidden; and the sālik sees his self, and works up his way. In the subsequent downward journey (safar-billah) from Wahdat to the stage of man, the sālik becomes the mirror and vanishes, and God alone remains. In safar-fillah, the attributes of sālik disappear, and the attributes *(ergo,* asmā') of God alone remain; the sālik works himself up in the attributes of God; the sifāt of *'abd* are the sifit of God in limitation:

> *Sūfi na shawad safi ta dar na kashad jami*
> *Bisyar safar bayad ta pukhta shawad kami*
>
> Sūfi does not become pure till he has drunk of the cup
> Much journeying is required for the unripe one to become ripe.

God has of His own accord, as it were, become accustomed to such limitations, and finds it against His will to throw them off. The sālik endeavours to throw off these limitations, and become absolute. The limitations cover God's absolutism, who estranges Himself from Himself. In this stage, the sālik retains only the most absolutely necessary *fard* and *sunnat* and discards even benevolences; as Shāh Muhiyyuddin Sāhib of Vellore[1] and, Saiyed Muhammad Makhdūm bin 'Abdul Nabi Savi[2] have remarked.

When the Sālik has accustomed himself to absolutism, he reverts to limitations in this Safar-billah and becomes Musā-wi-ut-tarafain *(i.e.,* equipoised between two extreme distances and forces); to whom creation is no veil from the Creator, and *vice versa;* and to whom necessary existence and possible existence are equal; and who has by the aid of Fikr, discovered the Hadrat-i-Khamsa, and their details in his individuality, and become the perfect man. This is the stage in which auliyā' and Prophets take their stand.

When the sālik after mujāhada, enters upon the stage of

---

1 Jawāhir-us-Suluk, p. 141.

2 Risāla-i-Hayāt-i-Jan (unpublished).

mukāshafa, he meets with photisms, epiphanies or *tajalliyyāt.* A tajalli means a disclosure, an opening out of certain mysteries. It is the manifestation of *Dhāt* without the instrumentality of Shuyūnāt, asmā', attributes and hypostases. The first is the sphere of colours; these are Satanic, *i.e.,* that in which the Sālik's nafs predominates. Mr. Meyer calls them hypnagogic and hypnopomic illusions. These are vivid illusions of sight or sound, "faces in the dark," etc. They may be remnants of the impressions of light on the retina in one or more of its seven primary colours, after the eyes are closed, or the impressions of a dawning light, when sleep is departing; or they may be the work -of an imagining brain—True photisms are, however, reflections from *Ālam-i-mithāl* (Veridical thought-world, which is a world of colours). The last sphere is a colourless region, or as the Qur'ān puts it, "With God, there is no morning or evening," *(Ma indillahi subh-un wa la masa un).* Abū Sa'id Abul-Khayr (ob. 1049 A.D.) has divided Illuminations into three kinds. First *burūq.* These are flashes of lightning (forked lightning) which leave appearances of stars behind. Then *Lāwamih* which may be compared to sheet-lightning; it is like the light of the Sun falling on the surface of transparent water. The third is Lawayah; it is compared to a shining lamp (*sirājan muniran).* The sulūk of the Patriarch Abraham is borne out by the Qur'ān *(Sūrā An 'am, Rukū 9).* The story that Abraham was brought up in a cavern; and at the end of three years brought out of it, is only an idea of the commentators; and similarly no more importance is to be attached to the story, that he made the remarks in his sixteenth or fortieth year as maintained by Maimonides and R. Abraham Zucuc;[1] or that he made them by way of argument to convince the idolators amongst whom he lived, as observed by Muslim commentators. The fact is that the remarks refer to the sulūk of the Patriarch. When he progressed in his sulūk, he saw a star in the dark recesses of his heart; and said: "This is ray Lord,". *(Haza rabbi)*;[1] and when

1 See *Sale's Note* on Sūra A'nām.

it set, he said: "I do not like that which sets." *(Lā yuhibb-ul-āfilin).* He saw the Moon rising and setting; and so also the Sun rising and setting, and made the same remarks. His conclusion was: "I turn my face towards the Lord who created the heaven and the earth; I am a unitarian and not a mushrik," *Inni wajjahtu wujhiya lil-lazi fataras samawāti wal ard hanifan wa ma anā min-al-mushri-kin*).

Shaykh Ahmad, the Mujaddid of the 11th century has, according to the progress of his sālik in the upward course, seen different colours at different stages. He, a Naqsbandi mystic, is the discoverer of six positions in the part of man's body between the neck and the navel, which he has called the six subtitles *(Latāyif-i-Sitta),* one encircling the other, much after the manner of Kundalini of Patanjali. The colour of *qalb* is yellow; of *soul,* red; of *ser,* white; of *khafi,* black; and of *ikfa,* green. It may be noted that these stages are according to the stages given in the doubtful Hadith mentioned in the Ihyā-ul-'Ulūm of Ghazzāli, *viz.,* that in the body of man, there is a lump of flesh; in this lump, there is *qalb* or mind; in mind, reason; in reason, fawad; in fawad, there is khalfi, and in khalfi, there is "I." *Ina ft. jasada ibn adama la muzghatun wa fi muzgatin qalbun. wa fi qalbin aqlun, wa fi aqlun fawad wa fi fawad khafi wafi khafi serrun wa fi serrun ana).* Some say that the colour of *Nafs* is blue, and of *rūh,* ochre. When the nafs entirely disappears, whiteness over shadows. The colour of soul often becomes green, the last stage is colourlessness, "everything disappearing, and leaving the sālik in a state of Fanā, the Transcendental wonder—spoken of, by Tennyson, which the Sūfis call 'Ālam-i-Hayrat. (There is no morning or evening with God, *vide* p. 100 *ante).* The colour of the cloth, specially the head dress, is indicative of the stage of the pilgrim's journey, e.g., if this cloth is of ochre colour, it means that his sulūk has reached the stage of *rūh.*

---

1 *Bahr-ul-Ma'ani* (19th letter on the'Mystery of Kufr' by Saiyed Muhammad Husayni.

Chapter VIII

THE FUTURE STATE OF MAN

In his "Principles of Sociology," Herbert Spencer, one of the deepest thinkers of the modern times, develops the idea, "that it is the dream that has given birth to the idea of a future life in the primitive man. In a dream, the primitive man saw that he had been elsewhere; and so necessarily thought that he had two individualities; one of which left the other, and presently came back; and thus he had double existence like many other things. Somnambulism serves to confirm this interpretation."

Saiyed Amir 'Ali, a Muslim exponent of Islam to the English-speaking public, thinks that "a more careful examination of the facts, however, connected with the infancy of races and tribes, leads us to the conclusion that the conception of a future existence is also the result of the natural development of the human mind."[1] The life after death is considered to be a mere continuation of life on the earth, a sort of Scandinavian Valhalla, in which the battles of life are fought over again, and the warrior drinks out of the skulls of his enemies.

Up to the time of Daniel and Ezekiel, the wandering Israelites of Moses had their punishment meted out to them, only in this earthly life; the idea of Sheol was not well - developed. Gehenna was only a rubbish depot infested with reptiles under the walls of Jerusalem; which was now and then burnt down. Hades, the intermediate stage (Barzakh), found prominence in subsequent

---

1. *The Spirit of Islam.* p. 381.

years; for we are told in the Acts of the Apostles, that Christ descended into hell (Hades). The Aryans had developed the idea of a future life more systematically. The Zoroastrian had his Hurān-i-Behisht, and Chinvat pretu (the Bridge of the Gatherer); and the Jewish Talmud inculcated the severity of punishment in Hell.

Amir 'Ali, therefore, says that the faith of Muhammad was electic.[1]

Gar hameen maktab ast o aein mulla
Kar-i-tiflan tamam khahad shud.

If thus is the school, and this the teacher
It is all over with the children.

He, however, throws a glimmering ray of hope, in as much "the joys and pains are entirely subjective; the description of these being only beautiful imageries."

With the Sūfi, whose mind's eye (ocūlus cardis) is opened, the future life instead being of such stuff as dreams are made of, is the real and tangible world; and life on the earth is a dream; for the Prophet has said *"Al-nasu niyamun fa iza matu intabahu"* (People are asleep, when they die, they awake).

This world is a projection from the next world; and will be reabsorbed into it.

Haq bi jan andar nihano-jan hi dil andar nihan
Ai nihan andar nihan, andar nihan, andar nihan
Aein chunin ramzi ayan khud bi nashan o bi guman
Ay jahan andar, jahan andar, jahan andar jahan ,

The truth is hidden in life, and life is hidden in mind
O "hidden" within "hidden," within "hidden."

---

1 *The Spirit of Islam,* p. 398.

The mystery is plain, itself without sign or symbol
O world, within world, within world, within world.

The Qur'ãn says : "On that day, this earth will be changed into another earth," *Youma tabad-dual ard ghairul ard.*[1] In his Revelations, St. John, the Divine, has said, "And I saw a new heaven and a new earth: for the first heaven and the first earth were passed away, and then there was no more sea."[2] Some refer the above Qur'ãnic verse to the Last Day, but as[3] this Day extends over a period of fifty thousand years, it obviously refers to the period that elapses between death and resurrection, *i.e.,* to the duration of the *mithāl* World.

When the Soūl, (Ruh-i-Jari) travels over the spirit world, leaving Ruh-i-muqim behind in the body, and brings back its reminiscenses of that world, it is a true dream. When it is a mixture of this world and of that, it is a Satanic dream; and when it is a transformation of the thoughts of this world, it is a Naf-sāni dream. Dreams are the precursor of Prophetship. Before the commencement of his mission, which lasted 23years, the Prophet had true or veridical dreams for six months. Hence true dreams are considered to be a one-forty sixth part of Prophetship. The Prophet's dreams were as clear as daylight; what he saw therein actually came to pass. Some dreams are such that an interpretation (*tāwil)* has to be put on them, *e. g.,* the Patriarch Joseph dreaming that eleven stars and the Sun and the Mọon bowed in worship to him. Some dreams go by their contraries, as the dreams of the Pharaoh's butler, in which he carried a basket of bread pecked by the crows.

Like Amir 'Ali, the late Sir Saiyed Ahmad Khān too believed in dreams having only a physical basis. "Yes it is said," he says,

---

1. Sūra xiv:49. 2. Rev. 21. 3. Sūra Ixx : 4.

"after some discipline *(Sulūk)* and pious life and *Mujāhada,* veils are lifted up; and the realities of nafs and Malā-i-A'lā' dawns upon the mind; but how do we know that whatever dawns on the mind is a reality and not the very thoughts of the man taking a similitude like thoughts in wakefulness. To us no other faculties are known than the nafs in man". He does not believe in 'ālam-i-*mithāl.* The king of Egypt had an idea based on the calculation of floods in the Nile, that there would be famine in the land; and this idea took the shape of the seven lean kine, in his dream."[1] How the mere material vibrations in the brain-centres could generate an idea is yet an unsolved mystery with the psychologist ; and it is still a greater mystery how a future event could set up such vibrations in the organ and produce a set of similitudes, which find their realizations in the future in a different shape. This explanation does not find a response in the general system of Islamic thought.

The future world is not the creation of dream stuff; it is as real as, if not more real than, this world. The investigations of the Society for Psychical Research have considerably changed the angle of vision of scientific men. The Prophet has said, "After me Revelation (wahy) will cease; but not true dreams." (*Inqataal wahyu badi wa la ruya-i-saliha).* In the diagram given in the chapter on the "Theory of Emanation," it has been shown that from Ism-i-Badi to Jawhar-i-Haba is the soul world; and from Jawhar-i-Haba down to the 'Arsh is *mithāl* world; from the 'Arsh down to the Insān-ul-Kāmil (Perfect man) is Causal world. The soul travelling down from Ism-i-Badi (which is also the reality of man—Haqiqat-i-Insāni) reaches Jawhar-i-Haba; and travelling down from Jawhar-i-Haba to the 'Arsh, it takes the colour of 'Ālam-i-*Mithāl*; and travelling further down from the 'Arsh to Insān-ul-Kamil, it takes the colour of the Causal World. When

1 *Tasanif-i-Ahmadiyyah,* Part I, Sūra Yūsufi..

the *Dhāt* dawns on all those, they are all annihilated; and there remains the *Dhāt* absolute (*Kulla man alay ha fan wa yabqa wajhu rabbika zuljalali wal ikram).* The *mithāl* body is a devolution from above, it is not, therefore, the creation of imagination or the child of a dream.

Death is a bridge that joins the beloved with the beloved. *(At mautu jasrun yu sil-ul habiba ilal-habib).* Before the natural death, the Sūfi dies to himself. There is first Maut-i-Aswad (Black death). This is to suffer at the hands of others. Then Maut-i-Ahmar (Red death); it is to work contrary to carnal desires. Then Maut-i-Akhzar (Green death), which is to wear ragged clothes. Fourthly is Maut-i-Abyad (White death), in which one suffers starvation, as that is said to create the light of knowledge in the heart. Sa'di has said.

Andarun az taam khali dar
Ta darun nur-i-marifat bini.

Corporal death is the death of the body, wherein the ego (nafs-i-nātiqa) transfers itself to 'Ālam-i-mithāl.

Jalāluddin Rūmi says:

In khayal aein ja nihan payda athar
Zin khayal an ja huwayda shud suwar.

This thought is hidden here and its effect is obvious,
By this thought, figures are formed there.

Thoughts lead to the formation of character; one's character is the crystallization of his own thoughts. The thoughts and actions of this world take their shape in the next world.

A Hadith says:

"Verily there is a market-place in the Paradise, wherein there is no buying and selling, except of the faces of men and women" *(Inna fil jannati la suqhan ma fina sharran wa baiun illa bi suratin min rijalin wa nisain).*

The author of Risāla-i-Mursad says that greediness takes shape as a rat in the 'ālam-i-barzakh, avarice as a pig, miserliness as a dog, pride as a cheetah, enmity as a serpent, craftiness as a fox, anger as a leopard and so on.

A Hadith says : *Hushirat-un-nasu ala surati ama-lihum* (the resurrection of men will be according to the shapes of their actions). If personality is to survive tendencies, literary and technical, must also survive.

The Shi'ahs and the Sūfi' believe in this. Sūra Wāqiya (Ivi: 60) says, "We have fixed death for you and we are not helpless in changing your attributes and creating those attributes, of which you are not aware *(Nahnu qaddarna bainakum al-mawt wa ma nahnu bemasbuqin ala an tubdila amthalahum wa nunshiukum fi mala talamun).* Such thoughts as one thinks and harbours here, take their shape and await him there. Imām Ghazzāli has the following explanation in his "Kimiyā'-i-Sa'ādat"[1] "When the Nafs separates itself from the body, it bears away with it, the faculty of fancy (Wāhima); and nothing else accompanies him from the life of this world. At death, it is cognizant of separation from the body and from the world. In the grave, the thoughts that he was thinking in the world, take their shape—virtuous thoughts take happy shapes, and wicked thoughts, shapes of calamities according to what he believed in this world. Hence the real grave is this world. The first appear as paradise possessing gardens, and rivers and honey. Hence said the Prophet (peace be upon

---

1 Under the heading, "Knowledge of the Future World" *Note*: The faculties of the *nafs* are four in kind. Retentive faculty (*Hāfiza)* imagination (*Khayal),* thinking faculty (*mutasarrifa).* Fancy *(Wehm).* The centrepetal force that keeps all these together, and the common ground of their meeting is commonsense (*Hiss-i Mushtarak)*; this is the analysis of the mind according to old Psychology ; it need not be here discussed in the light of modern researches. It is, however, the *Wāhima* (Fancy) that accompanies the n*afs* to the other side of the grave.

him) that grave is either a garden in the land of Paradise or a pit from the pits of hell."

The Nafs is the last devolution of the *Tanazzulāt-i-Sitta,* and it goes by four different names, according as it shows itself in four different aspects. The first is Nafs-i-Ammāra (*Sūra xii*:53). This leads man to evil, thus turning him away from the path that leads to perfection. It makes him participate in the attributes of the lower creation; and if he stops short here, he cannot attain that perfection, which a creature endowed with Nafs-i-Rahmāni (Holy Ghost or Spirit) was purposed to attain. Sūfis, like the Shaykh IbnĀrabi and Abū Muhammad Ruzbahan explain that virtuous actions consist in killing this Nafs.

Nafs-i-Lawwāma (Ixxv : 2) is the animus that reproaches a man who goes in evil ways. It is the conscience of the western psychologist. It is like the mirror on which the slightest breath of moisture is visible; it can so far lose its brightness under the influence of Ammāra as to be dead to all susceptibilities to good influences. "When the scale of virtue rises up, this Nafs will be in hell," *(wa amma man khaffat mu-wazinuhu fa ummuhu hawya);* the third is Nafs-i-Mulhima—the *Nafs* that is inspired (Sūra, Sabā : 2).

Wa nafsin wa ma sawwaha
Fal hamaha fujuraha wa taqwaha
Qad aflaha man zakkaha
Wa qad khaba man dassaha.

By Soul and Him who balanced,
And breathed into it wickedness and piety,
Blessed is he who kept it pure
And undone is he who corrupted it.

The fourth is Nafs-i-Mutmainna (Sura Fajr: 27)—the Nafs that has found rest in God. It has been addressed thus "O Nafs which hath found rest in God, turn back to thy Lord. He is pleased with thee; and thou are pleased with him. Mingle with my servants and enter into my paradise."

According to the nature of the predominating faculty, the *Nafs* itself is in heaven or in hell. As a Nafs cannot be wholly good or wholly bad, there are gradations of heaven and hell. Those who purify themselves (as gold from alloy in the heat of furnace) enter the paradise, for which they become fit. The different kinds of heaven and hell are according to the thoughts (which, of course, precede action) that a man had thought and harboured.

The first is Jannat-us-Salam, in which a man's actions take shape, and give him happiness. They take the form of hūrān-i-behisht, and rivers of milk and honey; for he had these in view in doing good actions; or in other words, his thoughts take beautiful shapes; and he enjoys the happiness of possessing Divine knowledge and perfect faith; for milk is a symbol of the former; and faith of the latter.

The second is Jannat-ul-Makasib. It is also called Jannat-us-swar (Jannat of thoughts); to this he attains, when he has had good expectations from his Maker. "I am near the fancy of my creature, let him entertain favourable hope from me *(Ana inda zanni abdi bi, fa yazunna bi ma sha).* A Hadith related by Abū Hurayra says: "Good actions take beautiful shapes, and accompany the departed"[1] *(Al amailu yat-taka ma al mayyiti fil qabri fi ahsani suratin).*

The third is Jannat-ul-Mawāhib; God's name is Wahhāb, the bestower of gifts without consideration—"without value received." This is God's blessings, to which people of every creed and faith will be admitted, for God has said: "My Mercy encircles everything" *(Rahmati wasaat kulla shayin).*[2] His Mercy is not focussed on good works alone of His creatures.

1 Sūra xxx : 8.
2 Chap. lxxxix : 27.

The Fourth—Jannatul-Istihqāq. As its name implies, it is for those who by their actions, by religious discipline, have earned merit, for God's name is 'Ādil (the Just). The Fifth is for those who have obtained gnosis of God, and who annihilated themselves in Him, and who have observed the beauty of His Creation. It is called Jannat-ul-Firdaus. The Sixth is for those who observed in this world the manifestations of His names; and they are admitted to Jannat-ul-Fazilat. These are auliyā (the Saints). The Seventh is Jannat-us-Sifāt—intended for Prophets and great saints; and the last is Jannat-udh-*Dhāt*. It is also called Muqām-i-Mahmūd, in which is the beatific vision or cosmic consciousness reserved for the Prophet alone; from this station he will plead for the "Salvation" of humanity. "In this state, individuality itself seems to dissolve and fade away into boundless being, and thus it is not a confused state, but the clearest, the surest of the surest, utterly beyond words. The loss of personality, as it were, being no extinction but only true life."[1] This is the transcendental wonder *('ālami-i-hayrat)*, to which Alfred Tennyson has referred. In consciousness, a centre appeared; and it became the point of devolution; this centre now dissolves itself, and becomes the entire consciousness, which cannot bear the stain of sin. There are thus eight heavens, the highest is the heaven of *Dhāt,* and the rest are those of asmā'-i-jamāi (Beautiful names). But there are only seven hells which are manifestations of seven of His asmā'-i-jalāli (names of glory). There is no hell corresponding to Jannat-udh-*Dhāt*.[2] for God's names are Rahmān (one who is merciful to all without distinction) and Rahim (merciful towards those who deserve mercy); and not Ghadban and Ghadub (Merciless in general, or Merciless in particular). Mercy and not anger is God's personal attribute (sifāt-i-Dhāti).

---

1. Tennyson quoted in W. Jame's *The Varieties of Religious Experiences. P.* 384.
2. Ibrāhim Gazūr-i-Ilāhi, *Kitāb-ut-Tasawwuf* (unpublished).

God created the light of Muhammad (also called Yaqūt-i-Bayda—the white Chrysolite) by his names (asmā') Badi (the creator) and Qādir (the powerful); and looked at it by the sight of the names of Mannān (the bestower of blessings) and Qahār (the wrathful). That light broke into two; the right hand side became Jannat (heaven) and the left hand side, Dūzakh (hell). His name Qahar brought the hell into existence; the secret of creation of this latter was to manifest His name of Ghāfir (the pardoner).

God's creation of the world is a manifestation of His mercy and not anger; for the world had never sinned before. Hence in His hell, comfort will appear for His Creatures. Shaykh Akbar derives the word *'adhāb* (torment,) from *'azb* (relish); for, from that torment, comfort will come; the fish is for water, and salamander for fire. These cannot change places. They are comfortable in their own elements. It is like scratching-to-bleediness of body to a man who is suffering from itch. Therein he finds his comfort. In hell, the names that are manifest are:

1. Muntaqim (The Avenger). Dūzakh, the manifestation of this name—is for those who have taken away the rights of others and oppressed them.

2. 'Ādil (One who is Just. (Jahim is the manifestation of this name, and is for those who have unjustly taken away the property of others.

3. Shadid (One who is severe). 'Usra, the manifestation, is for misers, the envious, harbourers of revenge; lust-worshippers.

4. Ghadab (One who is wrathfull). Hāwiya is for hypocrites, liars, etc.

5. Mudil (Leading astray). Saqar is for the proud, the haughty.

6. Dhil-Batsh (Hard-compressing). Sair is for the crafty, the apostates.

7. Zul'iqāb (One who torments). Jahannam is the manifestation of this name. It is for *mushriks,* those who join partners with God.

Are heaven and hell local? or are they mere state of existence for the departed souls, created by their own thoughts. This world is a projection of God's thoughts, according to Jili, *khyālun fil khayālin fil khayāl* (thought within thought within thought); but you see it very material; the Intermediate State is a projection of man's thoughts *quo* God's thoughts; and it is material in that sense. The projection or appearances will dissolve leaving the reality as it is.

Dr. Browne in his *Literary History of Persia* (vol. II, p. 498) says: "That he (Shaykh-Muhiyyuddin) believed in the value of dreams, and in man's power to render them veridical by his own. It behaves God's servant to employ will to produce concentration in his dreams, so that he may obtain control over his imagination; and to direct it intelligently in sleep, as he could control it, when awake. And when this concentration has accrued to a man, and becomes natural to him, he discovers fruit thereof in the Intermediate State (Al-Barzakh) and profits thereby : wherefore let man exert himself to acquire this state, for by God's permission it profiteth him greatly." They are therefore conditions as much as the Universe in a condition of Divine thoughts. As a man soweth, so doth he reap. This world is the harvest ground for the next; or as a Hadith puts it: *"Ad-dunyā muzra-tul ākhira."* It may be said that heaven or hell is the personal thought of each man. While it is the result of personal thoughts, it is as expansive as the whole thought itself.[1] "In my Father's house, there are many mansions," said Jesus Christ. A description of the twelve heavens is given in' *Revi. 21-16.* Each man's heaven or hell is, therefore, the result of his own thought, while it is situated in a background and surrounded by an all pervading atmosphere of similar kind.

---

1 St. John, 142

Imām Abū Sa'id Salmi says: The Prophet had a dream, in which he entered into a Paradise, in which was Ramiza, the wife of Abū Talha. He heard the footsteps of somebody, and asked who it was. They said it was Bilāl. He again saw a magnificent palace in the Paradise, wherein a river was flowing, and asked whose it was. They said it was 'Umar's. The Prophet intended to enter, but became shy. When 'Umar heard this, he wept and said: "O Prophet, is there strangeness between you and me." This shows how far the background is common; and how also each creature reaps the fruits of his own actions.[1]

The question arises, whether the dead retain their awareness. The Qur'ān (Āl-i-'Imrān) says: "Do not consider those dead who have sacrificed their lives in the way of God; they are alive and derive their subsistence from God. Surely God does not leave to waste the good works of the faithful," [2] *(Lā tahsabanna al-lazina qutilu fi sabilillahi amwātan bal ahyawun inda rabbihim yurzaqun. In Allaha la yuzia ajral muminin).* After the battle of Badr, the Prophet (peace be upon him) called out to each and everyone of the dead of the non-Muslims by name. So it was understood, that they heard the call. Again the Qur'ān says[3] "You cannot make the dead hear, and the deaf do not hear your call, ' *Innaka lā tusme-ul-mauta wa lā iusmeul summa-ad-du 'ā).* It may be that the spiritually dead and deaf cannot hear; but the comparison clearly implies that the corporeally dead and deaf also do not hear. The conclusion is that an effective voice alone could make itself heard as in the case of the witch of Endor; who had called up Samuel out of his grave, whereas an ordinary voice could not have this effect.[4] Christ also preached to the spirits

---

1 *Shar-i-Barzakh, Chap. 73 under the heading "the Prophet's dreams."*

2 *Sūra Āl-i-Imrān (iii: 169).*

3 *Sūra Rūm (xxx : 52).*

4 *Samuel, chap. 28-12-6.*

in hell or the bottomless pit, mentioned in Revi. Chap. 20.[1] A man of this world engrossed in some affair does not hear the voice of a caller; but when, at leisure, he hears the same. Abū Dina has related a Hadith on the authority of Sa'd bin Jābir that, "When a man dies, his departed relatives come to him and talk to him about the people on the earth." [2]

"The souls of the departed Muminin live in the crops of green birds, which fly about among the green trees of the Paradise" so relates 'Abdulla ibn Mas'ūd. This puts them on a par with the angels, who are able to fly about.

Shāh Walliyullah Sāhib of Delhi (ob. 1176 A.H.) who belonged to the Naqshbandiyyah Order of Sūfis says in his 'Hujjat-ul-Bāligha' that the 'Ālam-i-Mithāl takes any shape it likes. Things take their shape in that world before they appear here. He bases his arguments on the following Hadithes:

(a) Sūra Baqra and Āli- Imrān will appear in the shape of two clouds, between two convoys of birds and will plead for those who had read them.

(b) Good and Evil will take shape, and appear before people. Good will bring glad tidings, and evil will envelope those who had committed it.

(c) The world will appear in the shape of an old woman with rugged hair, blue eyes and a haggard face.

(d) Do you see things which I see? I see showers of mischief done by you, falling in the backyards of your houses.

(e) Heaven and hell took shape before me. I saw them between myself and the Qibla wall, and stretched out my hand to pluck a bunch from heaven, and receded from the heat of hell.

(f) Death will take the shape of a ram on the day of judgment, and will be sacrificed between the heaven and hell.

---

1. St. Peter, 3-19
2. *Shar-i-Barzakh,* chap. 49.

(g) An angel of God appeared in shape before Maryam (Mary).

(h) Gabriel used to appear in a body before the Prophet who talked to him, but the surrounding people could not see him.

(i) The works of the dead appear in a shape before them.

Shāh Sāhib says, "That three courses are left to us to understand these Hadithes. Their literal meaning is to be taken; in which case, we have to confess to the existence of a world which we have spoken about. The great historian and traditionist, Sayūti believes in the veridical existence of this supersensuous world. 'Abdulla ibn Mas'ūd believes in its falsidical existence *(i.e.,)* these things are not externally existent, but appear so to the seer. There is the third school which says that these statements have a different meaning from what is literally attached to them. These are brought in, merely as illustrations." The Shāh Sāhib further says: "that at death, *nafs-i-nātiqa* or the soul does not entirely leave matter." The Nafs sticks to *Nusma;* it is dissolved in the matter of *Nūsma.* This *Nusma is* perhaps the ectoplasm, spoken of by Sir Oliver Lodge, "Exudation of a strange white evanescent dough-like substance, which has been photographed by scientific enquirers in different stages of evolution, and which shapes itself into parts or whole of the body, beginning in a putty-like mould, and ending in a semblance. This is the spiritual body spoken of by St. Paul, a body that contained the Spirit and yet was distinct from the ordinary body."[1]

'Ālam-i-mithāl lends itself to the *Nusma;* and a body of light appears. The Qur'ān says: "Do not consider those dead who have sacrificed their lives in the way of God. They are alive. They derive their subsistence from their Lord; and they are kept protected by His Mercy." Those who sacrificed their lives as martyrs, are fed with the substance provided by the Lord; and

---

1 *Mystical Message,* pp. 79 and 109.

those of the non-elemental world, who are fond of a bodily shape, attempt to express themselves in that shape. There is a tendency in the 'Ālam-i-Mithāl which conjoins with the *Nusma* to assume a luminous body; those who had a desire for food help themselves with the food offered to them and their desire is satisfied. Some have mischievous tendencies and rotten tastes; and they clothe themselves in dark dresses; suitable to the stages of *Nafs,* and they do not sever themselves from their bodies in thought. When their body is ill-treated, they think they have been ill-treated. Shāh; Waliyullah Sāhib is also a believer in a world which is between *Mithāl* and the causal world, and which he calls *Barzakh:* the seeing of angels, revelation, Mi'rāj, heaven, etc., all take place in that world. Regarding angels taking shapes—this takes place in a world which is the effect of the mixture of *Mithāl* and *Shahādat',* and this is the reason why angels appear to some and do not appear to others. Regarding Mi'rāj (or the Prophet's Night Journey), such things happened to the Prophet's body in a state of wakefulness; but in that world which is between and betwixt *Mithāl* and *Shahādat,* and which is the borderland between the two.

The Prophets Ezekial and Moses have had the same experiences; and so also the *Auliyā* (Saints) have them.

In fine, after all these wanderings through *Mithāl*, Arwāh, andĀsmā', one returns to the *ism,* of which he was a manifestation, (whether *Jalāli* or *Jamāli)*; and the *Musamma* (the named) alone remains, or as "Gulshan-i-Rāz" puts it:

> *Kaz aan dar amad* awwal *ham bi dar shud,*
> *Agar chi dar maad az dar bi dar shud.*

> He enters the door from which he emerged,
> Although in his travel, he went from door to door.
> Only that he should realise this in his sulūk!

Chapter IX

THE FIVE PILLARS OF ISLAM

The tabernacle of Islam raises its head on the pole-staff of the formula, "There is no god, but God and Muhammad is the Prophet of God." *(La-ilaha ill-allah Muhammad-Rasulullah).* This tabernacle consists of four inner Courts, one within the other and a sanctuary, "Let them make me a sanctuary, that I may dwell among them."[1] Thus spake the Lord unto Moses. The first Court is the *shari'at,* into which one has to step, when one's goal is the sanctuary. "There is none worthy of worship except God." *(La ma'buda ill-allah)* Muhammad is the sent messenger of God. This is the Court of ceremonialism. Then one enters the second enclosure: this shows that the pilgrim has the intention of advancing in a particular direction, that he is bent upon advancing towards the sanctuary. This is the Tariqat (the way) ; Christ himself has referred to this stage, when he said : "I am the way, the truth and the life; no man cometh unto the Father, but through me."[2] When he enters upon Tariqat or Sulūk (the pilgrim's path), he does not leave his *shari'at* behind; for as "Gulshan i-Raz" says (line 350) :

Shari'at ra shar-i-khis-sazad
Tariqat ra visar-i'khis sazad.

1. Exo. 25-8. 2. John, 14, 6.

He makes the law his upper garment
But know very truth is the station of his nature.

Tariqat simply says: "None is the destination, but God *(La-muqsudu-il-allah),* and Muhammad is the manifestation of the Light of God." A Hadith says : "I am from the Light of God and all things are from my light." (*Ana min nurillahi wa kullu shayin min nuri).* You are then admitted into the third enclosure. There you find none existing but God himself *(La Mawjudu ill-allah)* and that Muhammad exists by the existence of God. Then you enter the sanctuary, and there you see none other than God Himself *(La Mushhudu ill-allah).* God Himself is self-evident in His work. The Nirguna is self-evident in Sarguna. The Nirguna, the Colourless, evidences Himself in His limitations. God is God without limitation and is *'abd* within limitations, and Muhammad is the reality of Himself in his first cognizance of Himself. The remaining four pillars of Islam are the Salāt, (Persian: Namāz), Saum (Persian: Rūza), Zakat (charitable contribution), and Hajj (the annual pilgrimage to Mecca).

SALĀT

The obvious or external object of Salāt (Namāz or ritual prayer) is to make oneself disposed towards goodness. "Read your prayers at the joining times of the day and night, and the early part of the night. Good works make sins disappear" *(Aqimis salāta ta ra fayin nahar wa zulfan min-al-layl, ˉIn al-hasanatu yuzhabnas sayyiat);* [1] this is the exoteric object of Namāz; the esoteric object is the ascent of the believer in his journey upwards *(As salātu mi'raj ul muminin).* When one stands for his prayers, he begins by saying "Certainly I direct my face or attention towards the One who has created the Heaven and the Earth; and we are

1. Sūra xi: 12.

not of those who join other gods with God *(Inni wajhatu wajhiya lil-lazi fataras sam-awāti-wal arda hanifan wa ma ana minal-mushrikin).* Here the four stages mentioned above are traceable. "I direct my attention to God" shows the object of worship. This is *shari'at* (none worthy of worship except God) "Who created the Heaven and the earth." This shows the course adopted by the worshipper. The goal to be reached is God *(La Maqsūd-ill allah).—Hanifan,* "We are unitarians." The worshipper realizes that none exists other than God. Then he says: "We are not of the mushriks" *i e.,* he sees that God alone exists and none else *(La Mushud).* Thus; the very introduction leads the worshipper through all the four stages. After this, he raises his hands up to the lobes of the ear, in-as-much as to say, "I have left behind all other than God." His hands are empty; when he makes his *niyat* (intention) to say the prayer of a particular time or kind and begins, "In the name of Allāh the Rahmān, the Rahim." Allāh is a conglomerate name, an aggregate of all His conceivable names. Then the worshipper descends lower, and becomes more specific and calls him Rahmān, one who is the sustainer of all His creation, who bestows His gifts on all alike—the saint and the sinner; who sends down His rain on the garden or on the desert land. The worshipper then descends still lower, and calls Him, Rahim—one who leaves nobody without his earned recompense; who bestows His gifts and blessings on those who have worked for them. The worshipper is thus absorbed in himself and calls upon His Maker. Then God answers him in first three lines of the *opening Sūra.* The answer is, of course, from the mouth of the worshipper himself. The Sūra Fātiha repeated by the worshipper runs as follows:

"Praise be to God—the supporter of the worlds; the Rahmān and Rahim, the controller of the affairs of the worlds. Thee do we worship, and of Thee we crave assistance. Direct us in the right way—the way of those on whom Thou hast poured down Thy blessings, and not of those, against whom Thou art incensed nor of those who have gone astray."

God utters His own praise: "He is the supporter of the World (Rahmān); and Rahim—the Recompenser of those who deserve recompense. Then He is the king of the Day of judgment, *i.e.* He keeps the balance even, between the counteracting and contradicting forces of the world. Hearing this answer from God, the *'abd* expresses himself in the succeeding four lines: "Thee do we worship," etc. So really this *sūra* is a conversation between God and *'abd* and is sealed by the word "Amen." Then one small *sūra* or two long verses of a *sūra* are conjoined with this. This posture in the prayer is like the rendering of the accounts on the Day of judgment. Then the worshipper bends horizontally. This is as if he prays to God in the stage of the lower animals; while standing he was praying as a man, like a slave before his master or servitor in the King's durbar. In this bending posture, he feels as if his back is bent down with the load of his sins and then repeats *Subhana Rabbiyal 'Azim* thrice pure is my Great Lord). Then he rises up from this posture saying: "God has heard my praises" (*Sami allahu-liman hamida).* If the prayer is behind the Imām, the *Muqtadis* (the followers) add *Rabbana wa lakal-hamd.* Then the worshipper bends down and then prostrates himself. Now *Sajdah* (prostration) means that the worshipper is in the posture of the lowest creature (the creeping animal), that he has left the whole world and his own individuality behind, and kisses the dust at the door of his Maker; the dust cleanses him from his sins. Now he repeats, "Pure is the Most Elevated Lord" (*Subhāna Rabbiyal-'Ala), i.e,* My Lord is above all praises. After his first *Sajdah,* which is the *Sajdah* directed by the inspiration of God, he goes down into another *Sajdah,* which is the *Sajdah* of thanksgiving. After repeating the same genuflections, he sits down *(Qa'da).* In the first sitting, he repeats the *Tashahud* (or *Attahiyyāt)* in a two *rak'at namāz,* and *Tashahud* with *darūd* and *du'ā* in a four *rak'at namāz.* The sitting posture thus assumed, indicates that from the posture of a man standing, the worship-, per has descended to that of the lower animal (bending); and from the position of the lower animal, he assumes that of the creeping animal (prostration); and then from the latter, he descends to the mineral kingdom (sitting); thus the worshipper worships his Maker in all the postures conceivable of created forms; and also in all the conceivable postures that he himself assumes for all practical. purposes of daily life. Standing before his Maker, he has performed all the obeisances; he has now received orders to sit, just as a King grants permission to his servitor. When the servitor sits down in the dūrbār, he has to say what presents; he has brought with him; the worshipper then says: "All good and pure things and praises are for Thee, O Lord," *(Attahiyyat-u-lilahi was-salawatu wat tayubat).* To which the Lord says: "Peace to thee, O Prophet" *(Was salamu alayka ya ayyuhan Nabiyyu).* The worshipper says: "Peace on all of us and on all worshippers." *(Was-salām-u-'alaynā wa 'ala 'ibadihis sālihin);* and then I bear witness that there is none else to be worshipped but God and Muhammad is His *'abd* and messenger," *(Ashhadu an la ilaha ill-allahu wa ash-hadu anna Muhammadan rasūlullah).* This is the chorus in which all creation joins with the worshipper in reciting the praises of the Lord. It may be remembered that Salāt was instituted in *Mi'rāj* (the Elevation of the Prophet to the presence of God, called the Night Journey). Gabriel who had accompanied him in the journey stopped short at the Great Fig Tree *(Sidrat-ul Muntahā), i.e.,* Reason could not soar beyond the tree of life. The Prophet himself had to progress into that non-spatial, region *(Wara-ul-Wa'a).* When he reached there, he had the injunction: "Sit down my beloved and utter my praises," *(Ijlis ya habibi wa khul sanai)* The Prophet replied: "Why do I sit down." The answer was: "God is saying His own Namāz." The Prophet sits down and says the *Attahiyyāt* (described above). This is repeated by the worshipper in all prayers in the manner described above. Salāt is thus the ascent of the believer; and the heart of the true worshipper is filled with light, of which outsiders can have no conception. There are five salāts to which minor salats are added. There is, however, an injunction to observe the middle prayer carefully (*Hafizu salāt al, wusta).* Commentators refer this to the midday prayer (Zuhr prayer); for in this busy part of the day, people are apt to overlook it. This may, however, be the constant contemplation of God in daily life, dependent on the outgoing and incoming breath. The chief point to be secured and laid stress upon, in Namāz, is concentration of Mind (Huzur-i-Qalb), according to a Hadith related by 'Uqba ibn 'Umar (Mishkāt p. 31). In the several genuflections, this may be lost sight of. To secure this, it is enjoined that the worshipper should deliberately and determinately attend to each and every word and each and every action that proceeds from him. If he says: "Holy is my Lord" *(Subhāna kalla hu),* he must concentrate his attention on the meaning or at least on the words that proceed from him and so on. Thus if he diverts his mind in one particular channel, it is not carried away in another. According to a Hadith related by Anas (Mishkāt, p. 83), he is to fix his attention on the point on the ground, which his forehead has to touch in prostration (*Sajdah).* These are the means to secure concentration in the ordinary Salāt. The devotees of several orders of Sūfis have, however, devised various practices for securing concentration in contemplation which will be dealt with separately.

SAWM OR RŪZA

Rūza is the third pillar of the building of Islam. *Sawm* literally means "to keep closed." The same reasons are given in the first instance to keep fasts in the month of Ramadān as for saying the prayers, *i.e.,* you will be kept back from several sins *Laalla kum tuflahun*)[1] In fasting, man shows the qualities of angels, who neither eat nor drink, neither marry nor are given in marriage. "Fasting is for me and I give its recompense." *(As sawm li wa-ana ajruhu).* In fasting, *'abd* attains the attribute of God who neither eats nor drinks and whose name is Samad (Allāh-us Samad).

ZAKAT

This is giving away one-fortieth part of what you possess, under certain conditions, when your savings are 52 $^1/_2$ Rupees at the end of one complete year, which is called *Hawl-ul-hawl.* In a Hadith-i-Qudsi[2] related in connection with David's query, "what were Thou, O Lord before the creation," it is said, "I was a hidden treasure. I loved to be known, so that I created the world to become known." God has thus distributed His treasure, and so his *'abd* also distributes his treasure; thus entitling himself to the possession of one attribute of God; in fact, becoming a manifestation of one of His names. The same essence is manifest in all forms. The limited *Dhãts* or Essences recognize their identity with one another in manifestation, and distribute their attributes amongst one another. "Verily, saith God," says a Hadith. "I became ill, why didst thou not enquire after me, I became hungry, why didst thou not feed me, I begged of thee, why didst thou not give me, etc." *(Inallaha yakulu mariztu, falam tu idni, rusitu falam tut imni wa saaltuka falam-tu-itni, etc.)*

---

1. Baqara, 23.
2. Hadith-i-Qudsi is a revelation in the Prophet's own words; whereas the Qur'ãn consists of the very words of God. This is the view of those who believe in Kalām-i-Lafzi, *i.e.*, the Qur'ãn as uncreated and eternal like Imām Hambal.

HAJJ

This is the annual pilgrimage to Makkah—the making of seven circumambulations around the Black Stone (Hajr-ul-Aswad) and performing other ceremonies, the details of which are given in all ordinary books of Ordinances. Sir Sayyid Ahmad Khān thinks that this was the attempt to keep intact the method of the worship of Abraham. He jocularly puts it, (though jocularity is out of the question in serious matters)[1] "Spending a few days in the same barbarous condition, which were in vogue in the time of the old grandfather creates a deep effect on the mind, of the love of God, and creates a sentimentalism in the minds of plain people" and adds, "There is no religious foundation for the killing of animals in sacrifice at the Hajj, to be traced in the Qur'ān. Makkah is situated in a desert, destitute of animal life, it was difficult to procure food for man in such a place. For this reason, people carried animals for food to such a place which are known as Budan and Khulayd. Those who did not carry them, had to purchase them at Meccāh, kill them there and feed themselves and others. This alone appears to be the foundation of sacrifice in the Qur'ān.

In those days, an untold number of animals were killed and left to be devoured by kites and jackals; this has no origin in the religion of Islam." Sir Sayyid Ahmad, it has to be remarked, was not in for the higher truths, underlying these institutions. The seven circumambulations are, no doubt, the revival of the worship of Abraham; and Muslims follow the cult of Abraham in several respects; but it is to be remembered that this worship is performed once a year, excepting, of course, the same worship, performed at other times known as *"Umrah.* But the question is why around a stone? Now the mineral kingdom is the lowest rung in the ladder

---

1. Tafsir-i-Qur'ān, vol. I, *Sūra Baqara,* 24.

of manifestation of the Divine attributes. It is the lowest emanation. The poet Mullā Jāmi says;

> *Bud kull-i-jahan daru mastur*
> *Karda dar kul bi Dhāt-i-khish zuhūr.*

> The whole of the world was hidden in Him.
> He descended into the whole by His Essence.

Then the next higher zuhūr was in the vegetable, then animal and then man, *i.e.,* in the Sarguna or the manifested God; from man, upwards again in the unmanifest world. The whole is put in a nutshell by Jalāluddin Rūmi:

> We have grown like grass often,
> Seven hundred, and seventy bodies have we taken.
> From the inorganic, we developed into the vegetable;
> Dying from the vegetable we rose to animal;
> And leaving the animal, we became man.
> Then what fear that death will lower us?
> The next transition will make us an angel.
> Then shall we rise from angels and merge in Infinity.

Now these circumambulations around the Ka'ba indicate that man realizes his true origin; and from this, he wants to rise higher and higher. That is the starting point of his life in the world. The spirit descended into clay, for its fuller manifestation. Such a recognition of his origin once in a lifetime is sufficient to give him an upward .or spiritual start. The kissing of the stone brings back the same state of things to mind, though Sayid Ahmad Khan has remarked that it indicates the goal of a circumambulation or the number of times it is done.

'Umar remarked to 'Ali:[1] "That the Black Stone could not hurt him or benefit him; that he would not have kissed it, had he

---

1. *Bahrul Ma'ani* (Letters.) by Saiyed Muhammad Husayn ibn Saiyed Nāsiruddin Ja'ffari, vide letters 2 and 3.

not seen the Prophet himself do so. It was a stone after all." 'Ali replied : "There is benefit in kissing it. The promises thatĀdam and his descendants had made are in the mouth of this stone; and the kissing of the stone is the kissing on the promises; and the Prophet had said that the stone is the right hand of God. *(Al hajaru yaminullah fil ard)."* When 'Umar heard this, he said: "Thou hast saved me, O 'Ali, from ruin." In the world of *mithal,* this stone has a form, and the kissing of it means the revival of the promise made by man to His Maker on the day of promise *(Roz-i-Mithāq) viz.,* "that when he grew out of the sodden earth, he would remember his Creator." The mineral Hajr-ul-Aswad has its prototype in the Mithāl World.—An esoteric Ka'ba exists behind the material Ka'ba; and this celestial prototype called Bayt-ul-Ma'mūr exists in the Fourth Heaven.

Chapter X

THE SŪFI'S ASCENT

The high road to the attainment of a knowledge of God traverses over what are called the "five foundations of Islam." This road is a long one; the Sūfis have devised short methods to attain the same object. In salāt, which is ascent to the highest stage for a Mumin, *(lā salāta illa bi hudūr il-qalb),* there can be no prayer, without concentration of thought. Man is the lowest point of devolution on the downward arc of *tanazzulat;* he has to ascend again from this to reach the highest point. His mind is assailed from all sides by *Khawātir* (plural of *Khatia,* an affection). Unless he stills these affections, he cannot see himself reflected on the serene surface of his mind; there should be no ruffling on the surface of water for one's image to be reflected in it. Sa'di has said:

Taammul dar ainayi dil kuni
Safai ba tadrij hasil kuni.

Observe yourself in the mirror of your heart
Get the clearness of reflection by gradual steps.

A khatra is an affection in thought that descends from Wahdat itself, and passes down through all the stages of *Tanazzulāt,* Wāhidiyyat, Malakūt, Arwāh, Amthāl and Shahādat, before it crystallizes itself and finds expression in human thought; and finally appears in the material world as action and solidifies in the character of man.

Nineteen hundred years ago, there went out the dictum "there is none good but one and that is God." If God is only good, then how can that which is reflected from Him be anything but good. As a matter of fact, the affections of our hearts are good as well as evil. In descending, the affections partake of the character of the asma,' through which they pass. (See the diagram in the chapter on "Emanation"). God is Hadil (guide in the right path), as well as Muzil (one leading astray); He is Muhiyy, (the Quickener of life), as well as Mumit (the Annihilator); He is 'Aziz (bestower of honour),as well as Mudhil (the causer of degradation). The pairs of contraries make up the manifestation of the world. God abjures thus:

Wa nafsin wa ma swwa ha
Faalhamaha fujuraha wa taqwaha.

By the soul and Him who balanced
And breathed into it wickedness and piety.

A Khatra is the illumination of God on the heart. It can but be neutral by itself. Khatrāt dawn upon the minds of auliyā; and they are fully absorbed or lost in them, so much as they become unconscious to their own existence, their consciousness is lost in the consciousness of God:

'Ilm-i-Haq nuqt ust wa 'ilmi Sūfi kat
Az wujūd-i-nuqt bashad bud-i-kat.

(Mathnawi)

God's knowledge is a point, and *'abd's* a line,
On the existence of a point depends that of a line.

When, however, the Khatra does not reach perfection, it becomes the Khatra of Māsiwāllah (*i.e.,* of other-than-God). The first kind partakes of the character of good, and the second of evil. In Sawm (fasting,) there is total abstention from food and drink; this is the sample of good Khatra, in which the idea of masiwāllah (other-than-God) is totally eschewed. Hence the reward for fasting is *As-sawmu li wa ana ajruhu* (the fasting is for Me and I am its reward.) In Sulūk (pilgrim's course) all Khatrāt, are to be annihilated; just as in fasting, food and drink are annihilated. When in manifestation, the Khatra manifests itself in desire for good action, it is called Khatra-i-Rahmāni (Divine). If, however, it is a good Khatra, but finds no permanence in the heart, it is Khatra-i-Maliki (angelic). If it develops evil tendencies in the breasts of men, it is Khatra-i-Shaytāni (Satanic). It is "the mischief of the whisperer who slily withdraweth, who whispereth evil suggestions into the breasts of men" *(Sharri-il-waswas-il-Khannās, a'-ladhiyuwaswisu fi sudūrin nās)*.[1] If, however, it fully discards all Shari'at, and all remembrance or fear of it, it becomes Khatra-i-Nafsāni (of Nafs). The first two kinds are of the nature of good; and the last two are of the nature of evil. Man is composed of four elements; earth, wind, water and fire. The four Khatrāt correspond to these in nature. Man is to obey all Khatrāt, as they descend from above. Khwaja 'Abdulla Ansāri, like Buddha, has said that all Khatrāt must be carried into practice, if they accord with Shara', if they conflict with it, they must be carried out only in fancy. In any case, they demand obedience. To regulate these Khatrāt, the Sūfis have devised several *afkār* and *adhkār;* and hence have arisen their several orders.

The Sulūk of Qādiriyyah, the order of sūfis, founded by Shaykh 'Abdul Qādir Jilani (561 A.H.— 1165 A.D.) whose sacred shrine is at Baghdād, is divided into three stages by Maulāna Rafi'uddin Naqshbandi.

1. *Ordinary.*—The Sālik recites silently or aloud the praises of God. By this, "those who have brought faith, are taken out of darkness into light *(Il-alladhina aamanu yukkrij hum min al zulmāti il al-nūr)*.

1. Sūra Nās, cxiv: 4-5

The Sālik consider's that every manifestation is His. He practises Hama ūst.

2. *Special.*—This has reference to the sight on Nirguna. Whatever enters the sālik's thought. God is free from it. It takes no cognisance of things. Objects have no reality. This is called Wilāyat-i-Wahdat-ush-Shuhūd.

3. *The Most Special.*—This is the sulūk of the Prophets—evacuation of the thought both of reality and non-reality. A colourless impression dawns on the mind; the impression of sameness. God being above thought. Some people were reciting the name of God vociferously in a mosque, the Prophet (peace be upon him), said: "Why are you so aloud, you are not addressing a distant God." It is also commanded: "Read the Qur'ān slowly and deliberately *(wa rat-tilil Qurāna tartila).* The idea in the beginning was to shut out Khwātir by deliberate and loud repetitions as in the case of Hadrat 'Umar. When one has practised this, he may have recourse to zikr-i-khafi as in the case of Hadrat 'Ali. After a man has practised himself in thus shutting out ideas by vociferous and then silent adhkār, he shuts his eyes and closes his lips and concentrates his thoughts on the out-going and incoming breath. When the breath goes out, he thinks, he says: "Lā ila ha"—he annihilates all external objects; and when it comes in, he thinks he says "Il-lallah" (but God): the point in his heart which is the seat of God (*Qalbul-mumin arshullahi* says a Hadith) expanding itself without limit.

The order of Naqshbandi was founded by Khwāja Bahā'uddin (719 A.H.=1319 A.D.). The ashghāl (practices) of this order were as many as eight, or as some say, eleven. The first eight were devised by Khwāja 'Abdul Khāliq; and the last three by Khwāja Naqshband. Out of the first eight, a few are noted below:

1. *Hush-bar-dam:* Awareness on breath. This is to observe whether one's individuality is aware of the Divine Existence or has become neglectful towards it; whether the Khatrāt have been shut out or not. This is taking count of each in-coming and outgoing breath.

2. *Nazar bar Qadam:* The appearences of different colours disturbs the mental equilibrium of the sālik. The sālik is aware of the footsteps of the Prophet in which he is travelling. The Prophet Ādam attributed action to himself; when asked why he had disobeyed, he said: "I have done an injustice to myself. Thou art merciful and forgiving" *(Zalamna anfusana anta ghafūr-ur-rahim).* Abraham had adopted the sifāt of God; he was a patron of guests. Moses had found himself a *ma'dūm* (non-entity), and saw the *Dhāt* of God. Christ annihilated himself in sifat. The "Seal of the Prophets" changed his character into the character of God; the last stage of the descent of khatrāt. These are the stations of the great Prophets; and the sālik sees towards what station he is treading with steady steps, and by the Will of God.

3. *Safar dar watan:* Journey within one's own land. This is journeying from human to angelic attributes.

4. *Khalwat-dar-anjuman:* Solitariness in an assembly; while busy in the affairs of the world, to concentrate one's thoughts on God.

5. *Baz ghasht:* To turn one's attention towards the soul.

6. *Nigah dasht:* To shut out the affections of mind, The fakirs of this order, who go about with lighted lamps, are supposed to be noted for healing diseases by touches of hand (mesmerizing), for hypnotizing, thought-reading, and for dispelling epidemics.

The sulūk of Chishtiyyah. This order was founded by Khwāja Mu'inuddin. The devotees of this order generally practise *chilla, i e.,* they shut themselves up in a room for forty days, put themselves "on short commons" and also sleepless. They hear music. With them, music causes the ascension of auliyā and Prophets towards God. It is the ascension of the qalb. With them, there are no hūrān-i-bihisht or young slaves in Paradise, nor rivers of milk and honey; there is only the beatific vision. *(In alljannata la fiha hurun, wa la khusurun wa la labanna wa la asia wa lakhaya tlla liqaullah),* an enchanting sound is the air from the breath of God *(saut-ul-hasana rihun min nafsir-Rahmān). Samā'* (music) is, however, the training ground of the beginner, as it works on thought. The adept has out-stripped thought, he is impressed by the unlimited effect of music—the music of the spheres; the voice of the musician and of the jackdaw have an equal effect on him; or as Sa'di has put it:

Kasani ki yazdan parasti kunand
Bi-awazi dulab musti kunand.

Those who indulge in God-worship
Get into ecstacy from the creaking of a water-wheel.

In the limited effect of music, one concerns himself with, either the flow of words, or of the sense underlying them or the art of the musician. For *sama'* three conditions are necessary—zamān (time), makān (place) and *ikhwān* (brotherhood). By time, is meant the time in which the audience is concentrated on the thought of God; by place, a secluded place from which strangers are excluded; and by brotherhood is meant the followers of the one and the same Pir.

Besides samā', the Chishtiyyah order practises *Nāsira* and *Mahmūda* which are practices akin to the Hindu Samathi, converging the two eyes on the tip of the nose, and then gradually carrying the point of convergence up to the middle of the forehead; or they are similar to the navel-gazers of the Middle Ages of Mount Athos in Germany. There are eighty and odd orders among the Sūfis; the nature of the short cuts adopted by a few has been shown; and a list of some others of them is subjoined:

	Name of the order.	Name of the Founder	Place of birth	Date A M.
1.	Alwaniyya	... Shaykh Alwan	... Jadda	... 149
2.	Bistāmiyyah	... Bāyazid-i Bistāmi	... Jabal Bistām	... 261
3.	Naqshbandiyyah	... Khwāja Pir Muhammad	... Qasr-i-ārifān	... 719
4.	Bnktasiyyah	... Hāji Buktas	... Khayr Shar	... 730
5.	Sūqtayiyyah	... Sarri Saqti	... Baghdād	... 295
6.	Qādiriyyah	... Shaykh 'Abdul Qadir Jilani	... Baghdād	... 561
7.	Rafā'iyyah	... Shaykh Ahmad Rafā'i	... Baghdād	... 576
8.	Suharwardiyyah	... Shaykh Shahābuddin	... Baghdād	... 602
9.	Shazliyyah	... Abul Hasan	... Makkah	... 656
10.	Manla viyy ah	... Jalāluddin Rūmi	... Qonia	... 672
11.	Jalwatiyyah	... Pir Uftādi	... Brussa	... 988
12.	Jamāliyyah	... Jamāluddin	... Constantinople	... 1164
13.	Chishtiyyah	... Khwāja Muinuddin	... Sistan	... 532

Chapter XI

PREDESTINATION

The controversy of Free-Will arose in the very beginning of the spread of Islam; but the people who discussed this question were discouraged by the Elders of the Church. The party that professed the freedom of man's will began and ended as a heretical sect. In A.H. 80 Ma'bad al-Juhani paid for heresy. He and 'Atā ibn Yassār went to Hasan Basri (ob. 110) one day and said: "Kings shed blood and assert that they do it by the Will of God." Hasan said: "They are liars, they do it by their own power." The question was also mooted before Hasan Basri whether a Muslim who committed a *kabira* sin (heinous) as opposed to *saghira* (trifling) continued to remain a Muslim.

Before Hasan could frame a reply, Wāsil-ibn 'Atā, one of his disciples stepped forward, and cut the Gordian knot by saying: "Such an one is neither a believer nor an unbeliever—Muslim is a praiseworthy word, and cannot be applied to such an one—such an one will be in purgatory, before he is admitted to heaven." Hearing this decision, Hasan said : *Itazala anna.* (He has seceded from us). Thus arose the sect of Mutazilites—which had the Shi'ahs on its side; and they denied that God had predestined the action of man. The Mutazilites were the men of Unity and Justice *(Ahl-i-Tauhid wal 'Adl).* Abū Hudhail Muhammad al-Allaf (ob. 226) was a disciple of Wasil in the second generation. He was a Qadarite and held that changes are by Divine necessity; it was God that was working man.

Al-Nazzām (ob. 231) then stepped in and asked whether it was God that did evil through man, he held that God had not the power to do evil.

Abul Hasan al Ash'ari (born 873 A.D.), a remote descendant of Abū Musā al-Ash'ari, who had played a part in the arbitration between 'All and Mu'āwiyyah at the battle of Saffin was a pupil of Al-Jubbai, a Mutazilite doctor. He broke away from his master on the question whether all that God does is best *(aslah)* for his creatures and then gave out (1) that the Qur'ān was uncreated, (2) that man shall see God with these very eyes, and (3) that we are not the author of evil deeds. These doctrines subsequently formed the belief of Ahl-i-Sunnat wal jamā'at. *Wal qudri khayri voa shurri min Allah-i-Taala.* (The power of doing good and evil is from God.

The doctrine of predestination was considered in its religio-metaphysical aspect by the Muslim sects. From a purely metaphysical aspect, it is the doctrine of Free Will and Necessitarianism.

In a note to Reid's "Works," p. 599, Sir William Hamilton remarks: "Liberty does not consist in the power of doing what we will, but in the power of *willing what we will."* Necessitarianism is denying freedom of will. "The proper meaning of free," remarks Professor Bain, "is the absence of external compulsion; every sentient under a motive to act and not interfered with by another being is to all intents 'free'; the fox impelled by hunger and proceeding unmolested to a poultry-yard is a free-agent. The motive of hunger is here therefore a compulsion."[1] "Given the motives, which are present to an individual's mind and given likewise the character, and disposition of the individual, the manner in which he will act may be unerringly determind. Religious

1. *Mental and Moral Science,* p. 398.

Necessitarianism is, however, a sort of Fatalism. A superior being overrides our wishes and bends us according to its will."[1]

All religions which admit the existence of God believe that God has Will; and He directs the world as He wills Islam is submission to the Will of God; your will must pass away into the will of God. "Thy kingdom come; Thy will be done in earth as it is in heaven."[2] Religion being dualistic in nature, while in its inmost depths it is monistic, its two phases are to be considered side by side. Qur'ãn, like all other religious books, contains verses showing dualism; otherwise during the peregrinations of the *mithāl* body in its upward course there could be no punishment for wrong-doing and reward for right-doing.

There are a large number of verses showing this, *e g.* Sūra Baqara—"God has fixed His seal on their hearts, and on their ears; and before their eyes, there is a curtain and for them is great calamity." Sūra Jāthiya—"Whatever acts you do, we cause them to be recorded (entered in your register.)

There are again verses which prove that man is not a free agent. Sūra Anbiyā', 3. 14 : "By way of trial, we shall tempt you to good and evil—you shall return to us."

When Abū Tālib refused to embrace Islam, the Prophet was down-hearted, and then the verse descended,[3] *"Innaka la tahdi man ahbubtu wa la kinnal-laha yahdi man yashau,* (Truly you cannot rightly guide those whom you like, but God can rightly guide as He wills). *Yahdi allāh bi nurihi man yashau,* (Whomsoever He likes. God directs him aright) There are thus verses showing that man is a free agent, and also that he acts out his destiny as pre-ordained for him; and it is left to those who have to understand them to find out their way.

---

1. Mill's *Logic,* II, p. 416.
2. Math, 6-10.
3. *Mirsad-ul-lbad* by Khwaja *Najmuddin-in-Kubra,* p. 142,

In a pamphlet named "Mir'atul-'Arifin," said to have been written by Imām Zaynul-'Ābidin at the dictation of his father Imam Husayn, it is said that God's knowledge was in the abstract—in the Pen, (the First Intelligence) called also Umm-ul-kitāb; and it became detailed in Lauh-i-mahfūz (the Preserved Tablet) also called Kitāb-ul-Mubin; or Imām-ul-Mubin[1] and what was still abstract in the latter, showed itself as detailed in Kursi—The former thus, in its turn became Ummul-Kitāb and the latter Kitāb-ul-Mubin; and the illustration is therein given of a seed and a tree; what is in the abstract in the seed, is detailed in the tree. That is what was in the abstract in the knowledge of God, has become detailed in the manifest world. Shaykh Muhiyūddin ibn 'Arabi (ob. 1241 A. D.) said "that God's knowledge is given Him by the objects which he knew (*a'yān*). He simply granted them their prayer to be what their nature required them to be—unless the thing to be known is there—the relation of knowledge cannot arise, and the three, viz., the knower, knowledge and the known cannot be." In the *Dhāt* all these three are hidden; Fate therefore is fixed. God certainly decreed that everything should be what its nature required to *be—Kun-fayakun—*" Be and it was." There could be no command "to be" unless there *was* something already there to receive the command. Shaykh 'Abdul Karim Jili (OB.1406 A.D.) however said: "That their (a'yān's) natures were necessitated by His knowledge of them before they were created and brought into existence. It was His knowing them; not the necessity inherent in them of being what they are, that caused them to become objects of His knowledge. After they were created, their nature required other than what He knew of them at first, and then He for the second time, decreed that they should be what their nature required, according to that which He knew."[2] Again to quote the

---

1. Sūra 36 : 12.
2. R.A. Nicholson : *Studies in Islamic Mysticism, P.* 101,

same synoptical translator of Insān-ul-Kāmil, "Ibn 'Arabi says God brought the world from being in His knowledge into actual being ; Jili argues that this is making the world co-external with God. It is not so, the judgment that God exists in Himself is logically prior to the judgment that things exist in His knowledge; and the former judgment implies the non-existence of things and the existence of God alone—God brought things from not-being, and caused them to exist in His knowledge *i.e.,* He knew them as brought into existence from not-being; then He brought them forth from His knowledge, and then to exist externally—Does it follow that because they were produced from not-being that they were unknown to Him, because He caused them to exist in His knowledge. No, the priority is of logic and not of time. There is no interval between the not-being of things and their existence in knowledge. He knows them, as He knows Himself, but they are not eternal as He is eternal".

The argument is simply on the first stage of Tanazzulāt-i-sitta (The six devolutions). The *Dhāt* of God is unknown and unknowable *(Kullu shayun halik illa wajhullah).* He is known only when He is manifest in sifāt. Then there are four *i'tabārat* (hypostases),'Ilm (knowledge), Nūr (Light), Wujūd (existence), Shuhūd (observation), and these four are i'tabārāt of Himself and not of any "Other" ; for the Other is not there. The a'yān (the realities of things) are Him as the tree is the seed; there is no necessity of the tree being co-eternal with the seed. While with Ibn 'Arabi Fate is unchangeable; with Jili it is liable to change, as Khwāja Hāfiz, one of his remote disciples, has said:

Dar ku-i-niknāmi mara guzar na dadand
Gar tu nami pasandi taghyir kun qaza ra.

On the road to good name, they allowed me not
If thou doest not approve, change my Fate.

If Fate is liable to change, man is a free agent. If, however, there is non-else but God to will, then his fate is determined for him.

The sifāt (attributes) of man are derived from or are circumscribed within the sifat of God; and man can have no idea of the sifāt of God which are infinite; the finite cannot comprehend the infinite, and the will of roan is derived from the will of God. The Will of God is free; and man's will so far as it is identical with God's is also free, but it is limited, as his other sifāt are limited and it partakes of his temporality *(Hudūth)* and then becomes predetermined. When man passes away in the stags of Fanā, the Will of God alone remains as *fons et origo* of the will of the *'abd.*

Fa il-i-harkat ast wu taskin ast
Wahdahū la sharika la ain ast.

The agent in motion and in rest is He;
This is the meaning of One without a partner.

Chapter XII

TASAWWUF IN THE MAKING

Mysticism in the world is as old as its hills. Ādam was perhaps the first mystic who had direct illumination; and that without an effect on his part, (*Zalik fauz lullahi yutihi man yashau wallahu zul fadl-il- 'azim*).[1] This is the grace of God, which He bestows on whomsoever He likes. There is a kind of mysticism, which is the result of acquisition (*In Allāha la yuziu ajral muminin*).[2] By leading life in a particular way, you open up the channels through which the grace flows.

Pythagoras had prescribed a five years' course of silence on his disciples, before they were admitted to his mystic path. The word mystic is derived from *mu,* to close. The secret rites and lessons of the Greek mysteries were things about which the mouth was closed.

Jalāluddin Rūmi has also said:

Labi band o chashm band o gosh band
Gur na bini sirri haq bar ma bi khand.

Close your lips, close your eyes and close your ears
Laugh at me, if you do not see the secret of the Truth.

Man araf allaha, kala lisanalahu, says a Hadith (who knows God, his tongue is tied). The word was again applied to inner esoteric doctrines of a religion. The disciple admitted to these

---

1. Sāra Mā'idah, v: 43.
2. Sūra Āl-i-Imrān iii : 174-176.

was a myst or mystic. The three mystic doctrines of Christianty are the Purification, Illumination, and Perfection, as materially illustrated by the Baptism, the Eucharist and the Unction. The Eucharist was transubstantiation, till Luther denuded it of its mystery, and converted it into consubstantiation. The mysteries were, on purpose, explained in parables and allegories, so that only those could hear that had ears to hear. The zest and relish of a doctrine is better realized, when it is presented in a foreign garb. The effort of the mind in realising it, brings its own reward.

Khush tar an bashad ki shri'dilbaran
Gufta ayad dar hadith-i-digaran.

(Mathnawi)

The secret of the beloved is better relished,
When explained in the language of others.

By closing every avenue of perception, one withdraws the mind from all external objects; and is able to concentrate it on a point within, when the heavenly light flashes on it. Behmen, the cobbler-mystic of Gorlitz, (in Germany) got into ecstacy, when in his presence a light flashed on a tin-jar. Inward contemplation solves the greater mysteries (Daqā'iq), while all other branches of knowledge (Haqā'iq) depend on a process of ratiocination.

With the Catholic mystics of the medieval ages, mysticism, was the religion of the heart *('Ilmi ladunni*, while knowledge obtained from observation and speculation was scholasticism *('Ilmi-lkalām.* knowledge on which disputation was carried on). When mysticism was applied to natural sciences amongst the Greeks, or when philosophy was correlated to mysticism among the Christians, it assumed the name of Theosophy, which is therefore a knowledge of the lesser mysteries. The word Theosophy cannot therefore be applied to Tasawwuf or Sūfism, in its entirety.

The German mystics had two kinds of words in the realm of this knowledge—*mystik* and *mysticismus.* The Sūfis too, have two words of similar import—the *Sūfi* and *Sufistai.* The Sūfi is the man who believes in the realities of things; his creed is *Haqāyiqul-ashyā thābitatun wal". 'alamu hadithun.* (The realities of things are permanent, the world is transitory). The Sūfistai is one who believes in the world being a delusion, a vanity. (Tasulluf).

"In the first year of the Hijra," says Ohsson in his *Ottoman Empire,* "forty-five citizens of Makkah joined themselves with as many of Al-Madinah. They took an oath of fidelity to the doctrines of their Prophet and formed a sort of fraternity, the object of which was to establish among themselves a community of property, and to perform everyday certain religious practices in a spirit of penitence and mortification. To distinguish themselves, they took the name of Sūfis. To the name of Sūfi, they added also that of faqir, because the object was to renounce the goods of the world" "*Al-faqqru fakhri*" said a Hadith (poverty is my pride).

Abul Fidā, the famous Muslim historian of ancient days also traces their origin to Ashāb-i-safā (sitters on the bench of the temple of Makkah). "They were poor strangers, without friends or place of abode, who claimed the promises of the apostle of God, and implored his protection. Thus the porch of the temple became their mansion; and thence they-obtained their name. When Muhammad (peace be upon him) went to meals, be used to call some of them to partake with him, and selected others to eat with his companions."

No doubt the sect of the Sūfis came into existence about this time; but they did not bear this name. The author of *'Awārif-ul-Ma'arif* (Shaykh Shahābuddin Suhrawardi, ob. 632 A.H) thinks that this name did not come into existence for two hundred years after the Prophet's death. This statement is borne out by the fact that the word, Tasawwuf does not find a place either in the Sittah compiled in 392 A.H. or even in the Qāmūs, the standard Arabic Dictionary compiled in 817 A.H.

These men are known in the Qur'ān by the terms Muqarrabin (Friends of God), Sābirin (Patient men), Abrār (Virtuous men), Zuhhād (Pious men)— some of them were known as Muqarrabin, for six hundred years in the region of Turkistān and Māvarā-un-Nahar (Mesopotamia).

The author of *Ghiyāth-ul-Lughāt* says, that Suffā, was the name of a tribe of Arabs, who in the time of Ignorance separated themselves from the world, and engaged themselves in the service of the Makkah temple—This Arab tribe of Suffā lived in Bani Muzar.

Thirdly, some say that they take their name not from Saf (bench), though they might have been bench-sitters as Abul Fidā says, bat from *sūf,* wool ; as they wore woollen garments; but this was repudiated, as wool is the garment of cattle (*as soof libā-sul anam.)*

A fourth sect derives it from suff, a row; (a far-fetched idea) ; as these men will stand in the first row of men on the day of judgment.

A fifth derivation is from the Greek, Sophia, wisdom; in which case they become *sophists*—an origin and a significance which they emphatically repudiate.

Most probably the word comes from *safā* purity. These were men of pure hearts and pure lives like the *hawāris* (apostles) of Jesus Christ. Baidāwi derives the word Hawāri from *hawara,* to be white (Syriac, *hewara).* They became *hawaris,* not because they wore white garments, but because of their pure lives ; and so the Sūfis were Sūfis because of their pure lives and pure hearts and spiritual elevation. No doubt they had their origin on the bench, but their appellation came to them on other considerations.

The Qur'ān has defined 'Ubbād or the subsequent Sūfis as "the true servants of God who walk on the earth with polite and courteous bearing; and who when they address the ignorant people give reply to their salām (*Wa 'ibadur Rahmān illadhina yamshuna 'alal-ardi hawnan wa iza khātabahumul jāhiluna qālu salāma*)[1]

A Sūfi has been defined in various ways.

Dhun Nūn Misri says that a Sūfi is one whose speech accords with his behaviour and whose silence indicates his state, and who discards worldly connexions. *(As-sūfi iza naūqa biana nāuqihi min al haqayiqi wa an sakata nutqata anhul jawarih biqatil alayiq).*

Junayd of Baghdād defines Tasawwuf as an attribute in which the *'abd* takes his stand, the substratum of which is an attribute of God, and the appearance, the attribute of the creature, *i.e.,* in Tasawwuf, the attribute of the *'abd* is annihilated and of God becomes everlasting, e.g. God has said: "Fasting is for me and I am its reward" *(As-sawmu li wa-ana ajzi bihi).* The fast is for God, who neither eats nor drinks; and its appearance as a ceremony is for man. Abul Hasan-i-Nūri defines it as renunciation of all pleasures of Nafs (*At-Tasawwufu taraku kulli hazzin nafsi),* thus emphasizing on asceticism. Further fā Sūfi is one who neither owns (property) nor is owned, i.*e.,* one who is not in limitations (*As-sūfi al ladhi la yam-liku vsa la yumlaku).* Abū Bakr Shibli has said: *Tasawwuf* is renunciation, *i.e.,* guarding one's self against seeing 'Other-than-God' in both the worlds." (*As-sūfi lā yarā fid dārain ma Allāh ghayrullah).*

Khafit If defines it as an Observance of the existence of God at the time of neglectfulness (*Wajid Alla fi hin il-ghaflat).*

Abū Sa'id Fadlulla thinks that it is concentrating the mind on God (*Al-Tasawwfu qiyāmul qalb ma-Allāh).*

---

1. Sūra Furqān, xxv, 63.

Tasawwuf consists of two duties— action (formalism which consists in conforming to the lines of the Shan'at; and the thinking and feeling—(Tariqat). There can be no correct feeling without correct thinking. First the idea that you form must be in the proper mould— before you can feel the existence of the idea in the correct way.

The mystical theology among the Catholic divines in Germany of the 14th century included Theopathetics (sulūk) and Theurgy (mashaikhi).

"What saith History as to mysticism," asks Vaughan, "Very plainly she tells us that the mystics have been a power in the world, a power for good, in proportion as their teaching has been in accordance with the Bible; that the instances, wherein they have failed have been precisely those in which they have attempted (whether willingly or not) to substitute another and a private revelation for it."[1] The first were *ba-shara'* (exoteric) mystics, *i.e.,* those who observed the rules and regulations of the religion; and the others were *bishara'*—(esoteric). Anselm, Bernhard, Hugo and Wicliffe were of the first type; the German mystics generally were of the second type like Tauler, Prior Rusybroeck, Suso, Eckhart. A similar distinction existed among Muslim Mystics— their names and doctrines will appear in detail later on. The lives of the general run of the Muslim Mystics were based on the teaching of the Prophet, for they maintained as Sa'di expressed it in Bustān:

Dar-in rah juz mard i dai na raft
Gum an shud ki dumbali-rai na raft
Khilafi payambar kasi rah guzid
Ki har giz bi manzil na khahad rasyd.

In this path none but the Dai entered;
Astray was he who left the trail of the shepherd.

1. *Hours with the Mystics*—I. 207.

Who sought a path contrary to the Prophet's
He will never reach the desired goal.

Those who gave up the path were those who had no liking for exertion, or those who were given to ecstacies. In a state of ecstacy, no blame attached to one's saying anything. The sayings were called *Shathiyyat,*—Mansūr ibn Hallāj said: *Anal-Haqqu* (I am the truth). Bayazid said: *Subhani ma azama shani* (I am Holy, how great is my grandeur).[1] The Prophet himself (peace be upon him) was in such a state and asked Hadrat 'Āy'esha: *Man anti* (who art thou)? She said: Ana 'Āy'esha. (I am 'Āy'esha); again asked: *Man* 'Āy'esha (who is 'Āy'esha)? the reply was *Ibnnatus Siddiq* (Daughter of Siddiq). Again, Mnnis *Siddiq? Sahūrul Muhammad* (Father-in-law of Muhammad) (peace be upon him). Again *Man Muhammad* (who is Muhammad) ? Here Hadrat 'Āy'esha stopped short; thinking that the Prophet was in another state.

In the beginning, the doctrines of Tasawwuf were taught by signs, as even now the occult part of it is similarly dealt with. The adepts could talk with each other by signs, nay, without uttering a single word (clair-audience). Dhun-Nūn was the first to put the doctrines in words; Junayd of Baghdād systematized the same. Abū Bakr Shibli was the first to preach them from the mimbar of the mosque. He brought them out from the innermost recesses of the heart which is the throne of God (*Qalb ul muminina 'arsh-ullah)* to the rungs of the mimbar, like Socrates who had brought down philosophy from the heaven to the earth. It was committed to writing by Abul Qasim al Qushayri, (437 A.H.) in his Risāla-i-Qushairiyah fil 'Ilm-ut-Tasawwuf.

Feeling again is connected with speculation, *i.e.,* getting above earthly things, and surveying them as if from a tower

---

1. Preliminary *Discourse to Kanzul Asrār il Qidam* by Mullā Mubārak 'Ali of Hyderabad, p. 5.

(Specula) flying to the dizzy heights of imagination, or it may be—being drawn up to the heights of illumination. It was on a mountain-hight that Christ had his transfiguration. The schools of Muslim speculative philosophers or idealists have already been dealt with. The men of action were those mostly concerned with moral and spiritual regeneration. Of course, the two sets cannot be separated were watertight compartments. Those who speculated were also those who ascended the ladder of certain phases of moral conduct. Junayd, for example, based his Tasawwuf on eight different qualities of the heart, viz , submission, liberality, patience, silence, separation (from the world, woollen dress, travelling, poverty—as illustrated in the lives of Isaac, Abraham, Job, Zackariah, John the Baptist, Moses, Jesus, and the Seal of the Prophets (on whom all be peace). The Sālik adopts anyone of the paths chalked out for him; and thereby attains his station *(Muqām), i.e.*, he stations himself on the attribute in which God manifests himself in him. He is a man of Mushāhada, e.g., Hadrat 'Uthmān's station was Bash fulness; Hadrat 'Ali's, liberality of heart; Imām Hasan's, patience; Imam Husayn's steadfastness in truth, etc.

Hadrat Abū Bakr and Hadrat 'Ali founded their own orders. Three important orders trace their origin to the first, *viz.*, Naqshbandiyyah, Baktashashiyyah and Bistāmiyyah; the remaining orders were the offshoots of the one founded by Hadrat 'Ali. On the demise of the former, his mantle descended on the shoulders of Salmān Fārsi; and on that of the latter, his mantle descended on Hasan al Basri.

Uways-i-Qarni (ob. 39 A.H.) who had no connection with the above two, founded his order of Uwaisiyyah. A Sūfi who has no *Pir* is said to belong to the Uwaisiyyah Order, since Uways of Qarn (a village in Nejd) had none for his Pir like the two founders, who had the Prophet for their Pir. Uways-i-Qarni is known only as 'Āshiq-i- Rasūl (Lover of the Prophet).

The Prophet (peace be upon him) has said: "The best of the times is my time, and then the one that succeeds it; and then the one that succeeds it" *(Khayr-ul-quruni qarni, thummal ladhina yalunahum; thummal ladhina yalunahum);* and hence the three generations of the best Muslims are the Ashāb, Tabis and Tabitabis.

In the first generation connected with Ashāb-i-Suffiā appear the names of Abū Bakr, 'Umar, 'Ali, Bilāl, Ibn Riyah, Abū 'Abdullah, Salmān-i-Fārsi etc. In the second generation appear the names of Uways-i-Qarni, Hiran ibn Heya, Abū 'Ali al-Hasan Basri, etc; and in the third of Habib-i-'Ajmi (disciple of Hasan), Mālik ibn Dinār, Abū Hanifa. Dāwūd-i-Tāi Bishr Hāli, Dhun-Nūn Misri, Ibrāhim-i-Adham, Abū Yazid Bistāmi, Sarri Saqti (Uncle of Junayd), Abū Hafa, Ma'ruf Karkhi, 'Ābul Qāsim Junayd, etc.

After these arose different orders of Sūfis who ascended the ladder through their moral and spiritual exertions.

The following are some of the schools of ba-shara' Sūfis:

Muhāsabiyyah—founded by 'Ābdullah Hārith Muhāsibi of Basra (ob. 243 A.H.). He distinguished Hāl (state of ecstacy) from Muqām (station). Hāl is secured by practice—(Mujāhada); and Muqām by the constant overshadowing of hāl. Hal is the gift of God, it is as fleeting as lightning. The beginning of *Muqām* is repentance. Hārith did not consider Radā (submission) as a maqarn; Radā is the disappearance of other-than-God (*Mā-siwāllah).* According to him, knowledge is superior to action. We know God by knowledge and not by actions.

Knowledge is an attribute of God and action that of *'abd, Tafakkuru sā'tin khayrun min 'ibāditis thaqalayn* (Contemplation of the moment is better than service in both the worlds). Sarri Srqti, the uncle of Junayd, arranged the system of

Muqamāt and of *Ahwāl* (plu. of Hāl).

Qaysariyyah—founded by Shaykh Qaysari ibn Hamdan. This sect was *Malamati, i.e.,* they covered themselves with opprobrium and calumny, while inwardly at heart they were pure.

Tayfuriyyah— founded by Abū Yazid Tayfūri of Bistām (261 A.H.). He was styled Imām-ul-'Ulāmā. The doctrines of the sect consisted of *Sukr* and *Sahw. Sukr* (intoxication) is a state of ecstacy—a dreamlike state, only that in a dream the senses are closed; and in *Sukr* they are active, *i.e.,* in *Sukr,*[1] one enters *the mithāl* world with his physical senses active and responsive to the Causal world, while in a true or veridical dream the avenues of his senses are closed. In *Sukr* of a lower kind again, one is lost in the observation of the manifestation of attributes and names, *i.e.,* the attributes that; he observes in and around himself, and also the *Dhāts* of self and others, he takes and feels to be attributes and *Dhāt* of God in limitation, *i.e.,* in manifestation; and thus loses the sense of materiality. In this state, Namāz is not incombent on him; which is the esoteric meaning of the Qur'ānic injunction *Lā taqrabus salāta wa antum sukara,* "Do not approach Prayer, when you are in intoxication." In *Sahw,* he returns to the normal state with his experiences of *sukr.* Ordinarily, the Zāhir (the external) covers the Batin (the internal). In *Sukr,* the *Bātin* overshadows the Zāhir; in *Sahw* both are equipoised—both are present to the mind's eye, at one and the same time so that while continuing to have his beatific vision, the *'abd* serves God as His slave :

Gulshan-i-Rāz (line 347):
Kasi Mardai taman ust kuz tamami
Kunad ba khwajagi kari ghulami.

He is a perfect man who in all his perfection
Does the work of a slave in spite of his lordliness. Junayd

---

1. *Bahr-ul-Ma'ni,* Letter 15th,

preferred *Sahw* to *Sukr,* as in the former, man is in a proper state. In *Sukr,* one is permanent in himself and annihilated in his sifāt. When the Prophet (peace be upon him) threw a handful of dust at the enemy at the battle of Uhud, it was not he that threw it būt God, *(Mā ramayta iz ramayta wa lakin-allaha rama).*[1] In *Sahw* one is permanent in himself as well as in his sifāt. When David killed Goliath, it was said *Qatala Dāwūdu Jāluta,* The action of killing is referred to David himself.

Junaydiyyah—founded by Abi Qāsim Junayd of Baghdād (297 A.H.). He was given the title of *Tāwūs-ul-'Ulāmā* (the Peacok of Ulāmā). His Tasawwuf was based on *Sahw* and love, and his practice was contemplation (Murāqaba) He discarded *Sukr,* "for," he said, "we have no need of the company of those who are unsound." There is necessity for exertion, for the grace of God to flow towards us. This appears to be a doctrine of salvation by grace, as opposed to Luther's doctrine of justification by works. "A free gift is not based on works. He also said. If you discard Satan, you give him an independent existence, which he has not."

Nūriyyah—founded by Abi Hasan ibn Muhammad Nūri (Born at Baghdād and lived at Bagsu between Hirāt and Merve, ob. 295). He said: "Know God through God." Solitariness is propinquity to Satan. He was called Nūri (one of light), because he had the faculty of "ending other people's thoughts, wherefore he was also called "Jāsūs-ul-Qalb" (spy of the heart); or because his proofs were clear; or, because, as some say, a dark room was illuminated, when he opened his lips. He was a disciple of Dhun-Nūn-i-Misri. His principle was self-sacrifice. According to him, the world was a place for sacrifice; "you cannot reach happiness, until you give up the best of what you have" *(Lan tanālul-birra hatta tunfiqu mimmā tuhibbun).*[1] When the Khalifa ordered

---

1. Sūra Anfāl, viii : 17.

Nūri, Ruqam and Abū Hamza to be beheaded, Nūri stepped forward to be beheaded first.

Junayd and Nūri, two old men could be seen, of an evening, wandering through the bazaars of Baghdād, taking away whatever they laid their hands upon; and delivering up, whatever was demanded of them. Like Socialists, they did not say "We are all hereby the equal permission of the Creator, we are all here by the equal title to the enjoyment of His bounty, with an equal right to the use of all that nature so impartially offers."[2] They felt that the property was God's, nobody has a title in it; let it change hands without a demur. Like Hobbes, they felt that property, rights and privilleges are the outcome of the artificial construction of Society. Their practice was neither utilitarianism nor Hedonism nor yet St. Simonism. It was "turn thy left cheek, whenever thy right one is slapped," for the abuser as well as the blesser are but the manifestation of God.

Suhayliyyah.—Founded by Suhayl ibn 'Abdullah Tastūri. His sulūk consisted of Mujāhada. "Those who labour in God's ways. We guide them to the right path." *"(Wal ladhina jāhadu finā lanhadiyannahum subulanā)*[3] His was the doctrine of salvation by work as opposed to Junayd's salvation by grace. The Prophet (peace be upon him) after a certain battle said : "We return from the lesser Jihād to the greater Jihād *(Rajatu anā min al jihād il asghari il-al-jihād-il-akbar).* Suhayl considered *mujāhada* as a high road to *mushāhada.* This is the way of shari'at. But Mujāhada is a fight with Nafs—which is a manifestation of God *Man 'arafa nafsahu faqad 'arafa rabbahu.* (He who understands his Nafs, understands his God.) You cannot kill Nafs; but you can divert it into other channels just like *khatras,* whose

---

1. Sūra 'Āl-i-'Imrān, iii : 91.
2. George's *Progress and Poverty,* p. 262.
3. Sūra 'Ankabūt, xxix, 69.

transmission can be diverted from one *ism* to another. He who understands his Nafs as transitory, understands His God as eternal. He, who understands his Nafs as *'abd,* understands his God as *rabb.* He who understands his Nafs as "Fed" (*Marzūq),* understands his God as the feeder *(Rāziq).* Suhayl was the man who correlated Shari'at to Tariqat.

Vilāyaliyyah.—This sect was founded by Abi 'Abdullah ibn Hākim Tirmizi. "Vilāyat" is derived from *vila* "Victory," "greatness" *(Alā inna auliyā' allahi lā khawfun 'alayhim wa la hum yahzunun)* .[1] "Beware, there as no fear for the friends of God, and they shall not be sorry."

Walis are those who are annihilated in their selves, and are an eternal in the beatific vision. There are always 4000 auliyā' in the world, who keep it going ; of these in the order of ascendency are 300 *akhyār,* and of these latter 40 are *abrār,* of these latter again, seven are *abdāls.* Then four *autāds,* three *naqibs,* and the head of them all is *Qutub* (the pole around which the existence turns), or *Ghaus.* These, in a way, correspond to the orders of spiritual existences explained by Iamblichus, the first Grecian theurgist (Mashāikh), and commented upon subsequently by Dionysius and St. Hugo, viz . gods, demons, heavens, principalities, angels, souls, also spoken of in Milton's *Paradise Lost.* The Mutazilites do not recognise the existence of these orders.

Kunnaziyyah.—Founded by Abū Sa'id Khunnaz. (ob. 890 A.D.). He thought that Fanā and Baqā were attributes. This subject has already been dealt with, in a previous chapter. This is the doctrine of ascent which was in vogue for the first time amongst the Catholic monks, led by John Scotus Erigena during the Middle Ages of Europe.

Khafifiyyah.— Founded by Abi 'Abdulla Khafif. He was

---

1. Sūra Yūnus, x : 62.

of royal blood, like Ibrāhim-i-Adham, a wali of a former period. His doctorine was Ghibat and Hudūr. This was to make the mind oblivious to *Mā-siwāllah* (other-than-God); so much so that you become oblivious of your own existence, your own thoughts, and your own will; which in turn become, the existence and thought and Will of God. When you disappear from yourself, (*Ghayb*), you appear before God (Hudūr). In Eckhart's system, "separate personality is a sin—a sort of robbery of God; it resembles those spots on the moon which the angel describes toĀdam as unpurged vapours, not yet into her substance turned'[1]—Eckhart would probably apply such expressions, not to actual self, for that he supposes non-existent and reduced to its true nothing; but to the Divine Nature which, as he thought, then superseded within him the annihilated personality."

Eckhart was irreverent; for with Khafifi, the vapours would remain as vapours on the Moon. The descendants of Ādam were in ghayb from themselves while in the spine ofĀdam; and in this condition they were in hudūr with God. The *a'yān* of the world which are the extremist realities of the world were similarly situated. Mullā Jāmi has expressed this idea thus:

Hubbaza rozi ki pish az roz wa shab
Farigh az anduh wa āzad az taab
Muttafiq bu dim ha Shahi-i-Wujūd
Hukm-i-ghayriat bakulli mahu bud
Bud ā'yani-jahan bi chand wa chun
Zi imtiyazi ilmi wa ghari masun
Na gahan dar jumbish amad parhi-jud
Jumla raz khud bi khud zahir namud.
Excellent the time before day and night
Devoid of trouble and free from fatigue,
United were we with the King of Existence.
The rule of separation was wholly melt,

1. Vaughan's *Hours with the Mysthus,* II, 282.

The *a'yān* of the world were without number and similarity
From distinction of knowledge and hiddenness protected.
Suddenly the ocean of existence broke into waves.
And manifested all in Himself and out of Himself.

The *a'yān* were thus in *ghayb* (absent) to themselves, but were in hudūr (presence) in the knowledge of God. Husain ibn Mansūr, Abū Bakr Shibli, etc. gave preference to *ghayb* over *Hudūr,* and so in their moments of ecstacy they gave out such expressions as "I am the Truth," *"(Anal-Haqq)."* "There is none under this cloak except God" *(Laysa jubbali siwallah).* Others and theirs is the vast majority—gave preference to *hudūr* over *Ghayb,* like Hārith Muhāsibi, Junayd, Suhayl and Muhammad bin Khafif. These latter are those who take care of this world as well as of the next.

Siyāriyyah.— Founded by Abi Abbās of Siyār (a village in Merv). They identified attributes with the *Dhãt* of God, and differentiated His actions from Him. This is known as the doctrine of Jama' and Tafriqa— assimilation and differentiation. In the matter of differentiation (Tafriqa), the Mutazilites differed from them, as they held that God sees by His own *Dhât*, knows by His own *Dhãt*, hears by His own *Dhãt*, etc.

There are some sects, which are Known as Sūfis : but which are removed from their inner court like the *Mujassamiyyah* (the Corporealists), the *Hulūlis* (Incarnationists), the *Tanāsukhis* (Transmigrationists), etc. The first of these sects traces its origin to Abi Halmān of Damascus; and the second, to Mansūr Abul Ghayd Hallāj (who lived in Iraq and was a contemporary of Junayd). The latter is to be distinguished from Mansūr-i-Fārsi of Baghdād, who was considered to be a Mulhid (atheist). The first Mansūr gave out *Anal Haqq* (I am the Truth). He was not, however, a Hulūli (Incarnationist) like the Phrygian mountaineer

Montanus (the founder of the sect of Montanists) who gave out that he was a subject of Divine possession, and taught among the Protestant peasants of Cevennes. Hallāj simply meant that he was a manifestation of the Truth. For this very reason, he was supported by Junayd. Although the fatwā of the former's execution was also signed by him, out of regard for the exoteric Shari'at, Junayd said "Mansur and I are one and the same thing, only that madness has saved me, and reason ruined him). *(Anā wal Hullāju shayun wāhidun fa khallasani jununi wa ahlakahu 'aqluhu).*

Shaykh Abū Sa'id Abul Khayr (6b. 440 A.H. 1040 A.D), the *Murshid* of the famous Wali of Baghdād Shaykh 'Abdul Qādir Jilani (Pir Dastagir) considered him to be "a man of the secret." The doctrine of Tanāsukh (Transmigration) was that the soul transmigrated into another body,—re-incarnation (Naskh); or into the bodies of animals (Maskh); or into vegetables (Faskh), or into minerals (Raskh). Ahmad ibn Thābit, and his disciples Ahmad ibn Yābus, 'Abū Muslim of Khurāssān, Shaykh-ul-Ishrāq, 'Umar-i-Khayyām were the exponents of the doctrine of reincarnation, basing their arguments on Sūra Baqara, (61:92), Sūra Mā'ida,55. Druses, whowere the followers of Darazi were also believers in it. They even went to the length of saying that Christ had reappeared in the person of Salmān-i-Fārsi; and that Hamza had reappeared in the person of a son of 'Ali 'Umar Khayyām even believed in Maskh. The following interesting story is reproduced in E.G. Browne's *Literary History of Persia.* (Vol. I. p. 254).

"It is related that there was in Nishāpūr, an old College, for the repairing of which donkeys were bringing bricks. One day, while the sage (Hakim, *i.e.,* 'Umar) was walking with a group of students, one of the donkeys would, on no account enter (the College). When 'Umar saw this, he smiled, went up to the donkey and extemporised the following quatrain:

Ay rafta, wu baz amada bal hum gashta
Namat zi miyan-i-namha gum gashta
Nakhun hama jam amada, wa sum gashta
Rish az pasi kun, amada wa dum gashta.
O lost and now returned *'yet more stray'*
The name from men's remembrance passed away,
Thy nails have now combined to form the hoofs,
Thy tail's a beard turned round the otherway.

The donkey then entered; and they asked 'Umar the reason of this. He replied the spirit which has now attached to the body of this ass (formerly) inhabited the body of a lecturer in the college; therefore, it will not come in, until now when perceiving that its colleagues had recognized it, it was obliged to step inside.

Was this a hoax or a *reductio ad absurdum* of the theory on the part of Khayyām?

The doctrine of transmigration was not however accepted by the Sūfi mystics, who held that "it was an abomination to all Muslims," as Dr. R A. Nicholson has put it.[1] The doctrine of *Baruz.* in which the *ruh* of a departed saint could foster and cherish and guide the *rūh* of a living man was in favour with them. The *rūh* is neither within nor without the body; only its vision is on the body, the *ruh* of a departed "friend of God" could guide the *rūh* of a living man on whom it has fixed its vision.

The Sūfis have a doctrine of their own which conflicts with the doctrine of transmigration, *viz., Tajaddud-i-Amthāl* (Revival of Similitudes). They hold that *tajalli* (illumination, epiphany) has no repetition, thus contradicting the statement that history repeats itself. God's power is infinite, and He is exhaling out of the deeps of His Existence ever new forms, and ever new lives; there is no

---

1. *Studies in Islamic Mysticism,* p. 225.

scope for the repetition of the same *tajalli.* This doctrine may be traced to the Grecian philosophers, Leucippus and Democritus who maintained that Non-being exists as well as Being. "The Being is that which fills space— the Full; Non-being is the Void."[1] "All atoms from eternity move downward in the infinite space." There is ever a change in the atoms of the Cosmos there is no reappearance of the same atom in the same place. *Balhum fi labsin min khalqin jadid (Sūra-Kahf:* 15). God manifests Himself in ever changing garbs. *Wataral jibala jamidathun wu hiva tamarru marras sahab.* "You see the mountain as solid, although it runs like a cloud." This points to the modes of manifestation and not to metempsychosis.

Some others of the Bi-shara' orders are Mādaiyyah of Zinda Shāh Madār of Syria (whose shrine is at Makanpur in Oudh), Rafā'yyah, Qalandariyyah, etc.

---

1. Zeller's *Outline of Greek Philosophy,* p. 78.

Chapter XIII

TASAWWUF AND THEOSOPHY

It would seem as if Sūfism (Hybrid form of the word Tasawwuf) and Theosophy have had a common origin. The word Theosophy *(Theos, sophia.* Divine Wisdom) was originally used by the Grecian school of Porphyry. Amongst the earlier Germans, it meant mysticism as applied to natural sciences; and later on, in the medieval ages, when scholasticism prevailed, it came to mean mysticism as applied to philosophy. The present day theosophy is an exposition of the phenomena of the world on esoteric basis; in India it is applied to an exposition of the mysticism of the Hindu sacred books; and acting out the truths underlying that mysticism. The word Tasawwuf or Sūfism is variously derived (*vide* chapter on "Tasawwuf in the Making"). It was originally applied to Ahl-i-safā (men of the bench) a set of the holy men (Safā) of Makkah, who had given up the world and lived on the love of God and His Prophet (peace be upon him); in fact who having had a *glimpse* of the Divine truths, had become obvious to the cravings of their creature-comforts. At any rate, the two systems seems to take their source at the same fountain-head *viz.,* the esoteric realization of religious truths, as Maulānā Rūmi has, unceremoniously, put it:

Ma zi Qur 'ãn maghs ra bar darteem
Ustakhan pishi saghan andakhteem.
We have taken the marrow from the Qur'ãn
And cast the bones before the dogs.

Like two rivers from the same source, they converge and

diverge at different points before they reach their final goal. The two having their origin at the same fountain, start with the same object—the realisation of an idea of God; but as they pursue their courses, they seem to fertilise different fields of thought. This chapter will set forth the points of divergence.

THE GOD IDEA

It is sometimes believed that Tasawwuf or Sūfism inculcates Pantheism, that the world is the manifestation of God, and that there is no place for *'abd* (creature) in it. If there is no *'abd,* then the whole super-structure of Islam must come down; for the Prophet always preached and taught that "Muhammad was His *'abd* and His Messenger."

Several Sūfi thinkers have no doubt given out in their moments of ecstacy: "I am the Truth," like Mansūr-i-Hallaj; "O Praised, how great is my Glory !" like Bāyazid. That which cannot be traced to the Prophet, before whom these thinkers licked the dust, cannot be taken as the genuine teaching of Islam. Besides there might be a special sense in these sayings other than that implied in Pantheism. Pantheism deals a direct blow to the extra-cosmic conception of God; but Sūfism is such that while it accepts the extra-cosmic conception, it also believes in His immanence. There are such verses in the *Qur'ān:* "Really God surrounds you";[1] "God is with you wherever you are,"[2] "God is in the East and the West, so wherever thou turnest thy face, there is the face of God,"[3] these show the extra cosmic conception. And again there are such

1 Sūra Nisa 116.
2 Sūra Hadid 11.
3 Sūra Baqara 128.

verses as: "He is nearer to you than your jugular vein;[1] "He is in your individuality, but you do not see;"[2] these show His immanence.

In Islam, the *'abd* is always kept in the forefront; and the Founder of Islam never proclaimed Himself as the Truth, or as an Incarnation of God; the motto of His religion was: "There is no god but God: Muhammad is His *'abd* and messenger." On account of these conflicting conceptions, the idea of God is to be searched for in a deeper depth. To quote the following expressive lines of Mullā, Jāmi to begin with:

Hubbaza rozi ki pish az roz wa shub,
Farigh az anduh wa azad az taab,
Muttafiq budim ba Shah-i-Wujud.
Hukm-i-ghayriat ba kulli mahu bud
Bud ayan-i-jihan bay chund wa chun,
Zi imtiyaz it ilmi wa ghayri masun.
Na gahan dar jumbish amad bahri jud
Jumla raaz khud ba khud zahir namud.

Excellent the day before day and night,
Devoid of trouble and free from fatigue;
United were we with the King of Existence.
The rule of separation was wholly null.
The *a'yān* (or realities) of the world were without number and similarity,
From distinction of knowledge and hiddenness protected
Suddenly the ocean of existence broke into waves
And manifested all in Himself and out of Himself.

Thus the realities of *'abd* remain for ever in the knowledge of the Supreme, who is everlasting. The manifestations are ever changing, the *a'yān* remain the same.

The *Dhāt* of God is ever the same; then come His four

1. Sūra ccvi: 16 and 20.
2. Sūra Dhāriyāt 19.

primary attributes: Knowledge, Light, Existence and Manifestation; to these are added three more: Speech, Hearing and Sight. These are what are called the seven primary attributes (the Ummahātus Sifāt, the mothers of attributes); and these are evolved the other innumerable attributes. The attributes subsist on the *Dhāt*, the one ever the same; and the other at no two moments the same. The Mutazilites and the Shi'ahs do not believe in the attributes as subsisting on the *Dhāt*. Their God is without His separate attributes. From the attributes come the names (asmā'). If speech is an attribute, speaker is a name (*ism*); for there can be no manifestation of an attribute (Sifāt) without the manifestation of action (fa'il) first; and there are four primary names (Ummahātul-Asmā', the mothers of names): "The first and the last—the apparent and the real"; [1] and out of these are evolved the other innumerable asmā'. The world is said to be a manifestation of asmā' of the Supreme; .but an *ism* (name) cannot be manifest -"without a *rasm* (its counterpart). And this *rasm* is the reality of *'abd,* which is its form in the knowledge of God. When He looked at Himself as Rahim (merciful), there was simultaneously in His knowledge the reality of murhūm (one on whom mercy is bestowed.) There was no duration of time between the two. When a seal is set, the words on the seal may be read one after the other; but in the setting of the words on the wax, there is no lapse of time. When He saw His own names as rabb. He saw the realities of the forms as murbūb. At this, the very first stage, the realities of '*abd* became separate. Before that, there was no *ism* and there was no *rasm*; "they were not separate from Truth or from each other"; but when these were there, they were separate in His knowledge. Thus began separation; the attributes of *Dhāt* (of God) are positive the attributes, and the attributes of the *Dhāt* (form) of *'abd* are negative attributes. Whatever one possesses, the other does not. The one possesses

1. Sūra Rahmān. 26.

His attribute of existence, the other is devoid of existence. Then the forms take their shape by, as it were, borrowing the attributes of the *rabb*. He manifests in them His own attributes. Now it must be remembered that no attribute exists without *Dhãt;* the attribute is only a manifestation of the *Dhãt*. So the manifestations of the attributes in the 'abd are the manifestation of the attributes (behind which is the *Dhãt*) of the rabb. Where therefore the world is a manifestation of the names of God, (*Dhãt plus* sifat), the unchangeable from *'ayn* is still there in His knowledge. The *'ābd* is there for ever. And hence the Prophet, the first *'ābd,* always gave himself out as His ' *ābd* and Rasul". There is, however, the stage of Fanā; the manifested *'ābd* annihilates himself in his thought, his own attributes and then his own *Dhãt;* and begins to ascend and ascend the ladder till he reaches the very form in the knowledge of God and annihilates his own form also in his own thought. From his own side, he annihilates his own form (his 'ayn); but from the side of the Supreme, the forms remain. When he annihilated his own *'ayn* from his side, his form from the side of the Supreme remains as it was; and thus the '*ābd* sometimes gives himself out: "I am the Truth."

Maulānāi Rūm says :
Chun pari ghalib shawad oar admin,
Gum shawad az mard wasfi murdumi
Her chi guyad aan pari gufta buad
Zin saray nay zan saray gufta buad.
Ruay ou rafta pari khud wu shuda
Turk bay ilham tazi gu shuda.
Gum ba khud ayad na danad ek lughat.
Chun pari ra hast aen dhãt wa sifãt,
Pụs khudawand pari wa admi
Az pari khi bashad dash akhar kami
Chun pari ra ain dam wa qanoon buad

Kirdagar-i-aan pari khud chun buad.

When a fairy overpowers a man,
Vanishes from that man the attribute of manhood.
Then what that man says becomes the saying of the fairy.

Neither from this side nor from that is said.
His nature gone, he becomes the fairy itself,
The Turk without inspiration talks Persian
When he recovers, he does not know one word of that language
When the fairy has thus its *Dhãt* and its attribute. Well the Lord of the fairy and man,
Why will He have any the less ? When the fairy has this faculty, How will the Creator of that fairy Himself be?

The question has often been asked whether the God of the *Qur'ãn* is a personal God. He is not a personal God in a material or anthropomorphic sense, that He is a big man sitting on His 'Arsh, surrounded by His angels, and regulating the affairs of the world; for He then becomes an idol. But He is a personal God in the sense that He has attributes. But these attributes are not like our attributes. We speak with our tongue, hear with our ears and see with our eyes.

In our case:

Na budi chun ki fi at afaridund
Tura az bahr-i-kari afaridund

(*Gulshan-i-Raz,* line 542.)

You existed not when your actions were originated.
You were appointed to fulfil a certain purpose.

The faculties manifested themselves through organs; but the faculties are not, or are not like, the organs themselves.

INCARNATION

The manifestation of God in flesh and blood for the salvation of humanity The Eastern Dispensation—whose apex Islam claims to be—was free from a working hypothesis of incarnation. The idea that the paschal lamb referred to the crucifixion of Christ was not accepted as a working hypothesis till the advent of St. Paul. Moses had his talk with God on Mount Sinā'i; Christ underwent transfiguration on the mount; and Muhammad had his *mi'rāj,* or elevation, or, as it is called, the night journey. Muhammad (peace he upon him) ascended from heaven to heaven, and saw the previous Prophets, till he was admitted into the audience hall of God. He is reported to have beheld God in the shape of a 'young beardless youth'. Thus the purdah still hung; the limitation still existed.

The *'ayn* of Muhammad (peace be upon him) was the last point reached by him. Some men like Muhiyuddin ibn 'Arabi, however, consider that the Haqi-qat-i-Muhammadi was the name of a rank. Viceroy is the name of a rank, irrespective of the individual who happens to hold that rank. So is the stage called Haqiqat-i-Muhammadi. That stage was fully, manifested in Muhammad. It had manifested itself in different and lesser degrees in preceding Prophets, like Ādam. Moses, David, Jesus; In that particular *ism* each individual had annihilated :his *'ayn*, and God alone was manifest, for the time being. This Fanā or annihilation results in everlastungness or Baqā. The martyrs in jihād are said to have attained everlasting life. When the soldiers in Badr had slain their enemies, it was said: "They have not slain them, but it is God who slew them."[1] When Muhammad (peace be upon him)

---

1. Sūra Anfāl, 18.

shot his arrows in the same battle: "Thou hast not shot (arrows), but it was God that had shot." The individuals had annihilated themselves, and had reached their *'ayn* in the ecstatic condition in which they were, when they fought *fi sa-bilillah* (in the way of God). The actions done by them were not their actions, they were not held responsible.

REINCARNATION

If there is no incarnation there is no transmigration or reincarnation either, *i.e.,* the individual souls taking different shapes, till they have exhausted their *karma*. Reincarnation appears to be a sound enough doctrine to explain the unevenness and aberrations and apparent injustices in the lot of people on this earth. Why is one man doomed to perpetual suffering and another destined to everlasting sunshine and happiness ? But it does not strike at the very root. It takes for granted that all souls must have started with the same capacity, and that they increased that capacities by reincarnating from time to time, till they obtained the full benefit of their earthly experience. They start as germs and by constant migrations attain their perfection; but their different conditions have been brought about by inequalities in their worldly careers; so that their different conditions are the outcome of their different careers; and hence the question of justice remains as much unsolved as before. They had no power over the inequalities of the mundane sphere; and therefore why the suffering kept in store for them? They begin their careers in the same conditions. A savage lives and dies, and the experience gained on the savage plane helps him to be born as a semi-savage, and additional experience in that life help him to the ladder of the civilised man. It is, as if he is destined to suffer to gain more knowledge till losing his interest in the fruition of his endeavours, he obtains Nirvana. Here will—an attribute of God given as a loan to this *'abd*—

clashes with necessity.

He is led to be born in a particular family or tribe according to his development; and that development could not accord with his environment, or he has to wait endlessly; he is thus helpless and shorn of freedom. Cannot this reincarnation be believed to be merely "The progress of the soul from one stage of existence to another, symbolised and vulgarly believed to be rebirths in animal bodies ?"[1]

"The metempsycho is must only be regarded as a supplementary doctrine, disfigured by theological sophistry with the object of getting a firmer hold upon believers through a popular superstition. Esoterically it is explained in the mystery of Kounboum, and relates to the purely spiritual peregrinations of the human soul?"[2]

Cannot therefore the different peregrinations merely be in the region of the *lokas*? After its disappearance from the world, the soul appears in the different *lokas* and gradually passes on to svarga, where he has the beatific vision. These *lokas* are the seven heavens of the Muslims; and the wheel of *karma* merely refers to its peregrination in the lokas.

"As the dweller in the body experienceth in the body, childhood, youth and old age, so passeth he on to another body; the steadfast one grieveth not thereat."[3]

Thus says Shri Krishna. This obviously refers to the future condition. Just as there are several stages in the development of the body in this world, so there are several stages in its development in the next. The man who has eaten something disagreeable has not to take out his stomach to purify himself and get better. He sends down a bitter pill on the top, and thus cures bis internal

---

1. *The Isis Unveiled,* i p. xxxvi.
2. *Ibid*. p. 289.
3. Gitā , II—13.

disorder. "As you sow, so you reap" forms the formula of all religions. A Muslim tradition has it, that "this world is the harvest-field of the next." After he has reaped the fruits of his actions, he passes on to the next higher stage. The hell is not a place of punishment but of correction. If the inequalities of life cannot be explained away by a doctrine of reincarnation—how else can they be and still establish the justice of God?

Before the creation of the world, it is said God brought together all the souls that were to find manifestation, and enquired:" Am I not your Lord (Rabb)?" The chorus went forth: "Yes, Thou art our Lord God." This is what is called the Roz-i-mithāq (the day of promise). Esoterically speaking, when the *ism* found itself—it found itself with its corresponding rasm, as given in the simile of the seal *(supra);* the *ism* was the rabb (the ruler) and the *rasm* was its murbūb (the ruled). In a higher plane, the plane of the three Logoi, (or as they are called ahdiyyat, wāhdat, and wāhidiyyat by the Sūfis), the *ism* and *rasm* are the same; in the lower plane, the one is the counterpart of the other. Each ism was the *'ayn* of each rasm, which was a centre in Divine Consciousness; and that centre had to find its manifestation by externalisation. Each *'ayn-i-thābita* had to become an *'ayn-i-sāhira.* When the *ism* providence found its local habitation, so to speak, in the Divine consciousness, its rasm (*i.e.,* one who would be provided with) was there in Divine Knowledge, and of its own free-will and accord (in other words, of its own tendency) prayed to its rabb for its minifestation. There was no compulsion. It was perfect willingness to please its Lord. When the differentiation between rabb and murbūb occurred, the murbūb, as the servitor of its rabb deliberately chose its role to please its rabb. It the leper (the muqhūr. *i.e.,* one on whom wrath falls), chose its own role on that day to please its rabb, the qāhir *(i.e.,* the wrathful), he is not to blame his rabb for being His muqhūr in manifestation, though he might blame Him in his manifestation, forgetting his previous history. The Prophet Job suffered without complaint, because he had reached his *'ayn* in his suffering. The distress, the agony, are past and gone, when once the true origin is realised. The merest beggar on the roadside with festering sores becomes as contented and happy as the veriest Caesar in his palace. He submits to the will of his rabb, submission being the key-note of Muslim theology, which of course, is the exoteric form of Muslim philosophy.

Further the hope lies in the changing manifestation: "Verily after sorrow, there cometh joy," says the Qur'ãn. The leper has had this suffering; in this world; and he enters upon the next, better equipped to travel higher up. This is why people who die from lingering painful diseases are called martyrs.

The following verses from the Qur'ãn are quoted to give a denial to transmigration.

When death comes to anyone of them, he says: "O Preserver, send me back that I may do good works in the world that I am leaving—the answer will be 'never'.[1]

There will be barzakh in their front, till they are raised again."

"When the trumpet will be blown, then there will be no relationship between them. Nobody will care for another; whosoever has his scale heavier will have good reward, and those whose scales are light are those who have ruined themselves, and they will be ever in Jehannum (*gehanna*)."[2]

Curiously enough, there have been people, though very few and far between, who think that reincarnation can be traced in the *Qur'ãn.*

"What are we tired and fatigued after first creation? But they (the unbelievers) are in doubt and error as regards new creation?"[3]

---

1. Sūra Mūmin, 11.
2. Sūra Ma'ida, 112 and 114.
3. Sūra 'Kahf 50.

"Tell. O Muhammad, all praise to God, but many of them do not understand it. The life in this world is play. The home of the future is real living. They do not understand it."[1]

"We created man in trouble."[2]

"We swear by the declining day (afternoon), man is in similar decline."[3]

"Say, O Muhammad, He who created them first, will revive them. He knows about all creation."[4]

Muhammad's dispensation, (peace be upon him) like the dispensations which had preceded it, included the doctrine of the resurrection of bodies on the Day of judgment. References appear to be made to this throughout the above verses.

Authority is again quoted from the Mathnawi of Jalāluddin Rūmi:

We have grown like grass often,
Seven hundred and seventy bodies have we taken.
From the inorganic, we developed into the vegetable ;
Dying from the vegetable we rose to animal;
And leaving the animal we became man.
Then what fear that death will lower us?
The next transition will make us an angel,
Then shall we rise from angels and merge in Infinity

Have we not been told
All of us will return,

The first part refers to material evolution, on this side the grave; the second part to evolution beyond the grave, through the different spiritual planes.

The third point at which Tasawwuf parts company with Theosophy is

---

I. Sūra Ankabūt 29.
2 Sūra Balad 34.
3 Sūra Asr 20.
4. Sūra Yāsin 23.

SYMBOLISM

The Muslim mosque is a vacant space—nothing to touch or see—a symbol of the house of the Supreme. The Muslim fixes his eyes on the point of space in front of him, at which he performs his sajdah (prostration); and thus concentrates bis attention at that point, according to Baidāwi who was a Shāfi'. When he prays, he is ordered to assume an attitude as if he sees God; and if he cannot do this, to imagine that God sees him. There is no symbol required to attract and concentrate his attention.

It may be remembered that the Arabs had worshipped gods and goddesses in the temple of Makkah. There were 360 of them. They were the embodiments of the different asmā' (names) of God. Muhammad (peace be upon him) emptied the temple of those graven images. Though the asmā' of God are recognised, the *Dhāt* or individuality of God is not to be ignored and hidden behind the asmā'[1]. The extinction of the deities as intermediaries in the temple was the extinction of the embodiment of names in worship. The worshipper always stood face to face with the Supreme. Each *ism-i-kiyāni* is directly under the influence of its own *ism-i-ilāhi* and indirectly of the other asmā' *(vide* diagram on page 54. *Wa ma min dabbatin fil ardi illa hua akhizun bi nasiya-tiha, hazy,rabbi ala siratin mustaqim* (Every creeping creatury on the earth has its forelock in hand of the its rabb, and that rabb is in the right path), *vide* page 57-58 *ante.* Each *ism-i-kiyani* is guided by its rabb in other words, each marbūb seeks the help of and worships its rabb whose form it is: *lyyaka nabudu wa iyyaka nastayin*[1] (Thee do we worship, and of Thee we seek help) This is the prayer of each murbūb to its rabb; and this is the line of barzakh between the two sets of names, according to Mir'atul-'Ārifin—a treatise written at the dictation of Imām

1. Sūra, Fāthia : 3.

Husayn. Man is a conglomeration of all the conceivable *asmā'-i-kiyāi* and he is to seek the help of, and worship the Being, whose form or "own image"[1] he is, (vide pp. 70 and 76 *ante),* and who is the possessor of all the conceivable asmā'-i-ilāhi. *i.e*, who is the Rabb-ul-Arbāb—God; and he is to worship none else. This is *his* prayer of *lyyaka nabudu.* Man is not to confine himself to the worship of one particular *ism.* This particularization of one name to the exclusion of other names, (for the name Allāh is *ism-i-jāmi*—it comprises all names) militates against and mars the perfection, which should be characteristic of a perfect being like man—the vicegerent of God on earth, and is a source of bis degradation; and is a shirk and therefore a sin.

In the case of aūliya, it is different; they realize the named, through the name—look through Nature up to Nature's God,—drop materiality altogether in their outlook of life, according to the advice of Rūmi:

Dar guzar kun jumla tan ra dar nazar
Dar nazar rau dar nazar rau, dar nazar
Drop the material body out of sight,
Go into sight, go into sight and go into sight.

No doubt, there are intermediaries working in this mundane sphere, *e.g*, if there were not the forces called gravitation and cohesion, the existence of the world would have been impossible. These could be symbolised and embodied in figures. Man lives and works under the natural forces, and he does not thank them; he thanks only the Supreme Power who keeps them going. There are archangels and angels for the administration of the world; but no Muslim worships anyone of them. They have their own functions and duties, as we have our functions and duties. Besides the angels, there are functionaries on the material plane, through whom and by whom the affairs of the world are regulated. (For an account of these see pages 161-162 *ante.)*

1. Genesis, 1-27

Their administration is said to be carried on, on the same lines as the administration of worldly Kings and Governors. With all that, there is no worship for them from anybody. The Muslim has not got his household deity. A Hadith runs as follows:

When the latchet of your shoe is lost, ask it of God.

Mediation in this world cannot, altogether, be done away with; but the thought should always be directed to the moving spring of all actions, as the poet Sa'di says:

Dar ain nout az shirk poshida ast
Ki Zaydam bi azurd wa Amrum bi kast

There is a sort of shirk hidden in this:
That Zayd has injured me, and 'Amr has ruined me.

This is *shirk fil-af' āl. Shirk* also consists in giving the attributes of God to other-than-God. *Mā-siwālla),* which is *shirk fis Sifāt.*

An attack is, however, levelled at the Muslims that there is a stone in the temple of Makkah. It must be remembered that this is not a graven stone. It is there as a historical monument, and to commemorate a historical event. It is said to have been placed thereby the Patriarch Abraham; and revolutions that are made around it commemorate the form of prayer that was practised by Abraham and his followers. Since Muhammad was a descendant of the great unitarian Patriarch, he wished to keep green the holy practices of his forefather. Besides he wanted to congregate bis followers in one and the same place at least once a year, for social and religious intercourse. The stone of Ka'ba is after all a stone, regarding which 'Umar said :

"I know that it is a mere stone, but I kiss it, as it was kissed by the Prophet" (peace be upon him).

(For an esoteric explanation see pages 132-133 *ante.)*

There is no doubt that the human mind takes all means to be ends themselves; and hence the religion and philosophy of Islam have eschewed the worship of means altogether.

APPENDIX I

SŪFI ORDERS IN THE DECCAN[1]

The Faqir is not such a simple individual as he appears to be at first sight. At first blush, it would appear that one has to take a bowl of clay or wooden tray to play the role of a Faqir ; but the history of the individual would reveal that he is the product of a well-organized machinery, a member of a society, a Monastic society with regular rules and regulations, the breach of which involves his being "drummed out"—a way of ostracism that appears to be popular amongst them as in the army. According to some Jurists, every Mussulman, man or woman is bound to follow the lead of a spiritual director—a Pir answering to a *guru* amongst the Hindus. There is no direct authority in the Qur'ān enjoining the following of a Pir. In fact, the democratic spirit of Islam would appear to be against all confessional and *guru*-worship;[1] but texts are quoted as supporting the ceremonials connected with the *bay't* such as "Obey God and obey His Prophet, and such as those placed in authority over you."[2] *(Ati 'ullaha wa ati 'ur-Rasūla wa ūlil-amri minkum.)*

"O believers, fear God and seek a means to approach Him." *(Yā ayyuhal-ladhina amanu-atqul-laha wabtaghu ilayhil-wasilata.)* [3]

Whoever did *bay't* to you (O Prophet) has verily done *bay't* to God, for verily God's hand is on their hand." *(Innal*

---

1. Reprinted, from the Author's book *The Philosophy of Islam.*
2. Sūra Nisā, iv : 59.
3. Sūra Mai'da ,v : 35.

ladhina yubāyi'unaka innamā yubayi'unallaha, Yadullahi fawqa aydihim.)[1]

"O believers who have brought faith in God, bring faith in God (once again) and in His Prophet and the Book He sent down to His Prophet." *Yā ayyukal ladhina āmanu, aminu billahi wa rasūlihi, wal kitābil-ladhi nuzzila 'ala rasūlhi.)*[2]

The ceremony of *bay't (i.e.)* placing the palm of one's hand on that of another person appears merely to have been the sign of sealing an agreement. The Prophet took under a tree the allegiance of some of the people of Madina, who had invited him to their city; and performed this ceremony.

He had the ceremony of *bay't* performed for the following purposes:[3] When people adopted Islam, they had to perform *bay't* to the commander of an army. When *jihād* or the holy war of Islam was undertaken, the people performed *bay't,* to the effect that they would risk their lives. When a Caliph was elected, they performed *bay't* or took the oath of allegiance. Lastly, when a man repented of his sins, and had made up his mind to lead a life of righteousness and piety, according to the Shari'at of the Prophet, he had to perform *bay't* or take an oath before a holy man who is walking according to the Shari'āt, that he would not go back on his promise. No *bay't* was ever performed with the object of learning occult knowledge or seeking intercession.

However, the *bay't* in vogue in Islam is based on the *bay't* mentioned last.

The spirit of Islam seems to be for man to have direct communion with God. so much so that all the intermediaries whose existence is acknowledged are lost sight of, in the communion of man with God. There is no angel-worship in Islam, otherwise Islam,

1 Sūra Fath, xlviii: 10

2. Sūra Nisā. iv : 13.

3. *Tasānif-i-Ahmadiyyah,* pp. 84, 86.

like Hinduism, would have its 33 crores of gods (or *devas or* the intermediary beings who manage the affairs of the world). Such being the case it would seem incredible that Islam should enjoin saint-worship. The *Ghayri muqallidin* do not believe in the *bay't*, if it means more than the making of a promise to a saintly person, to keep away from the ways of sin. However, most Muslims perform this ceremony and attach themselves to some one Pir or other.

The ways in which a man performs the *bay't* are different. The murid performs two *rak'at* namāz.[1] If he is illiterate, the Pir leads in the namāz, and the candidate simply follows him. Then he sits before his Pir four-square, and they join hands. If a woman is to become a murid, she takes hold of one end of a turban-cloth, while the Pir takes the other end; or a basin of water is put in front of them and they dip their hands at the same time and say the same prayers. The Pir says: "I take you as brother or sister in religion and ask you to accept the allegiance of all the Pirs up to the Prophet." Then he reads the Fātiha and concludes the ceremony. Then again there is a stage at which a man renounces the world and joins some order of Dervishes or Faqirs.

Asceticism is foreign to the teaching of Islam which openly proclaims that "there is no asceticism in Islam." Still several order of Faqirs have arisen. There are people who have honestly given up the world; and there are people who have made a show of doing it, with the object of gaining, more of it:

Ay basa Iblis ādam rnya ast,
Pus bihar dusti na bayad dad dust.

(Mathnawi)

O, there are many an Iblis in the form of man
Do not strike the palm (of hand) on that of everybody.

---

1. Murid is one who has attraction towards God; and Murād is one whom God attracts towards Himself.

When a person wishes to become a Faqir, he must become a murid (seeker after God) first, and then present himself before the chief of some Order, called *Sirguru.* He has first to prove that he is circumcised. The Pir takes a pair of scissors and cuts off three hairs from his forehead. This is cutting of the three vices of ignorance, pride and selfishness. The latter then gets himself completely shaved and has a bath. The Pir then gives him a strap of leather—$2^1/_2$ hands long, also a *lungutee* ($3^1/_2$ hands by $1^1/_2$ hands), and a *lungi* (lower garment) and a long cloth like a shroud and a cap for the head. If-all these latter are not within his means, he merely gives him a *lungutee.* The ceremony is then performed before the assembled Faqirs The murid is then clad in these garments, while the necessary texts are chanted aloud. A cup of *sharbat* already partaken of by the Pir is then given to the murid to drink. A dinner is to be given to the assembly by the candidate or the Pir; if this is not possible, they are satisfied with a mere cup of *sharbat* each. After this, the candidate becomes a regular Faqir. The Pir then teaches him the names of the four Pirs and fourteen *Khānwadas,* and how the different ceremonies connected with the initiation arose and on what authority they are based. The shaving of the eye-brows originated with Jamāluddin Sawochi and is based on the text "Am I not your Creator, they all said 'Thou art our Creator. "(*Alastu birabbikum, Qalu bala)*[1] The binding of the strap originated with either Belool or Meran Khil or Hadrat 'Ali. The *lungutee* arose with 'Abdulla. the standard-bearer, and is based on the text, *Al-ladhina āmanu wa 'amilus salihati sanadkhiluhum jannatin tajri min iahti-hal anharu).* [2]"They shall enter into it (the Heaven) for ever, etc.

The 'lung' arose with Khwaja Uwais-i-Qarni and is based

1. Sūra Araf, 9 :17.
2. Sūra Niā. iv : 47.

on the text, "You will never reach virtue, unless you spend all of what you love." *(Lan tanālul-birra hatta tunfiqu mimma tuhibbun).*[1] The ceremony of bathing arose with Khwāja Hasan Basri, and is based on the text, "Thou art to die and they are to die. And verily on the Day of judgment, you will not quarrel before your Lord."[2] *(Innaka mayyatun wa innahum lamayyitun, wa innakum yawmal-qiyamati inda rabbikum lā takhtasimun).* The ceremony of wearing the *cap* and giving *sharbat* arose with the Prophet, and they are based on the text, "God is the light of the heavens and the earth," (*Allahu nūrus samawāti wal ardi)*[3] and "Then gave them their Creator the purest wine" (*Saqahum rabbuhum sharaban tahura)* and so on.[4] Every ceremony is traced to some saint and is supposed to be based on some text of the Qur'ān.

The chief seat in this Presidency where the several bands of Faqirs are organised is Penukondah, a Qasba town in the Anantapur District. Each year on the 1st day of Jamādi-ul-Ākhar, the Faqirs of all orders Banava, Rafā'i, Madari, Malang, and Shāh Jalāl congregrate at this place and select their office bearers to go on a two-year pilgrimage to the tombs of the saints in the Presidency. The Banava order was founded by Ghulām 'Ali Shāh of Delhi, and is traced to the Saint 'Abdul Qādir Jilani. The Rafā'i order was founded by Saiyid Ahmad Kabir Rafā'i (ob. 756 A.H.) and is traced to Khwāja Junayd of Baghdād. The Madāri Order was founded by Shah Budruddin Qutub-ul-Madār. He seems to have come from Syria and to have travelled over a large part of North India and made thousands of converts to Islam, (ob. 840 A.H.) His shrine is in Makanpur in Oudh. His order is traced to Tyfūr of Syria—said to have been a disciple of Jesus Christ. The

1. Sūra Ali-'Imrān, iii : 85.
2. Sūra Zamar, xxiv.
3. Sūra, Nūr, 35.
4. Sūra Dahr, xxvi: 21

Jalāli Order was founded by Saiyid Jalāl Bokhari (ob. 699 A.H.) They wear a sash and bear a horn of deer, and the seal of Nabuwat on their shoulders. The selection of the chief of each of these orders was so long in the hands of the Faqirs themselves. Now it appears that the *Sajjāda* of Penukondah has this selection taken into his own hands. The latter is said to be descended from a brother of the local saint Bābā Fakhruddin and has got nine villages attached to the tomb. Out of the proceeds of two of these, he has to celebrate the annual festival. The *Sirguru* is the ruler of each Order, and "has dominion over all Faqirs of his Order in whatever part of the Presidency. The *Sirgwu* of Banavas must be a bachelor, and must have some knowledge of Tasawwuf; but as often as not, he is a mere ignoramus. He has the power of drumming out or excommunicating a Faqir from his Order, for breach of discipline.

Next in rank to *Sirguru* is the *Bhandari.* He is the Prime Minister of the Order, collects and spends money in behalf of the band. He is the money-bag man and distributes the money-share of each Faqir to him. Then comes the *Upkari.* He looks after the cooking and meals; the *Kotwāl* has to look after discipline and to accompany the *Sirguru* in his itinerations. The *Nakqib* has also to accompany and chant verses all along. Out of a collection of Rs. 100 (say), the *Sirguru* takes Rs. 5 and two shares; the *Bhandari* has no commission, but is entitled to 1 $^{1}/_{2}$ shares, the *Upkari, Kotwāl,* and *Nakqib* each take 1 $^{3}/_{4}$ shares; and one share is allotted to each Faqir in rank and file. These bands go on their two-year round in the Southern Presidency starting from Penukondah. The Sirguru holds four *chouks* or darbārs, *viz.,* at Penukondah, Matarwangal, Trichinoply, and Nagore.

At Penukondah there is the tomb of Bābā. Fakhruddin. He is said to have been a king of Sistan, a province of Persia, and a disciple of Nathar Auliyā (Mazharuddin), the saint of Trichinopoly.

He is the saint of cotton-carders (Panjaris).

On the 11th Jamādi-ul-Ākhar, the *sandal* ceremony is performed at Penukondab; on the 12th, the *urs;* and on the 13th the *asas* (staves) are taken round. From Penukondah, visiting small tombs *en route* and collecting their fixed *mamools,* the Faqirs go to Matarwangal, 22 miles from Kolar. Here is the tomb of Hayder Safdar, another disciple of Natbar Auliyā of Trichinopoly. Some of the Orders fall off from this place, the Banava Faqirs, however, proceed further. A times some of the Faqirs of the remaining Orders select their own chiefs for the remaining journey. At Trichinopoly there are the tombs of Nathar Auliyā and his two disciples Shumspurran and Shumsgoyan; Nathar Auliyā is also said to have been a king who became a saint. From Trichinopoly they go to Nagore, where there is the tomb of Qādir Wali. The last stage of the journey is the tomb of Buddū Shahid, near Pallavaram. The Faqirs have their *mamools* in each place, *e.g.*, at Dindigul (at the tomb of Saidāni Bi), the *mamool* is one dinner and Rs. 10. At the mosque of Tirumangalam, they get Rs. 5; at the Sivaganga mosque Rs. 30; at Tinnevelly, 5 day's meals and Rs. 150 and so on. A curious ceremony in connection with the four *chouks* mentioned above is that they make the Malang *Sirguru* sit foursquare, and tie raw thread round his toes, so that he is not to go even for the calls of nature for five days at Penukondah and Matarwangal ; and three days at Trichinopoly and Nagore; and then the Faqirs tread on fire in his presence. The practice of the visit from Penukondah to Trichinopoly appears to have arisen out of the custom of Bābā Fakhruddin paying an annual visit to Nathar Auilyā his Pir, during his life-time.

The salām amongst these bands is not the ordinary Mussulman salām. Amongst Banavas, it is "Love of God." Answer "Love to all." Amongst Malang and Madāris, it is "Huqq-Allāh Muhammad Madār" Answer "Dum Peer Shāh Madār." Amongst the Rafā'is "Love of God." Answer—"Love of Muhammad, the Prophet." When an order is on the move, the *Naqib* leads the band and calls out' 'Hush bar Dum," "Nazarbar-Qadam" *(i.e.,* wakefulness on breath and eye on foot).[1] These two are the terms of the Naqshbandiyyah Order. "Wakefulness on the breath" is akin to the Hindu Pranamaya. Each breath that goes up is said to voice forth, *"Laillāha"* and the one that goes in "*Illallah,*" "No god, except God," *i.e.,* in breathing out they negative all existences, and in breathing in, they acknowledge the only existence of God. "Eye on the foot," appears to be a fitting watchword in marching, and has for its objective the concentration of attention. Esoterically it is intended to put each man on his guard regarding the observance of the footsteps of the particular Prophet, he may have chosen for his model.

---

1. Vide page 137. ante

APPENDIX II

GHAZZALI "ON THE SOUL"[1]

"We equalised, breathed into it with our Breath."

The action that produces the highest degree of purification and moderation of temperament that is possible for the soul is called *equalisation;* the place of lodgment of the soul of Ādam was moist clay, with which his skeleton was built; that of his descendants is the germ of life within the man. In the world, there are solid substances like mud and stone, or liquids like water. Fire does not kindle either of these or the compounds of these. Fire has no effect on mud, till it undergoes modification, and becomes by natural process a regular vegetable. Man eats and assimilates the vegetable; it becomes his blood and humours. By a process of extraction, the essence of that blood becomes the germ within man. Within the womb of the future mother, the constitution of this germ is still further tempered, so that it becomes suitable to be the habitat of the soul. This process is very like the ignition of the wick of a lamp, which when soaked sufficiently well in oil, becomes fit to hold a flame. In short, when the germ attains its highest perfection and equalisation of temperament, it becomes deserving of a soul that might take possession of it. Then what is lacking that the great Benefactor and Giver who gives to every one his due, should not give to the embryo the soul that it is fit to hold? By equalisation is thus meant the process that the germ undergoes, till it becomes fit to hold the soul.

1. A free rendering from *Haqiqat-i-Ruh-i-Insāni*

The Breathing.—This refers to the cause by which the wick (embryo) becomes lighted with the flame of the soul. When a blower blows on a burning piece of tinder, it bursts into flame. Breathing therefore is the cause of the flame. The cause that is thus fixed is an unsuitable expression in the case of God, and therefore the effect is here taken for the cause.

The Qur'an says: "God became wrath with them and thus took vengeance." Now anger is an emotion that affects the temperament of the angry person, so much so that he feels distressed at it. This is impossible in the case of God. Here therefore the effect of anger is meant; the person who is the subject on whom the anger is vented is annihilated. Thus the effect of anger is taken for the cause. Similary the cause from which the effect (breathing) is brought about is taken for the breathing itself. There is no actual blowing in of breath.

The Wick and the Flame.—This is the conjunction of two attributes. One attribute is that of real acting or creating, and the other the existence of a temperament fit to receive the soul. The name of the Actor is the Great Bestower; and He bestows things on those who really require them and are fit to receive them. He gives existence to that which has the fitness to receive existence. He has another attribute called the Power. He is like the sun which lights up things which have the fitness to show themselves off, when there is nothing between them and the sun. The attribute to receive is thus the transparency of the thing itself. A mirror is tarnished. There may be faces in front of it, but they are not reflected in it. The furbisher begins to furbish the mirror and removes the tarnish. As the tarnish disappears, the faces opposite to it gradually appear in it; in fact, the faces are created in the mirror. Similarly, as the germ develops into an embryo and the embryo attains its equalisation of temperament and perfection, the soul too appears in it from the Creator of the soul. There is no change in the Creator, just as there was no change in the face that was reflected in the mirror, immediately the mirror became bright. To say that the soul was created then only, and did not exist before, is a mistake. The non-reflexion of a face in a mirror does not point to its non-existence before the mirror became bright.

The Great Beneficence.—When water falls on the hand from a vassel, the particles of water separate themselves from the vessel and fall on the hand. This is not an apt illustration of God's beneficence. It is however comparable to the sun, which lights the walls of a house. People incorrectly assume that the rays separate themselves from the sun, and attach themselves to things or spread themselves on the walls. The light of the sun is the cause of the appearance of a thing which is a fit receptacle for the sun's rays, though it might be less reflected on a wall. It is like the reflexion of a face in the mirror. The face does not detach itself from the person, and attach itself to the mirror. The face of a man becomes the cause of exigence of the face in the mirror, which is fit to reflect it. There is no detachment on one hand, and attachment on the other. In things that have aptitude to assume existence, the cause of their existence is the *beneficence* of God.

What is the Soul?—This is a question, the answer to which the Prophet was prohibited from giving in the case of unfit persons. To those that are fit to understand, there is no prohibition. The soul is not a substance that has been poured into the body, like water into a vessel. It is not an extension that exists in the heart and brain of man like blackness in a black thing or knowledge in the knower. It is, on the other hand, an essence that knows itself and its Creator, and enquires into causes and effects.

Knowledge is extension. If the soul were extension, then the existence of extension upon extension would become possible. This, however, is an impossibility in the view of philosophers. There is another proof that it is an essence and not an extension. An extension possesses one attribute, being one dimension of a thing; but the soul has two opposite attributes; while it knows itself, it knows its Maker also. It is not a body. A body is capable of being divided. If soul were capable of division or breaking up, there would be knowledge in one part of it, and ignorance in another. It would thus be cognizant and ignorant of the same thing at the same time. Knowledge and ignorance of one and the same thing at one and the same time is impossible.

Thus it is one; it has no parts, and it is a thing that cannot be divided. The word *part* is unsuitable, for part implies a whole, and no whole exists here. It may be a part in the sense that one is a part of ten; for when all parts are taken which exist in ten, then one will be one of the parts. Take the whole creation, or those things that constitute the existence of men; their soul will be one of them.

How it exists.—It is neither within or without the body; it is neither separate from it nor connected with it. It has been proved that soul is neither corporeal nor spatial. When it is neither of these, then the question of its connexion or separateness is as much unconnected with it as the question of ignorance or knowledge with a mineral. A mineral is neither cognizant nor ignorant; for knowledge and ignorance, life is a condition; and when life itself is denied to a mineral, then whatever is dependent on life should also be denied.

The Soul's Direction.—it is free from all the qualities of being contained in a space, connected with a body or particularised in a direction. These are the attributes or dimensions of a body; and when it is proved that soul is neither a body nor an extension of a body, then it is free from all those attributes.

The Forbidden Explanation.—Common people cannot have the understanding of this. There are two sets of people—the common and the elect. The former cannot understand the attributes of God; how then can they understand the attributes of the soul ? The Karāmatians and the Hanbalis who are overshadowed by materiality have become Corporealists, have denied the attributes of God Himself, and cannot understand how God can have no body. Those—advanced a stage further—have no doubt denied cor poreality; but could not deny the attributes dependent on corporeality. They have fixed a direction. Then come the last—the 'Asharis and Mutazilites, who have advanced the furthest, and believe Him to be existence free from direction and dependence.

Why mysteries are not for the common people.— An impression has gained ground amongst them, that the attributes ascribed to the soul are impossible except in the case of God. One runs the risk of being labelled heterodox, if he ascribes these attributes to the soul. They would think that the attributes peculiar to God are assumed not only for the soul, but for the personal self.

How the attributes are common to God, and others than God.—They think it impossible that two things in space can occupy one and the same place at one and the same time. Similarly they think it impossible that two things can do so in non-space. In the first case (of two things in space), they think that their distinction would disappear, and they would coalesce into one. In the second case, they think that if one of the two things in non-space requires no space, their distinction would disappear. Two dimensions cannot occupy the same space. The objection is seemingly valid. It is a palpable mistake to suppose that distinction between two objects is made known on account of space. The distinction may be from three sources: from *space*—two things in two places are distinguishable; from *time*—two extensions in one essence in two different times are distinguishable; and the third from *definition.* Different extensions of one and. the same object are distinguishable at one and the same time by mere description or definition, as, for example, saltness and moisture in a particular object. Time and space are one; but by mere description they are distinguishable. Knowledge and intention (Divine)—these are distinguishable by themselves by mere description or definition; otherwise the whole is one only. When extension of objects is imagined and distinguished, different objects, though they may not be in space, can be imagined and distinguished. It would appear that to give such attributes to soul is to bestow the attributes of God on it, and to make the two similar. This is not so; no similarity is established between man and God, when we speak of man as living, knowing, powerful, hearing, speaking, although those attributes belong to God also. Similarly to be non-spatial is not a peculiar attribute of God. The special attribute of God in which no one partakes is His everlastingness. He is, by His essence, everlasting—by His essence, living, and so on. The essence of all things is nothingness; their existence is borrowed from God. God's existence is His essence and is not borrowed; everlastingness is the special attribute of God.

Breathed with our Breath.—The question arises: "Why with our breath? and why is the breathing specified?" All things owe their existence to God; why this particularity in regard to soul ?

In one place, God has said: "I created man out of putrid mud, and told the angels, 'I am going to create man out of mud; and then again He said: "When I properly tempered it, I breathed my spirit into it." What then is the meaning of this breathing? If it means that breath left God and joined man, then division in the nature of God becomes possible; but this cannot be. The answer to this question may be illustrated from the sun. If the sun says, "I have given light to the earth," this will be correct. The earth, although there might have been little light. in it, was not like the atmosphere. Thus Soul was free from space and dimensions; to become cognizant of everything was potential in it, although it has no comparison with God; but in other bodies there was nothing of the sort, and hence the particularity.

Spirit, the Command of God.—The "world of command" is simply the world in which there is no measurement, estimate or delineation; and the world of creation is the world in which these qualities exist. It does not necessarily mean *invention.* The "world of command" is therefore the world which is above sense, thought, direction and space. There is no quantity in it, it does not come within the purview of measurement; but the world of creation is just the opposite of this. The souls of men and angels belong to the world of command.

Whether Soul is Created.—Although a set of people believe that the soul is uncreated, I do not believe it. We say "the soul is not created" in the sense that it is not subject to measurement or division. But all the same, it is created in the sense that it is not original and not everlasting. When the embryo becomes fit and suitable enough, the Spirit manifests itself in it; just as in the mirror, a face manifests itself immediately the mirror acquires sufficient brilliancy.

A face may be existent previously, but it does not appear in the mirror till the latter becomes fit for it. Immediately the mirror is burnished, it reflects the face.

After Separation.—In virtue of connexion with bodies, souls acquire certain qualities, such as knowledge, ignorance, purity, impurity, good morals and the reverse. On account of the acquisition of these, their separateness will remain, which was not the case before their connexion.

The Image of God.—The word *'sūrat* (image or face) has different meanings in Arabic. It means shape or combination of shapes, as of bodies which we sense. Sometimes it means *proposition;* one might speak of the *sūrat* or shape of a problem in Euclid. It may mean the image of a combination of circumstances. Here shape or *sūrat* is the metaphorical shape of the thing. It means the connexion between essence and attributes and actions. We have explained that soul is an essence; it is neither a body nor an extension. It is not an essence contained in space or direction ; it is neither connected with nor detached from body; is neither within nor without the body. These things are in God also. Consider the attributes of God. The soul is living, knowing, powerful, willing, hearing. seeing, speaking. These are God's attributes also.

The Source of Man's Actions.—It is *will* or intention. It manifests itself in mind, and then with the aid of the animal soul (which is a term for ethereal vapour). it circulates through the system and rises to the brain. From there it acts on the nerves which emanate from it, and reaches the arteries, veins and muscles. When the nerve absorbs it, the finger moves, and through the finger, the pen; then there is motion in ink, and then a form appears which originally was in will or intention. This form is according to the form in the treasure-house of our thought. Whoever has dived into the actions of God, and pondered over them and considered the skies and stars and their influences, cannot but be struck with the thought that angels play the same part in the macrocosm as do our faculties in our microcosm; and that man's control over his body is very like God's control over the world.

Man has the same control over his *qalb* (mind), as God has over his *'arsh;* the brain corresponding to *kursi* and the senses to the angels, who by nature are obedient to the Owner and do not disobey Him, just as our senses do not disobey us. The organs and the muscles correspond to the skies; the power in the fingers corresponds to the nature with which the Creator has endowed every living creature. The paper, pen and ink (in our simile) are the element through which combinations and dispersions manifest themselves. The mirror of our thought corresponds to the *Lauh-i-mahfūz* (the preserved Tablet).

He who has understood this will grasp the meaning of the tradition: "God created man in His own image." "He who understands his *Nafs* (soul) understands his God." If the relations and correspondences, described above, are not understood, man cannot, from a knowledge of his *Nafs,* understand his God. If God had not concentrated in man all the things that are in the world, and had not made him a small model (microcosm) and had not made him the rabb (the ruler) of this microcosm, he would not have understood the great world and its rabb (ruler) who controls it with knowledge, power and wisdom; and would not have become cognizant of any of the attributes of God. By such a relation, nafs becomes one of the rungs of the ladder to the knowledge of the Maker of the nafs.

The Reaction of the Prophet.—The Prophet has said: "God created souls two thousand years before the bodies." "I was before all the Prophets, but in mission the last of them all." "I was a Prophet when Ādam was in clay and water." The first Hadith clearly shows that the soul is *non-eternal* and is a created object. At first blush, it would appear as if the souls were created before the bodies, and they existed before them. It is however possible that the souls of angels are meant, and that the bodies referred to are *'arsh, kursi,* the heavens, stars, mud and water. Remember that the bodies of men *en masse* are insignificantly small in comparison with the body of the sun. The body of the sun small beyond comparison with that of its heaven and with the heaven about it; and so on until finally we reach the *kursi* in which all are contained, This latter is so small in comparison with the *'arsh* of God, that there can be no comparison between the two. When all these are considered, the bodies of men *en masse* are so insignificantly small that they cannot be thought of. Remember also that the souls of men *en masse* are also as small, in comparison with the body of the *'ālam* (from man to *'arsh).* Their appearance would manifest to one endowed with the light of illumination as the flame of a wick in comparison with the fire that has enshrouded the whole *'ālam.* That fire is the souls of angels. There is a gradation amongst the angels. They are separate, and no two of them are in one rank, as in opposition to the souls of men; which in spite of their multiplicity are all one in kind and rank. Each angel is *sui generis.* God has made the angels say (in the Qur'ãn*):* "There is no one of us but hath his known place." "We are those having purity." The Prophet has said that none of those who are in *rukū'* perform the *sajdah;* and none of those who are in *qiyām* perform their *rukū'.* Verily there is none amongst them, who hath not his appointed place. Thus the souls and the bodies mentioned in the hadith are the angels and the bodies in the creation. As for the second Hadith, "I am the first, in creation, of the Prophets; but the last of them all," hereby creation is meant the same estimate, plan or forecast which I have mentioned above. It does not mean "the bringing into existence"; for the Prophet never existed till he was born. The excellences and perfections that manifested themselves in him were first in the forecast of God, though last in point of manifestation, amongst the Prophets. This is the same as the Arabic saying: "First thought, then action." An engineer thinks of constructing a building. In the plan in his mind, there exists a fully constructed and finished building; but it is only then that actual construction begins. So far as he is concerned, the fullyconstructed house already exists in his thought; although material construction is his last act, there have been many stages from start to finish—the digging of foundations, the collection of materials, the raising of the walls, the putting up of the roof. These are mere intermediaries to bring his thought into full material existence.

What is the Object of Man's Existence—To know the excellence of proximity to God. This becomes known to us from the teaching of the Prophets. The foundation-stone is first to be laid; when this is done, the construction progresses upon it from stage to stage, till the building is complete. InĀdam, the foundation was laid, and the finishing touch was given in the Prophet (peace be upon him). This is the meaning of the saying, "he is the seal of the Prophets"; for an addition to perfection is a defect. The perfection of our hand consists in one palm and five fingers. Just as a four-fingered man is defective, so is a six-fingered man. Perfection consists in five fingers and five alone; the sixth is an additional appendage and a defect. The Prophet has compared Prophetship to a building, which is all but complete for want of one brick. He was the last brick to give perfection to the building. Thus we see there cannot be an addition to a complete building, and that (if there were) such an addition would be a defect. These things were in the forecast of God first, although they came last in the order of existence. As for the third Hadith: "I was a Prophet whileĀdam was in mud and water," the explanation of this in the same strain.

The creation of the children ofĀdam could not he complete, until a perfect man was born amongst them—one who perfected the object of creation. In him, we believe creation reached its perfection, when it accepted the blessed soul of the Prophet, God first makes an estimate, and then brings it into objective existence; just as an engineer draws up a plan on paper or on slate. The engineer draws up the plan with his pen; but it is the knowledge of the engineer that sets the pen in motion. Similarly God draws up his plans with the pen of His Power on the tablet of His knowledge. Remember that a tablet is simply an object, which has the aptitude of being engraved upon ; and a pen is the object which draws up figures on this tablet. This pen and tablet are not a reed and an oblong board. Materiality is not a condition of their existence. The pen and tablet of God must be suitable to His hand; they are free from material existence. The truth is they are spiritual essences,

APPENDIX III

TECHNICAL TERMS IN TASAWWUF

'Ārif; One who observes the *Dhāt* and attributes and actions separately, and in conjunction with each other in his state *(hāl);* and not merely talks of these. One who has lost consciousness of these himself in the *'irfān* or knowledge of God.

'Abd: That which is manifest. The first *'abd* is "I"—the stage of Muhummad (peace be upon him). With one *rabb* (God), there is one '*abd* (the Prophet); and from this first 'abd other *'abds* are manifested; the first *'abd* is, therefore, a barzakh between God and the creation. Tauhid therefore is a reality, in which there is no rabb and no 'abd *(Tauhidu haqiqa-tun lā rabba wu lā 'abda).*

Abdāl: These are the seven auliyā who guard the seven continents. They arc called abdāl (those who change), because they can change into any form they please. They can be present in one place, and show themselves in their causal bodies in different places.

'Ādam: Nothingness. This is of two kinds: Real and Relational. Real *'ādam* does not exist; for if it did, it would be the opposite of God and would no longer be *'ādam.* Thus its existence is impossible. Excepting the letters A, D, A, M, nothing exists are externality. It has no *Dhāt* behind it; it is only an *'ādam* in words *('ādam-i-malfūzi).* It is a name without the named; merely for the purpose of argument, a name is given to it.

Relational 'adam *(ādam-i-idāfi);* this is the reality of *a'yān*—which are clothed in the existence of God (according to the Shuhūdiyyah School); or according to which God manifests Himself (according to the Wajūdiyyah), *i.e.,* the relation that exists between God and forms of *'ābd* in His knowledge is God's own existence. The *a'yān* are forms which are not differentiated from Him in the very first stage of Tanazzulāt.

Ahwāl: (sing. *Hāl),* conditions to which the 'ābd is transferred by purifying his *Nafs;* conditions that overshadow one's being spontaneously like fear, happiness, zest, love, etc.

Allāh: Al-Ila (Ar. and Sanskrit. El. Hebrew, Eel "the worshipped") One who is worthy of worship; one before whom we humiliate ourselves. Name applied to God, implying all the attributes of perfection (the attributes of imperfection and defect being applicable to the *Dhāt* of 'ābd, nothingness ('ādam). Shah Kamal of Cuddapah has said :

> *Mayn hun asam, shunwa hay haq, mayn bey basar bina hay haq*
>
> *Mayn gung hun, goya hay haq, mayn nay hun, haq mawjud hay.*

I am deaf, the Truth is Hearing
I am blind, the Truth is seeing
I am dumb, the Truth is speaking
I am nothing, the Truth is existing.

The word is used in the first stage of Infinity where all indications are dropped (*Al-Tauhidu is-qātul-ishārāt);* in the second stage, the attributes of perfection are predicated, and in the third, where such attributes become detailed, they indicate the named *(musammā).*

'Anāniyat: The ego of God. Gulshan-i-Rāz says:

Haqiqat kaz taiyyun shud muiyyan
Tu wu ra dar ibarat guftai man.
Truth by limitation, became limited
You call it "I" in your common parlance.

In the lower creation, it is limited; in man it is unlimited. When a man is conscious of his unlimitedness and infinity, he becomes Insān-i-Kāmil (the Perfect Man). If he does not. he is *zālim* and *jāhil.* The 'anāniyat of 'abd is the 'anāniyat of God in limitation. An Apostalic Hadith says: *Inna fi jasadi adama la-muzghatun wa fi muzghatin fawadun, wa fil fuwad ruhun wa fir-ruhin sirrun wa fi sirri kafi, wa fil kafi akfa wa fil akfa anā.* The 'anāniyat is thus hidden under seven sheaths, akfā (most secret) *kafi*, (secret), *sirr*, rūh (soul), *fuwad, muzga* (lump) *jasad* (body). Shaykh Ahmad Sarhindi has located his six subtitles (Latāyef) thus; akfā in the head-plate, kafi in the forehead,, rūh in the right-side, qalb in the left, *sirr* above the navel, and Nafs in the navel.

Asmā (sing. *Ism*), An *Ism* is the *Dhãt* looked at from a particular view-point; which view-point becomes a shan and then a sifat. This aspect or sifat of the Dhat comes into operation (fā'il) and appears in form, and the form is that by which it is sensed.—The iorm of ism-i-kiyāni, ergo of ism-i-ilāhi, *i.e.,* an aspect of the *Dhãt* is just what is sensed; or as Ibn Arabi has put it, *Al-Haqqu mahsūsun wal khalaqu ma'qūlun* (the Truth is sensed and the creation inferred). Imām Ghazzāli in his "Asmā'-i-Husna" (the Beautiful Names) gives the illustration of water and its thirst-quenching quality (attribute). This shān is inherent in water, becomes potential in your imagination, before it becomes kinetic in its proper place (the animal system). It manifests itself in operation, but it is the eternal aspect of water. God is creator and rabb, whether or not there is the creation or marbub. The Names are applicable, when their counter-aspects are in manifestation, and are sensed in their aspects of forms.

The Ism-i-ā'zam (the Great name) of God is Allāh. Some consider it to be Rahmān; and some consider it to be either Rahim or Hayy (the Living one) or Qayyūm (the eternal one). It is the

Shem-hamphorash of Talmud. The asmā' are either of *Dhãt* like Quddūs (Holy), Salām (everlasting or of sifāt, which are of limited aspect, like 'Ālim (all-knowing), Murid (the willer). To remember God (in *dhikr)* by the *Dhãt* name is to show honour to all His other names; whereas to remember him by the sifāt name is to limit Him to that name. When you remember Him by a particular name that name must manifest itself, e. g., if a sick man calls out "Yā Shāfi" (O Healer) he must get well at once; but in most cases this does not happen, because, says Ghaz-zāli (in his Asmā'-i-Husna), he does not know the exact name and the exact way and circumstance in which he has to call out that name, *e.g.* a healthy man calling out "yā, shūfi," must become sick before that name manifests itself. Hence it is safer to call Him by His personal names than by His sifāti names.

Auliyā: (sing. *Wali).* Those who have obtained proximity to God. They are those who have ascended from the lowest to the highest rung of the ladder. Some like Ibn 'Arabi, consider that the state of wali is higher than that of prophet in the Prophet Muhammad (peace be upon him); because Wilāyat is proximity to God and Prophetship is proximity to the Creation. A wali is an Abul-Waqt (father or controller of the time) as opposed to an Ibn-ul-Waqt (son of the time—one who swims with the current of time). An Abul-Waqt is one who has annihilated his will in the Will of God; and in him the Will of God alone manifests itself; and he does what God wills—he works wonders and miracles. An Ibn-ul-Waqt is one who observes the manifestations of asmā', and adjusts himself to the requirement of those asmā'.

A'yān: Thought-forms of the *Dhãt*. Forms of jug, saucer, etc., are the bodies in which clay appears; and these exist only in imagination; their peculiarities come into display by means of clay. A'yān are similarly the outlines in which the existence appears. Hence it is said that a'yān never smelt the smell of existence *(ma shummu rahiyatul wa-jud).* They are realities, so far as God's knowledge is concerned; they are unrealities, so far as their externality is concerned. They are called *Thabilah* as they are *permanent* unrealities externally. Philosophers, call them non-existent *shay* (thing desired) and *mahiyyat.* Since they are permanent in God's knowledge as *adam-i-malfuzi,* they are called A'yan-i-Thabita. They are thus eternal in God's knowledge; in externality their manifestation is fleeting. They cannot be said to be non-eternal in their inward aspect; for then God's knowledge will have to be considered non-eternal, which is impossible. A'yān begin after the stage of Wahidiyat, where their manifestation begins, and when they are called A'yān-i Kharija which are subject to annihilation.

Ayniyat: 'Sameness.' When two things are identical it is 'Ayniyat, like ice and water, wave and sea. This 'ayniyat holds good in the case of the *Dhāt* and sifāt of God and servant. This is a real identification, as in the identity of words and ink: the number one and ten, etc. The 'ayniyat is real *(haqiqi)* as is proved by such verses as "I am in your Nafs, you do not see me" (*wa fi anfusikum afala tubsirūn).*[1] "We are near you. but you do not see" *(wa nahnu aqrabu ilayhi minkum wa lakin la tubsirūn).*"[2] As opposed to 'Ayniyat, there is Ghayriyat, which is suppositional or in fancy. This is owing to i'tibārāt in existence. God is independent in the worlds. *(Inn Allaha lā ghaniyyun anil 'ātamin.)*

Burūz : The influence of one soul on another, both being where they are. The soul is neither within the body nor without it. Its sight is on the physical body. When it sees 'Izrā'il, the Angel of Death, it is so enamoured of him that it shifts its sight to the mithāl body; and the physical body dies. When it shifts its sight to the

1. Sūra li: 22.
2. Sūra lvi: 27.

body of rūh, the mithāl body also disintegrates. In Burūz, the soul of one individual influences the soul of another (and consequently the physical body of the latter), both being where they are, (there being no change in the influencing soul).

The soul of Sanā'i influenced the soul of Rūmi in this way; or the soul of Abū Sa'id Abul Khayr influenced the soul of Ibn 'Arabi. This is different from Tanāsukh (metempsychosis), in which one soul peregrintates from body to body; which doctrine is "abominable to the Muslim." This is the same as *Tamassul,* (spiritual resemblance) in which angels or saints take shape in different places, being where they are in their original places, *e.g.,* the angel Gabriel appeared before the Prophet (peace by upon him) in the form of Dihyā Kalbi, or a sahābi, or in that of an Arab of the Desert being in his own sphere. God appeared to Moses in a burning bush or to the Prophet (peace be upon him) in the shape' of a "beardless youth" *amrudin khatat).*

Barzakh: A barrier of separation between two things or states, whether allied to each other, or not; as anthropoid ape is barzakh between man and beast; coral is barzakh between the vegetable and mineral kingdoms, the date tree is barzakh between the vegetable and animal kingdom; *mithāl* is barzakh between the causal and soul worlds.

Shāh Waliyullah Sāhib has used the term Barzakh for the state after the earthly life, confining the term *mithāl* to pre-natal condition, although the two terms are promiscuously used ordinarily. In barzakh, one assumes a garb befitting the character that had predominated him in the earthly life, e.g. If one had the character of using a sharp and stinging tongue (or a similar quality) in this life, he assumes the form of a scorpion, while he still retains his earthly self-consciousness (*vide* p. 108 *ante).* This prevents him from disclosing himself to his former earthly relatives and acquaintances already living in the barzakh world, who have retained or regained their earthly form, or who have acquired a luminous form or body there. If one assumes a particular unhuman form, he draws to himself similar forms already existing there, for according to the *Mathnawi*:

Nariyan mur nāriyan ra jaziband
Nūriyan mur nuriyan ra taliband.
Ahl-i-bātil bātilan ra mi kashund
Bāqiyan ba bāqiyan hum sur khusand.
The people of fire absorb the people of fire,
The people of light draw the people of light.
Pepole who are in darkness draw similar people towards them
Those who are saved are happy in the company of the saved.

If one is transformed into a scorpion in the barzakh, the other scorpions of that region or even his own verdical thought forms so transformed,[1] draw or are drawn towards him and ply their stings on him that being their character, and he being a new arrival in that region.

Similarly, if he has assumed the form of a dog (retaining his former identity), the other dogs of that region bark at him and bite him. This is the treatment accorded to a new arrival in the barzakh; and this is why a burial in the vicinity of the tomb of an auliyā or in the compound of a mosque is much preferred by Muslims to burial elsewhere; the influence of the auliyā or the holy magnetic atmosphere of the place serves to keep these old K.D's of this region at a distance from the new arrival. The auliyā's holy influence transforms the *mithāl* body of the new arrival into a luminous body. The Qur'ān says: *Khalaqal insāna fi ahsani tāqawim summa. raddad nahu asfaha sāfilin.* "We created man in the

1. *Shari-Barzakh* of Abū Sa'id Salami (translated by Maulavi 'Abdul Ghaffaf Sahib of Bangalore). chap. 58.

best of forms, and sent him down to the worst plane," In the *mithāl* world (prenatal), he had a heavenly form; having appeared in this world, he by his behaviour made himself eligible for another form (suitable or unsuitable as the case may be to his dignity as man). *Ad-dunyā mazratul akhira.* This world is the harvest-ground of the next. If he assumes an unsuitable form in the barzakh, a form unbefitting his humanity, he remains in it till the Day of judgment. It is only the luminous bodies that hear calls and prayers; and the dark bodies engrossed in their own character do not.

Bay't: Paying homage by laying the palm of one's hand on that of another—a Pir by preference. In the beginning, the Prophet used to receive homage from the people accepting Islam. The homage that was received from some people of Tā'if near Madina is called Bay't-ul-Ridwān. Secondly, it was a promise taken from those who volunteered for Jihād; and thirdly it was taken from searchers after truth. It was, however, a question whether it is sunnat or mustahab or wājib or fard. Those who consider it fard bring in the Hadith, "Search after knowledge is fard on all Muslims, male or female." *Talabul 'ilmi ' faridatun 'ala kulli Muslimin wa Muslimātun.*

Baqā: A condition in which the *'abd* is not hindered from seeing God on account of materiality, which is only *'ādam.*

Bātin: The interior of every from or world, e.g., the bātin of 'ālam-i-nāsut (the material world) is 'alam-i-mithal (the world of similitudes), the bātin of 'ālam-i-mithāl is 'ālam-i-arwāh (the soul-world), the bātin of 'ālam-i-arwāh is 'ālam-i-a'yān (which is Wāhidiyat); and *Dhāt* or Ahdiyat is the bātin of 'Ālam-i-a'yan

Haq bi jan andar nihan, o jan bi tan andar nihan,
Aynihan. andar nihan, andar nihan, andar nihan.
Ain chuni ramzi ayan khud bi nishān o' bi guman
Ay jahan, andar jihan, andar jihan, andar jihan

The truth is hidden in life and life is hidden in body,
O hidden, within hidden, within hidden, within hidden.
This is a mystery—obvious without doubt and sign,
O world, within world, within world, within world.

Sometimes *bātin* is applied to all the worlds from mithāl upwards and *zāhir* only to the causal world.

Durratul-Bayda, or *'Yākūt-ul-Abyad:* The first Intelligence; a Hadith says: *Awwala ma khalaquitahu Durratul-Bayda;* the next name is Nafs-i-Kul, which is called Durratul-Ahmar (the Red Chrysolite).

Dhāt: The Wūjudiyyah school considers the *Dhāt* (Reality) itself is wujūd (existence); so also do the Ash'aris (which include the Sunnis), the followers of Abu Hasan al-Ash'ari The Shuhūdiyyah school considers that it is separate from *Wujūd, i.e., Dhāt* in the first stage is without "be-ness" *i.e.,* without any indication *(ishāra)* whatever. The *Dhāt* of Wujūdiyyah appears to be wujūd-i-idāfi (the additional existence), which comes within cognizance and which is a reflection of the *Dhāt* of Shuhudiyyah; for in Tauhid there is no indication (*at Tauhidu isqāt 'ul-ishārāt).*

Dhikr: Repetition of God's name or names. It may be vociferous, as in the case of a beginner (*Dhikr-i-Jali);* it may be silent, in which the Dhakir forgets the words, and thinks only of the named. In another kind, both the Dhākir and Dhikr disappear, and the relish of Dhikr alone remains *(Dhikr Rūhi).*

In Dhikr-i-Qalbi, the sālik disappears by himself and fancies God to be in his form. "I am not and God is." In Dhikr-i-Rūhi, the salik sees his *Dhāt*, sifāt and af'āl, as the *Dhāt*. sifāt and af'āl of God.

Didār: (The Vision Beatific). When the *'abd* reaches his *'ayn*; he loses his egoism and then his vision becomes God's vision of himself. He becomes *Hū Hū* (He, without attributes) in the highest stages; in the lower stages, he has illuminations like lightning, etc. The *'abd* cannot vision the absolute; the finite cannot realize the infinite except through the screen of sifāt; but in his journey on the upward are, the sālik travels towards the absolute and infinite; one who ascends the successive stages of the absolute by Mujāhada, has vision according to that stage. In the limited, the vision is of the limited; in arwāh, the vision of arwāh. While the absolute sees the limited, the limited cannot see the absolute, or to put it in the profane words of Prof. Huxley, you cannot feel how a cray-fish feels, until you become the cray-fish itself. To see the absolute, one must merge in the absolute itself.

But this is a matter to be felt and realized and not talked of:

Dhawq-i-aein bada na dani
Bi-khuda ta na chashi.

This intoxication is not realized

Till you have tasted of the wine.

This part of the esoteric doctrine of Tasawwuf is inculcated by means of signs and symbols and not by words. The limited can see only the limited; the figures of our friends in 'ālam-i-mithāl are seen by us in real dreams. If they have progressed upwards to 'ālam-i-arwāh, they are not seen, unless we in ajsām have also progressed to a higher stage by Mujāhada or by the special grace of God. A Yogi in his physical body who has attained to a higher state of consciousness can see in his Samathi what another in his ordinary physical body cannot; what wonder then that the Prophet (peace be upon him) being in his physical body had his *mi 'rāj.*

The Didār of *Dhāt* in this life, however, lasts for an infinitesimal part of a minute in the case of ordinary sālik, and a little longer in the case of auliyā. It flashes on mind like lightning (*vide* p. 99-100 *ante).* A Persian poet says:

Hayf dar chushm zadan suhbat-i-yar akhar shud
Ruyi gul sayr na didim wu bahar akhar shud.

Alas thy companionship departed in an eye's twinkling.
The beauty of the flower was hardly seen when the spring departed.

Didār is the special privilege of man, as the Khalifa of God on the earth *(Inni ja'lnaka khalifatun fil ardi);* for even angels of the *Malā-i-a'lā',* who support the 'Arsh (throne) of God are still in search of Didār. A hadith of the Prophet (peace be upon him) quoted by Ibn 'Arabi[1] says: *Innallaha ihtajaba anil absari wu annal mala il a'lā' yātlumu nahu kama tatlubunahu antum.* God is Hidden from the Intelligences (angels) as He is hidden from our eyes. The angels are in search of Him, as you are in search of Him.

It is only the man who searches for totality in the Total, the All in the all, that has the vision; and this is to be in this world only, for, as the Qur'ān says, he who is blind in this world is also blind in the next. *Man kana fi hazi hil ama fa hua fit akhirati ama wa azullu sabila.*[2]

This eye is, however, the mind's eye : *La tudrikuhul absar wa hua yudrikul absar wa hua lateefun khabir.* The sight does not see Him, He sees the sight. He is the subtle and nice-discerning. The bodily eye becomes the mind's eye.

Emān: The Qur'ān says : *Yā ayynhal ladhina amanu, aminu billahi wa Rasūlihi wa kitabil ladhi nuzzila 'ala Rasūlihi.*[3]

"O believers who have brought faith, bring faith in God and in His Prophet and in the Book that He has sent down to His Prophet." The bringing in of the first faith is Islam; and that of the second is Emān. In the first, it is simply making a profession of the Creed *(Emān-i-Taqlidi)*; and the second is making a profession after investigation (*Emān-i-Tahqiqi).* In what is known as the

1. Futūhat-i-Makkiyah, vol. I, chap. Ill, sec. 5.
2. Sūra Bani Isra'il, xvii: 72.
3. Sūra Nisā,' iv : 13.

Hadith-i-Gabriel, which is the opening Hadith of Mishkāt-ul Masābih, it is stated that a stranger made his appearance before the Prophet (peace be upon him) and asked him some four questions. What is Islam? What is Emān ? What is Ihsan ? and when is the Qiyāmat. "Ihsān," the Prophet said, "is worshipping God as if you see Him or if this cannot be done, it is worshipping Him as if He sees you." This is Emān-i-Haqiqi, in which the devotee worships Him as if he sees Him, *i e.,* his mind's eye is opened, and he sees the 'ālam-i-mithāl and ālam-i-arwāh, and even penetrates as far as the Haqiqat-i-Muhammadi. The certainty obtained is Real Faith (Emān-i-Haqiqi). Hence the injunctions of the Qur'ān to bring faith once again. The Emān of the Muslim is concerned with his sight, and not with his hearing, such as it was in the case of the Israelites who had the injunction to hear, "Hear, O Israel, Jehovah our Elohim is one Jehovah" A Muslim advances up to the soul-stage, the characteristic of which is sight, while audition is perceptible and that feebly in the *mithāl* stage only.

Imām Ghazzāli has given three stages of the progress of certainty or knowledge. First 'Ilm-ul-Yaqin (knowing certainty). This is like your seeing smoke and inferring the existence fire. It is the lowest kind of Emān. The second is 'Ayn-ul-yaqin (ocular certainty) when you actually see the fire and believe in its existence. The sight is at times delusive, as in the case of a mirage; and hence the third is Haqq-ul-Yaqin, (certainty of certainty), when you approach the fire and experience its warmth. This precludes all doubt. The Qur'ān invites the believer not only to experience the faith of the second kind (to see 'ālam-i-mithāl and 'ālam-i-arwāh, etc.) but also to travel through these regions by sulūk and mujahada and thus bring in a faith founded on the bed-rock of personal experience. (Emān-i-Haqiqi).

Fāna (fis-Shaykh): To consider one's self as existing in the form of one's Pir; and to annihilate one's self in him. *Fanā fil-Rasūl,* to do the same in the case of the Prophet. *Fanā-fillāh,* the same in God. '*Abd* is '*ādam* and does not exist; for non exists but God. The existence of '*abd* is only the manifestation of the sifat of God. In fanā, the Sālik loses consciousness of himself; hence here is the '*ādam* of cognition, and not the cognition of 'ādam.

Farq-ma'al'Jam; To differentiate '*abd* from rabb is Farq; and to identity '*abd* with rabb in existence is jam. To see 'abd in *rabb* and *rabb* is '*abd* is Farq-ma'al-Jam.

Fayd-i-Aqdas : Manifestation of a'yān in *Dhāt*, before external manifestation; and Fayd-i-Muqaddas is manifestation of asmā' externally, according to forms in God's knowledge.

Faqir: A person who has subsistence for self and family for sometime; and *Miskin* is one who has no subsistance even for one time. In Tasawwuf, a faqir is one who has lost his self. An Apostolic Hadith says : "I take pride in faqiri and faqiri is from me" *(Al-faqru fakhri wal faqru minni).* Another hadith says: "Faqr is the blackening of the face in the two worlds" *(Al~faqru sawādul wajhi fiā-dārayn).* When the face is blackened, it disappears. Hence a faqir is one who is self-annihilated, even in this case.

Fikr: To think on the attributes of God and the identification of rabb and '*abd*. "Do not think on sine Dhat of God, but think on His attributes and His blessings." *Lā tafakkaru fi dhātittah, wa tafakutu fi sifāt-illah wa fi muama'illahi.* "To think for a moment is better than service in bath the worlds" (*tafakkura sā'tin khairun min 'ibādati-th-thaqalayn).*

Ghayriyat: Being of different sort. *The* Ghayriyat between rabb and '*abd* is only suppositional, and is brought about by I'tibārāt God is *the* "worshipped" in every limitation. Hence drop off the worship of the "limited"; and worship only Him who is manifest in it. *Lā-ilaha illallah.* In this, the ghariyat between idols and God is dropped off. The idols are the limitations of God. If one could overlook the "limited' for the time being, he worships the unlimited God through His manifestation. Once in a way only, worship through (and not of) "the limited" is permitted, as in the case of circumambulations around the Ka'ba. Here it is not to be lost sight of, that this is the worship of the Rabb-i-Ka'ba and not of the Ka'ba itself.

Ghauth: The axis around which the world turns. He is the chief functionary of the hierarchy which controls and manages the world.

Hama-bi- ūst: This is the tauhid of sifāt (Tau-hid-i-Sifāti). No sifāt can exist without the *Dhāt*, since all sifāt inhere in *Dhāt*. "He is with you wherever you are" (*wa Hua ma'kum ayna mā kuntum).*[1] The giver and the taker are one and the same in different, and sometimes in contrary manifestations.

Hama-az-ūst: This is the tauhid of af'āl. (Tauhid-i-afali). In actions also tauhid underlies; good and evil, profit and loss proceed from God (*wai qadri khayrihi wa sharri minailahi taala).* If evil and good are from God, to whom will the punishment be meted out, and where is the necessity for heaven and hell? The Qur' ān has verses, showing that man's evil actions proceed from himself. *Mā asābaka min hasa-natin famin allahi taala wa ma asābeka min sayyatin famin nafsika.*[2] (Whatever you have got out of goodness is from God; and whatever you have got out of evil is from yourselves). So long as Ghayriyat-i-I'tabāri remains, the distinction between good and evil must remain; when it disappears as in the case of Fanā, the distinction also disappears.

Ilama- ūst: (Tauhid-i-Dhāti): The manifestations of sifāt (attributes) and af'āl (actions) of God are not separate from God.

---

1. Qur'ān, ivii : 4.
2. Qur'ān, iv : 79.

God is present in every sifāt and fā'il. Hence the existence of every sifāt and fā'il is the existence of God. He is manifest in all, but each object is not to be considered as God, for this is limiting Him in that object. If the worshipper loses sight of the manifestation; and keeps the *Dhāt* in view in worshipping before an object, in fact, if he is "looking through Nature up to Nature's God," his worship does not become idolatry; but this is impossible for the *mobile vulgus* and is repudiated. The author of "Gulshan-i-Rāz" says:

Biahmin gar bidanisti ki but chist
Na danisti ki but ghayr az Khuda nist.
If the Brahmin knew what the idol is,
He would have known that idol is no other of God.

Hāba: The dust-particles, such as you see in a stream of the sun's light in a dark room. It is the *prima matrix,* the substance *(hayulā)* of the Divine Thought. There is the *hāba,* the soul-world and the causal world.

Haqq: Truth—Proven. This is applicable to the first three stages of the Tanazzulāt. *Ruyat-i-Haqq* is envisaging God in His Creation.

Hulūl: One thing entering into another like water in a tub. When "other than God" is not existent; the doctrine of the Hulūlis like Hallāj does not hold water.

Ḥaqiqat: The reality of a thing. The causal world is thing the *mithāl-world* is its Haqiqat. The latter again is *thing,* and the soul-world is its Haqiqat; and so on with 'ālam-i-a'yān and *'Ilm* up to the *Dhāt* which is the innermost "Haqiqat" "Haqiqat is opposed to *i'tibār.* The *Dhāt* is the reality of everything; and *i'tibār* is the idea of a thing. Whatever conception is formed by us of a thing is its *i'tibār.*

Indrāj: Entry of one object into another in its highest aspect, *e.g.* Fire is the manifestation of the *Ism,* Al-Qābid (the contractor); the quintessence of Qabid is the *Dhāt*. Water is the manifestation of the name Al-Muhiyy (the life-giver). The inner aspect of this name is the *Dhãt*. There is differentiation of contrariness in the lower stages. In essence, therefore, the one is the other in its highest aspect. This is the doctrine of *Indrāj-i-kul fil Kul.*

Indimāj: Entry of one object into another in its lower aspect, as in the case of the seed and the tree, the yolk of an egg and the chicken.

I'tibārāt: <u>Suppositions or fancies</u>: Hypostasis of the German monks. When you observe a mountain from a distance, one whole aspect of it is in view. 'This corresponds to Ahdiyyat. A nearer approach and a closer observation reveal the aspects of this one aspect in detail. These aspects correspond to *I'tibārat,* Hypostases which are four in number, *viz.,* existence, knowledge, light and self-observance. The *Dhãt* was thus in existence, and the discovery was His 'Ilm (knowledge). Knowledge involves the knower and the known. The knower is the *Dhãt* and the known, His *a'yān.*

According to Jili, the *a'yān* have come out in manifestation like an inscription in ink, which is hidden in darkness but comes out on exposition. According to Ibnul 'Arabi, they have not smelt the smell of existence, Ma *shummat rahiyat al-Wujud.* The Dhat manifested Himself according to them. God is sensed, and the creation is inferred. Clay is sensed, its shapes—jug, pot—are inferred. Ibnul-'Arabi again says that the peculiarities of the *a'yān* were with them from eternity; Jili says that they were bestowed by God. Hence with the one. Destiny is unchangeable; and with the other, it is changeable.

According to Ibnul-'Arabi, God's knowledge is given him by the objects which He knew; knowledge is a relation between the knower and the known *(Al 'ilm nisbatun tabiatun lil ma'lū).* God decreed that they should be what their nature required them to be, This makes God and objects co-eternal— a mutiplicity in God, which multiplicity *'ādam* as the *a'yān* had no knowledge of themselves or of each other. *(Zi imtiyūz-'ilmi wu ghayri masun)* Jili therefore maintains that it was His knowing them that caused them to become the objects of His knowledge God was self-absorbed "I am and there is none beside Me." When He introspected. He found his potentialities (*shuyūnāt).* These *shuyūnāt* are therefore second in point of consideration.

When one introspects, he finds that he has mercy, anger, etc.; till then these latter are only potential. Jili therefore says that the existence of God is logically prior to the existence of a'yan, which are forms of His manifestation.

Ishq: Love—God is 'Ishq. In answer to David's query. God said *Kuntu kanzan makhfiyyan fa-ahbabtu an 'urifa khalaqlui khalqa li 'urifa.* "I was a hildden treasure, I loved to be known, and created the world to be known." God's first impulse was : "To Love to know Himself. The author of "Man Lagan" says;

Eh nafs agar na chuibulata,
Keun khol kiwar bahar ata.
Rahta mohan apni mari meyn
Apus ki qadim kithri meyn.

If this nafs had not stirred up,
Why would it have opened the door to come out?
The lover would have stayed in his parterrie
And in His old, old room.

The first bātini (internal) manifestation was, therefore, "Love to know Himself"; and the result was the "form of the First Intelligence" in His knowledge, which was Haqiqat-i-Muhammadi (the Reality of Muhammad). This latter therefore was the beloved of God; hence the title of Muhammad (peace be upon him) came to be Habibulla (the beloved of God). *A'yān,* and Arwāh come on in the later stages of Tanazzulāt, and Love comes in the very first among internal manifestations. Among the Rafā'i Faqirs the salutation is 'Ishqalla (God is love); and the answer: 'Ishq-i-Muhammad "Rasūlalla (Muhammad the first manifestation is love). The first manifestation or intelligence took two aspects, *viz.*, of glory (Jalāl) and of beauty (Jamāl). Jamāl became the lowest manifestation of the Reality of Muhammad in the name of Hādi (True Guide): and Jalāl became the lowest manifestation in the name of Mudhil (one who leads astray)—the Iblis. The sight of Haqiqat-i-Muhammadi, or Rūh-i-ā'zam as it is otherwise called, was on the *mithāl* and causal bodies of the Prophet; whereas the sight of a lower manifestation, viz., the differentiated arwāh is on the mithāl and causal bodies of the other beings of the earth. Hence *Lau laka, lama khalaqiul aflak.* "If it were not for thee, we would not have created the heavens." If the Rūh-i-ā'zam had not manifested itself, the arwāh of the world could not have manifested themselves.

Izdiwaj: The gamahea of the Greeks: "God was a hidden treasure. He loved to be known and created the world to be known" (*Kuntu kanzan makhfiyyan fa ahbublu an 'urifa fa khalaqtal khalaq.)* His *Dhāt* was hidden. The Internality joined with Love of self, and produced manifestation. The first joining was of Ahdiyat and Wāhidiyat; and thus there was *conjunction* between names.

Jalāl: Glorious (attributes). The attributes and asmā' that draw to the centre, and tend to the contraction of the circle of manifestation.

Jamāl: Manifestation of the attributes of mercy, love; expansion of the circle towards the circumference—Evolution as opposed to Involution, in the words of Herbert Spencer. In Jalāl, Jamāl is hidden and *vise versa.* Rain, for example, is a manifestation of Jamāl. Too much of it becomes a manifestation of Jalāl; and again out of inundations, fresh fields and new populations arise—a manifestation of Jamāl.

Kalām-ullah: Word of God—the Qur'ān. It is considered in its two aspects—sense and word— Kalām-i-nafsi and Kalām-i-lafzi. Some consider that as *nafsi* it is eternal; and others consider that as *lafzi* also, it is eternal—Imām Hanbal held that as Kalām-i-lafzi, the Qur'ān is uncreated, and Caliph Māmūn and his successor brought the weapon of Inquisition (Mehna) to prove that Kalām-i-lafzi is created. The Qur'ān as it existed in the Lauh-i-Mahfūz was eternal. *Bul hua Qur' ānin majidun fi Lawhin Mahfūz.* When the Angel Gabriel brought it down, and the *Wahy* was expressed in the words of the Prophet it was called Hadith-i-Qudsi. It was something like the difference between the Catholic and Protestant Churches; the former holding that the words of the Christian scriptures are the very words of God, and the latter that the sense was expressed in the words of the inspired writers.

Kalima—Word: The reality of every object; its *ayn* is a Kalima (Logos of the Greeks).

Khalq: Manifestation from alām-i-arwāh to 'alām-i-nāsūt.

Khirqa: Gabardine. Torn cloth of patches, which the Faqirs wear; it is rent in the middle, so as to be worn around the neck. A Pir bestows a khirqa on his murid or khalifa The Prophet had sent such a khirqa to Uways-i-Qarni; and had bestowed one on Hadrat Ali. A murid assuming the garb of his Pir is supposed to have assumed the garb of his sifāt, and also to have assumed the *hāl,* in which the Pir was—when he last wore it.

Khatra: Whatever dawns on the mind from the useen; an invitation to '*abd* from his rabb.

Kiyāni: Realities of objects, and the manifestations of the names of God (Ilāhi); and these asmā'-i-kiyāni are twenty-eight in number.

Kitābul-mubin: The Preserved tablet. That which is general in God's knowledge is detailed in this. There is no addition to or substraction from this *(La ratbin wa la yābisin illā fi kitābin mubin).*[1]

Lāhūt: "The hidden treasure." The stage of *Dhāt*. The world of asmā' and sifāt is jabarūt, and the stage of arwāh is Malakūt, and the last stage is Nasut. These terms are said to have been first used by Mansūr-i-Hallāj. They are called manāzil (stages) of the upward arc in sulūk.

Latifa: Anything that is only understood and cannot be expressed in words. There are six Latifas *(Latāyif-i-sitta).* The first latifa is nafs located near the navel; the second latifa is Qalb, located above the heart; the third is latifa-i-Rūh, on the right side of the chest; the fourth, latifa-i-Sir near the mouth of the stomach; the fifth, latifa-i-Khafi in the forehead ; and the sixth latifa-i-Akfāh on the top of the head. The faqirs of the Naqkshbandi order and the followers of Shaykh Ahmad of Sirhind practise on these points; other Sūfis have not faith in them. These resemble the Kundalini (the circles) of Patanjali.

Maqām: Station: Locus standi. Till one has fulfilled the duties of a station, he should not advance forward, *e.g.,* Patience is a station from which the sālik does not stir towards the next higher stage, *viz.,* contentment, till he has completed its duties and got accustomed to it. Then in order come Dependence on God, Submission, etc. If the sālik stirs out without completing his course in it, the station is changed into *hāl* (state) in his case.

Murāqaba: (Literally to keep under sight; to hang down one's head). This is to free the qalb from the Khatarāt of duality: to make the eye of the body and the eye of the heart (Oculus cordis) one and the same. When this is done, there is no necessity to close the bodily eye. If not, one has to do this, till he sees the picture of the universal idea of God in bis qalb.

---

1. Qur'ān. vi: 59.

Muraqaba-i-Huduri: In this, the sālik thinks he sees by God, eats by God, works by God. "He lives and moves and has his being by God" (and not *in* God as St. Paul has said). When a Muslim begins a work or takes a step, he says, *Bismillahir-Rahmān ir-Rahim.* "I begin in the name of (by) God, whose mercy extends to all and whose compassion extends to His friends or the chosen" The Muslim is thus in Murāqaba at every step. Murāqaba-i-Nazari is when the sālik thinks that God has appeared in his own form, sees through his eyes, hears through his ears.

Mujahada: To strive against Nafs against desire. An Apostolic Hadith says : "Srive against desire." *Al-mujāhidu ma jahada nafs.* The Prophet after the battle of Badr said: "I have turned from the lesser jihād to the greater jihād. *(Ruj'ana minal-jihad-il-asghari ilal-jihad il-akbar).*

Mukashafa: (Lifting of the veil): In this, the secrets of Divinity break on the heart. The salik sees lights and illuminations. He sees the realities of 'alam-i-mithāl with his bodily eyes; in fact by means of his five senses, he perceives the realities of that world; the lower animals sometimes display this perception.

Mushahada: It is to see illuminations without the mediation of objects, *i.e.,* to put objects out of sight and have direct illuminations. The *Mathnawi* says:

Dar guzar kun jumla tan ra dar nazar,
Dar nazar raw, dar nazar raw, dar nazar.

Drop all objects out of sight,
Go into sight, go into sight, go into sight.

Muayanah: Is when the salik loses his self in these illuminations.

Maut-i-Ikhtiyari: The sālik annihilates his self and makes God permanent. When the sālik dies to his self, he lives by the

Eternal Life.

Mazhar-i-atamm: The perfect manifestation, the perfect man. The Reality of the Prophet was the First Manifestation of God; and the realities of the *'abds* are the manifestations of that reality. Each object is a manifestation of some one name; but all the other names are therein it potentially. Hence each object is a perfect manifestation in itself. The Prophet was the embodiment of Jalāli (glorious) and Jamāli (beautiful) attributes. The first were only potential in him, and the second were in evidence. He was thus a blessing to the worlds *(Rahmatan lil 'ālamin).* In fact, his Reality co-ordinates and harmonizes the contrary and conflicting asmā' manifested in this and the next worlds.

Nafs-i-Rahmāni: The influence that an ism-i" ilāhi exerts on its opposite ism-i-kiyani. The human breath keeps the body alive and active; so also each ism-i-rabb keeps its ism-i-murbub in activity. Both these are the manifestations of wujūd-i-idāfi (Derivative Existence). The worlds are the manifestations of this Divine breath; just as all the words of a language are the manifestations of one simple human breath.

Nay': A reed: Jalāluddin Rūmi represents the "Insān-ul-Kāmil" by Nay'. Every Muslim author begins his book with the hallelujah (*Hamd)* of God, and praise (*Thanā)* of the Prophet. The Maulānā, begins his *Mathnawi* with an account of the "Reed."

Beshnu az nay chūn hikāyat mi kunad

Uzjudai-ha shikāyat mi kunad.

Kuz nayaslan ta mara bi burid-and

Uz nafiram murd wu zan nalid-and

Sina khahum sharah sharah az firaq,

Ta bugoyam sharah-i-dard ishtiyāq.

Listen to the reed when it narrates its tale.
It complains about its separation.
From the time they cut me from the reed-forest,
Men and women have wept from my plaintive
voice.
I wish my breast were rent to pieces
When I make my commentary on the pain of my Love.

There is no direct *hamd* and *thanā* in this; but in a hidden way it contains both these. The reed-forest, herein referred to, is the stage of Wahdat. wherein the *a'yān* of the world he hidden; Insān-ul-Kāmil is removed from this stage down to the lowest stage, wherein he is using a plaintive voice. He has to adjust the jarring asmā' through which he descended; and the asmā' are weeping for having been brought down to the same level by the adjusting hand of Insān ul-Kāmil; *akhizun bi masiyatiha* (who holds them by their forelock); hence the males *(Āba-i-'Ulawi)* and the females *(Ummahāt-i-sifli)* referred to, Hidāyat 'Ali Sāhib in his Commentary of the 'Mathnawi' named *Kashful* '*Ulūm* says thatĀbā-i-' Ulawi are Asmā'-i-Ilāhi, and Ummahāt-i-sifli are the Asmā'-i-Kiyāni *(vide* p. 4). This cannot be; since the former being the direct asmā' of God are not under the. control of anybody or of the Insān-ul-kāmil. It is only the latter that are under his control. Again it is only the latter twenty-one asmā'-i-kiyāni that have their opposites. There could be no manifestation of the world without the display of the opposites. Hence Ābā-i-'Ulawi and Ummahāt-i-sifli are these twentyone asmā'-i-kiyāni. By their interplay, the world is manifest. The reed (Insān-ul-kāmil) by its sound (the Qur'an) has brought these jarring *asmā,'* into harmony; and hence, being refractory they bemoan in the grip of a compelling hand. Thus the Maulana has brought out both *hamd* and *thana* in his opening lines about the famous reed.

Qada: In God's knowledge, there were the aptitudes of A'yān; and He commanded the A'yān to become what they were—this is Qadā. Whatever they were ordered to become, they had to become through their own medium—their own activity and not by an external agent. This is Qādar.

Qiyāmat: The State of Stability—a static state as opposed to dynamic. This is the appellation given to the Last Day. When the soul severs its connexion with the body, the faculty of *Wahm* accompanies it, according to Ghazzāli, to the other side of the grave;[1] and renews, in kaleidoscopic forms and with a hundredfold vigour, the changes wrought and nurtured in it during the man's life-time on the earth; and he takes the form of the predominating characteristic of his life,[2] still retaining the identity of his earthly ego, which links him on to resurrection in the next life. These changes, whether pleasant or unpleasant, go on recurring till a fixed time *(qiyāmat),* when he feels his proximity to God and is lost in Transcendental Wonder; for God is with His *'abd* even in Hell, which is one of His asmā'-i-jalāli. This *qiyāmat* is not the *pralaya,* spoken of in Hinduism ; when one cycle ends, and there is stationariness before another begins. For the God of Islam does not "take rest." He is the God "whom neither slumber nor sleep seizeth"[3] *(La lakhuzuhu sinatun wa lā noum).* The changes are in His activity of creation, He is ever the same—*Wa hua al ana kama kana.*

The time of *Qiyāmat* is not known to any creature. In the Hadith of Gabriel (*vide* page 223 *ante),* the stranger also asked the Prophet (peace be upon him) to enlighten him regarding the day of judgment. The answer was, "the questioned one is himself no more enlightened than the questioner." "Then," said he,

1. Vide p. 109-11 *ante*
2. Page 109 *ante.*
3. Sūra Baqara 255.

"enlighten me regarding the signs that shall precede it." The Prophet said: "It shall be when the maid-servant shall give birth to her master," and "you see the naked and barefooted, and the grazer of sheep enjoying themselves in palaces." According to 'Abdul Karim Jili:[1] "Man is compared to Maid-servant and the Occult Truth to her Master," This, therefore, means that Qiyāmat will be when Divinity will manifest itself in Man. This world is where God observes through man ('Ālam-i-Shahādat); and the *Mithāl* world is where He does not observe through man but direct, which is therefore called *ghayb.* When man reverts to the *mithāl* stage, and God sees through him there, then this world becomes *ghayb* and the *mithāl* world becomes shahādat. The Wujūd-i-Bātini (the interior or real existence) of Man is God. The nature of this existence will become more apparent, and the reality of *'abd* will become more clear in that state; *(vide* "Qurb-i-Nawāfil)," and the naked (the interior) will enjoy in 'palaces' (illuminations). When the ' āriff will become aware of asmā' and ignore them in the light of *Dhāt*; and when also, he will ignore sifāt and envisage *Dhāt*, he will be like the shepherd; who is enjoying himself in a palace, *i.e.,* the human man will enjoy the light of epiphanies.

These are the minor signs.—The major signs are that Yājūj and Mājūj which appear on the earth. These are the Seditious Thoughts and Evil Intentions overpowering the Nafs of man. They will be finally killed; and in their places, Rahmani Khatras will appear. The second major sign is the appearance of *Dabbatul-ard,* a talking beast who will warn people against evil impulses. Jili considers that this refers to Rūh-ul-Quds (the Holy Ghost). The third is Dajjāl, who will wander over the earth, but would avoid the direction of Makkah and Madina; he will stop short at Ramilah, a village built of mud near Jerusalem. Here Christ will descend

1. Insān-ul-Kāmil, chap. 61.

and kill him with a lance. This Dajjāl will have hell on his left-hand side, and heaven on his right-hand side. Jili considers that Dajjāl is the Nafs-i ammara, which is the repository of evil thoughts. On its left is the hell of ascetic life; and its right, the heaven of licentiousness. Whoever is put into hell will at once find a place in God's heaven, and *vice versa.* The Christ referred to is the Soul that will scotch the Nafs. The two cities that Dajjāl will be unable to enter are the cities of Sukr and Sahw, and the village Ramilah that will obstruct his path is the stage of Causal body. The fourth is the appearance of Mahdi. The fifth sign is the rising of the Sun in the West and his setting in the East. This means that man will have illuminations from a quarter least anticipated. All these signs mean that the *ghayb* world will become the apparent world. This is the expected Millennium, wherein evil will disappear from the world before the coming of the Judgment Day. Jili's explanations are more or less on rationalistic rather than on *Kashfi* (illuminationists) lines and these are not acquiesced in, by literalists, such as Ahl-i-Sunnat are.

Qurb-i-Farā'yad: In this. God is the externality of *'abd.* God is the actor and instrument of *'abd.* He becomes the sight and hearing of *'abd.*

Qurb-i-Nawāfil: 'Abd becomes the externality of God, and the actor and instrument of God. In such a condition, Isaiah said: "Harken unto me, O Jacob, Israel my called: I am He, I am the First, and I also am the Last." Isaiah 48. See also Psalms, 46-10, for David.

Qalb: (The heart.) This is not the lump of flesh of pine-shape, located near the nipples, which is the soul of motive power, and is shared in by the lower animals. It is really the borderland between Rūh and Nafs, between light and darkness; it is so-called because it turns and directs itself to the *ism* that presents itself

---

1. Reve II,.7.

before it, or because it takes an inverted image of the world. The retina of the eye takes an inverted image of things, by the laws of refraction of light in the crystalline lens; but actually we see things upright; for Qalb has again inverted an upturned image, and made it upright. The Western psychologists simply say that we have an upright view, because of the force of habit. Qalb again is a drop in the ocean of rūh, which has manifested itself in limitation according to the nature of the physical body. It is compounded of the subtle ruh and the coarse body; and has thus established connection between the two. It receives impressions from the external world through the five external senses, and then from the internal world through the five internal senses *(viz..* Thought, Instinct, Memory., Reasoning and Fancy). 'Abdul Karim Jili describes Qalb "as the eternal light and sublime consciousness (Sirr) revealed in the *'ayn* of created beings, he is the throne of God (Al-'Arsh), and His temple in man *(Qalb-ul-Mumin 'Arsh-ullahi).* It is the centre of Divine consciousness in man. It reflects all the Divine names and attributes at once, and turns its face under the influence of different names, like the needle of a compass. The mercurial coating of this mirror is the body. The heart reflects the world of attributes. "The earth and the heaven do not contain me; but the heart of my beli eving servant con-taineth me." (*La yasuni ardun wa lā samaun wa yasuni 'qalbu 'abdia muminin).* When one perceives an object, an impression is carried to the brain, one or more of the five senses contributing their quota through their respective channels. The commonsense *hiss-i-mushiarak),* one of the five internal senses, then adjusts these impressions and forms the required images and these images are carried to the ruh (soul) through one of the other four internal faculties (*quwā-i-bātiniyyuh), viz.,* imagination *(khiyāl).* Thinking *(mutāsirrifa*), Instinct (*wahima)* Retentativeness *(hāfiza).* An adept does not see an object as an object; he sees it as the manifestation of God's attributes and names; and so the impression that his Qalb, which is the mystical commonsense, carries to the rūh (soul) is the manifestation of Divinity without. Qalb is really the photographic plate that takes on the picture of God's manifestations, and not merely of the outer shell of materiality, through the x-rays of the five internal faculties, so to speak. An Urdu poet has said:

Dil ke āyine men hay taswir-i-yār
Jab dharā gardan jhukā'i dekh li

In the mirror of the heart is the picture of the Friend
When for a while, I hang down my head, I see Him.

There are three aspects of this Qalb; one is Qalb-i-Munib. from which good Khatarāt manifest themselves, and another is Qalb-i-Salim which displays love of God and fondness for *'irfān;* and the third is Qalb-i-Shāhid, which discerns the presence of God in every object.

Rasm—as opposed to *Ism:* It is the effect and manifestation of *Ism*. It means the attributes of creatures (the created). All that is considered as other-than-God *(Mā siwāllah)* is really the effect of Āsmā.'

Rabb: Particular name of God in reference to each 'ayn-i-thābita The name Providence requires as its opposite, some one to be provided; the name "merciful" requires "some one to whom mercy is shown." The one is rabb and Ism-i-Ilāhi, and the other is murbūb and *Ism*-i-Kiyani. The name Allāh is conglomerate of all asmā'.

Sālik: One who enters on sulūk (pilgrimage); he is in the middle stage between a beginner and an adept. Firstly, there is pure sālik as defined above. Then sālik-majdhub, one who has attained *jadhba* in his sulūk. The third *majdhūb-sālik,* one who has attained *jadhba*, purely by God's grace, and without his Mujāhada and who then enters upon sulūk. The fourth is pure *majdhūb* who has attained *jadhba* without sulūk, and who never afterwards enters upon sulūk. Some consider that the second is the best.

Sirr: The first tendency to manifestation of a wave in the calm ocean—the first tendency to motion in the calm ocean may be likened to the first recognition of "I" by God in His *Dhāt*. That is the first 'ayn-i-thābita which is called Haqiqat-i-Muhammadi, the First Intelligence. From this one wave, several waves broke up and manifested themselves, and became the a'yān-i-thābita of objects. Qādi Husām-uddin of Gujerat has said:

Zi daryā mauj-i-guna gun baā āmad
Zi bichuni bi rang-i-chun bar āmad
Gāhi dar kiswat-i-Laylā faru shud
Gāhi bar sūrat-i-Majnūn bar āmad.

From ocean rose waves of different kinds,

From incomparableness, they assumed the colour of comparableness.

Now they appeared in the garb of Laylā,

Now they assumed the form of Majnū

Thus "you understand the 'I' of God, when you understand your own 'I'." *Man 'arafa nafsahu faqad 'arafarabbahu.* The first sirr contains this "I" *(Al-insānu sirri wa anā sirruhu)*. Man is my *sirri* and I am his sirri." Since man is a microcosm (Kawn-i-Jami), he has all the attributes of God as well as the, *sirri* of God. Every atom of the creation is crying out "I"— "I".

Shirk: To consider another existing beside God. Shirk-i-jali is to join "another" in the *Dhāt*, sifāt, and action of God, to consider the sifat of God as separate from His *Dhāt*. Shirk-i-Khafi is to consider that "other than God" is existent,

Shuyun: (pl. of Shān) Potentialities—like the potentialities of a tree in the seed.

Shathiyyat: Words that come out of the mouth of a Wali in

his state of ecstacy, like *Anal Haqqu* (I am the truth) from Mansūr-i-Hallāj; *Laysa fi jubbati siwallahi.* (There is none underneath my garment but God) from Junayd ; and *Subhāna ma a 'zama shāni* (I am holy, how great is my position) from Bāyazid-i-Bistāmi; *Anā nuqtatuba-i-bismillah.—Anā qalmun wu anā Lauhun Mahfuzun anā 'Arshun wa anā Kursiyun wa ana samawātun* (I am the point of the Bay of Bismillah, I am the Pen, I am the Preserved Tablet, I am the 'Arsh. I am the Kursi, I am the firmaments) from Hadrat 'Ali.

Sidratul-Muntahā: The Great Fig-tree on the outermost border of Space. It is the stage in the upward arc of ascension, at which spatial region with its manifestations of diversity ends, and the non-spatial expanse of Pure Being begins. A tree is a symbol of diversity in Unity (Kathrat dar Wahdat), the ramification of its branches, its innumerable leaves, flowers and fruits are but the outcome of one seed. At this stage, names and attributes (asmā'-wa-sifāt) drop off; and *Dhāt* alone remains. In the night of Mi'rāj Gabriel who had accompanied the Prophet (peace be upon him) stopped short here, saying, as Sa'di has put it:

Agar ya sari mui bar tar param
Farugh-i-tajalli bisuzad param.

If I fly higher by a hair-breadth
The splendour of Glory will singe my wings.

Reason (of which Gabriel is the first embodiment) could not ascend higher than the outermost limit of diversity. It is only Nūr-i-Emān, the light that lights the inner recess of the heart that could do this—*Iz yagshaus-Sidrata ma yaghsha, ma zaghal basaru wa ma tagha.*[1] When that which overshadowed the Sidra overshadowed it (*i.e.*, the Nūr), the Prophet (peace be upon him)

1. Qur'ān liii, 17-18.

did not glance aside, nor did his sight go astray.

Sifāt: Attributes in the *Dhāt*; manifestations of *Dhāt*: sifāt are essential to *Dhāt*, which is known only from sifāt, and without which it is "unknown and unknowable".

Saul-ir-Sarmadi: The Eternal and Incessant voice without sound and direction,—answering to the Logos of St John: "In the beginning was Word, the Word with God and the Word was God." It is a voice that is heard in jungles as well as in crowded market places. It is the voice of God that Moses heard. It forms a *Shaghal* by itself with some adepts.

Suwar-ul-Haqq: Forms in the knowledge of God. When God looked at Himself, He saw Himself in a form that became the Form of Muhammad (peace be upon him) Haqiqat-i-Muhammadi.

Ti'yun: Limitation. God's consciousness of Him-self was His first tai'yun. A tai'yun is an 'ādam in itself. The second tai'yun was consciousness of His attributes. These are the internal tai'yunāt. Arwāh, mithāl and ajsām are external taiyūnāt.

Tauhid: Losing one's self in the *Dhāt* of God.

Tajalli: The illumination of *Dhāt*. *Dhāt* as such is darkness. The two extremes of the spectrum of light end in darkness. Darkness is really light, which the retina of the eyes is incapable of appreciating. The 'Mathnawi' says:

Tajalli gar tu khah nur-i-dhat ast
Bi tariki darun ābi hyat ast.

Tajalli, if you say so, is the light of *Dhāt*
Within darkness lies the fount of eternal life.

When *Dhāt* dawned upon itself. Nūr appeared. This was Nūr-i-Muhammadi (Light of Muhammad (peace be upon him) as stated in the Hadith-i-Jābir. "O Jabir," said the Prophet "know that the first thing created was the light of thy Prophet." *Tajalli* is the appearance of *Dhāt* in tai'yunāt (limitations). God appears to the devotee in the form most eagerly sought for, by him. Moses was in search of fire in a desert on his way back to Egypt from Shu'ayb's (Jethro's) house in Midian (Madayun); God therefore appeared to him in a "burning bush." If one seeks Him in an image, the image appears to fulfil bis desires; thus there is no disappointment even in idol worship. God has said: *"Anā 'inda zanni 'abdihi."* "I am with the thought of my servant." If the devotee supplicates before an image, he is never disappointed, because image also is a *tajalli*, idolatry consisting in thinking it to be the *Dhāt* itself 'Gulshan-i-Rāz' says:

Barāhman gar bi dānisti ki but chist,
Na danisti ki but juz az Khuda nist.

If the Brahmin knew what the image really is,
He would have known that it is not other-than-God.

Tashbih: The manifestation of the attributes of God in limitation. The attributes of *'abd* are the attributes of God in limitations. When there is thus comparison between God's attributes and *'abd's* attributes. God is said to be in tashbih.

Tanzih: Since His attributes are infinite, we cannot form an idea of them from our limited attributes. His attributes are incomparable to our limited attributes, God in His own attributes is in Tanzih. *Subhāna Rabbika Rabbul 'izzati umma ya sifum.* "Pure is thy Lord, the Lord of Honour, from all that you attribute to Him."

Tariqat: Pilgrimage of Sālik towards God by inner purifications.

Taqdir: That which is measured and "estimated." The estimate of creation in God's knowledge (Ummul-Kitāb). Is liable to change or not? If it is liable, then God's knowlegde or His omniscience becomes defective or incomplete. If it is not, what is

---

1. Qar'ān xi, 60.

the good of prayer? The Qur'ān has said *Ud'uni astajib lakum.*[1] "Pray unto Me and I shall accept your prayer." With lbn-ul-'Arabi, the realities of A'yān are eternal in God's knowledge, which also is eternal; and He granted their prayer, by manifesting Himself in their form. He only wills what they have in them to become; for knowledge is dependent on the known. *Al-'ilmu nisbatun tabiatun lil-malum.* Thus human actions are self-determined God did not determine them; only in His name of Jawād (the gift-giver). He manifested them. Neither did the *a'yān* determine their own qualities, these latter were inherent in them. A draughtsman makes a triangle on paper. He did not propose the three sides and the three angles, and the three angles being equal to two right angles; these qualities were there in a triangle (according to the Laws of Thought). If the draughtsman makes four angles, and four sides, the figure will become a square or anything else and not a triangle. It may, however, be that Ibn-ul-'Arabi, the chief exponent of the doctrine that God is knowledge itself, thought that the knower, knowledge and the known are one and the same; in which case, knowledge depending on the known comes to be the *Dhāt* depending on Itself, for there is no *mā-siwāllah* (Other-than-God) in the first *bātani* stage. In the third stage or still lower down, ghayriyat-i'tibāri begins, and the *Dhāt* controls the asmā' and a'yān.

'Abdul Karim Jili, however, differed from this Shaykh. He says A'yān became what they were by His knowing them before their creation, *i.e.,* by His knowing, they became the objects of His knowledge. He knew the angles and the sides and put them in a particular way and they formed a triangle. This leaves taqdir in His hands. There are many Qur'ãnic verses to this effect.

Wa tuizzu man tashau wa tudhillu man tashau biyadikal khayr, wa huwa ala kulli shayin qadir.[1] "He elevates whomsoever He likes. He degrades whomsoever He likes. In His

---

1. Qur'ãn iii, 26.

hand lies goodness. He is omnipotent over all." *Yef'alu ma yashu wu yahkamu ma yurid.* "He does what He likes, and orders what He wills."

La tahdi man ahbabtu wa la kinnallaha yahdi man yashau. "You cannot rightly guide whomsoever you like, but God can guide whomsoever He likes."

This controversy appears to have arisen by making a'yān co-eternal with God, like Aristotle having made matter co-eternal with Him. If the a'yān are brought down to their proper place in the scheme of Tanazzulāt, that is, below asmā', they need not be co-eternal in point of time; they are co-eternal in His knowledge. In the regular ascent in the upper arc of *'Urūj,* a'yān disappear in asmā', asmā' in sifāt and sifat in *Dhāt* and the *Dhāt* alone remains. *Kullu man alayha fan wa yabqa wajhu rabbika dhul-jalali wal-ikram.*[1] "All are annihilated, except the face (the *Dhāt*) of thy Lord with His glory and mercy." Sifāt are of secondary consideration, so also are asmā' and a'yān. Just as one cannot say that sifāt (which are aspects of *Dhāt*) are co-eternal with the *Dhāt*, for they are sometimes so hidden in the *Dhāt* as to be annihilated, like tree in a seed; so also one cannot say that a'yān, the forms of sifat in God's knowledge are co-eternal with the *Dhāt*; the *Dhāt* has priority in rank. It, therefore, controls the sifāt and a'yān. In this case, man simply manifests the asmā' that play upon him. One of the names of God is Al-Ghani (the independent). When this name is manifest, man appears to be a free agent; while really in his own *Dhāt* he is an '*adam.*

The 'Mathnawi says':

Darya bi wujudi kwish mauji darad,
Khas pindarad ki kasha kash ba ust.

Ocean by itself has waves and billows,

---

1. Qur'ān Iv, 26, 27.

Straw on the top thinks that it struggles with it,

In the three Internal *(bātini;)* stages, there is no foreknowledge; for with God there is the "Eternal Now." *Laysa indallahi sabahun wa la masaun* (with God there is no morning and no evening) In the three manifest (zāhiri) stages, or more correctly in the last stage (' ālam-i-zāhir), there is succession of events, and this gives rise to the idea of priority or of cause and effect.

Uluhiyat: This term is used for the stage at which the rabb (ruler) and marbūb (ruled) come into play. This is the line of separation between asmā'-i-ilahi and asmā'-i-kiyāni. Taqdir has its source here, where change from one *ism* into another takes place.

Ummul-kitāb: The First Intelligence, the Reality of Muhammad, (peace be upon him).

'Urūj: This is to reach the station of Wahdāt. The Sālik travels from 'ālam-i-ajsām annihilating his body in sight or in thought, to ' ālam-i-mithāl. He annihilates ' ālam-i-mithāl and travels to 'ālam-i-arwāh; thence to 'ālam-i-a'yān, thence to Wāhidiyyat, and Wahdat, in the reverse serial order in which he descended; and thus reaches the point from which he had descended. The *'Urūj* of the sālik is up to the Light of Muhammad (peace be upon him) *Man raani faqad raul Haqq* (Whoever has seen me., has seen God) says a Hadith; and the 'Uruj of Muhammad (peace be upon him) is up to God Himself (Ahdiyyat) for the Prophet is the barzakh between Ahdiyyat and Wahidiyyat. In this sense, said 'Urfi the Persian poet, in praise of the Prophet:

Taqdir bi ekk naqa nashanid du mahmil
Salma-i-hudusi tu wa Layla-i-qidam ra.
Taqdir has placed two litters on one camel,
The Salma of thy Transitoriness and the Layla of Eternity.[1]

1. These are the heroines in the love literature of the Arabs of the Days of Ignorance.

'Unsūr—(Element): The doctrine that there are only four Elements, *viz.,* air, water fire and earth is now an exploded doctrine; Chemistry has proved these to be compounds.—The four elements out of which, substances are formed are different; although they go under these names; they are beyond the confines of the three dimensions. By air is meant the Divine Breath, *La tasubbur riha fa innaha min nafsir Rahmani.*—"Do not abuse the wind, for the wind is the breath of God." *Nafakhtu fihi min ruhi.* "We breathed into him (Ādam) from Our breath."— It approximates to *khāli* or ether. By water, is meant the Surging Ocean *(Bahrul-Musjūr)* above the 'Arsh—*Wa jaalna min al mai kullu shayin hayyun.* "We made all things, living—by water."—This perhaps is the Ocean of Nebula. Fire—is the "blazing fire that leaps up to our hearts."—*Nar-ullahi muqatul lati ta'.taliwu alal afyida* (Sūra 110 : 4.) This is the fire of Nafs-i-Lawwāma, the conscience that reproaches; or perhaps the fire which Prometheus stole out of Heaven, to animate his men of clay. The earth is the earth above the 'Arsh—the mithāli earth, on which the Jannat is situated and on which the Judgment Day will take place.—*Yuma tabaddulul ardu ghayrul ardi.* "On that day. We will change this earth into another earth." This is the Ard-ul-Wasia' (the expanded earth) and is "the new earth" which St. John the Divine speaks of—(Revelation 21: 1)

Wahdal-ul-Wujūd: There is only one existence which is the *Dhāt*; and limitations are like billows and bubbles on the surface of water which are not realities. This is the belief of the Wujūdiyyahs as led by Ibn-ul-'Arabi and Ash'aris led by Abul Hasan Ash'ari. The Shuhudiyyahs led by Shaykh 'Alā-ud-Dowlah Samnāni and Shaykh Ahmad Sirhindi believe in two existences *(viz.,* of God and a'yān) and one *Dhāt*; and the Mutakallimin believe in two existences and two *Dhāts* (of God and creation.)

Wujūd-i-Idāfi: Also named Zāhir-ul-Wujūd, manifestations of God with the forms and attributes of A'yān. Wujūd is from *Wajd* "to find out".

Wajd: Attraction towards God, it is also called *jadhba.*

Wajh—Dhãt: "Wherever thou turnest thy face, there is the wajh (*Dhãt*) of God." *(Fa aynama tawallu fa samma wujhulla).* If wajh is *Dhãt*, is it *shay* also? The Qur'ãn says : "everything is, or is to be annihilated, except His visage" (*Kulla shayin halika illa, wajhahu), i.e.,* the face or the *Dhãt* is not, or is not to be, annihilated. When an exception is made, it must be from a group of its own species. There is only one *Dhãt* and that is of God. There are three internal stages of Tanazzulāt, *viz.,* Ahdiyyat, Wahdat, Wāhidiyyat, *i.e., La bi sharti shay;* (without the condition of 'thing'); *bisharti shay* (with the condition of no 'thing') and *bisharti la shay* (with the condition of 'thing'). In the third stage, the *Dhãt* comes under the category of "thing" and hence the exception. The Qur'ãnic saying *Laysa kamithlihi shayin* (He is not like the pattern of a thing), refers to the first of *La bishari shay* (Ahdiyyat).

Zāhir: External. When *taiyun* becomes more and more in evidence, Externality becomes more and more pronounced. Words written in ink are not seen in darkness. As more and more light is thrown on them, they become more and more prominent, *i.e.,* they become Zāhir—*i.e.,* come into Externality or Manifestation—Zāhir screens the *bātin* (internality). The more the attributes are manifest, the more the Reality becomes hidden; the more a fire-brand is turned round and round, the more is the fire-circle *in evidence,* and the fire-brand hidden from your sight. Hence it is said:

Al- 'ilmu hijāb-ul-akbar

Knowledge is a great screen.